M000318319

Credit And The Two Sources From Which It Springs:

The Propensity to Save
&
The Propensity to Consume

A Treatise On Gold, Interest And Discount

VOLUME IV

BY

PROF. ANTAL FEKETE

Credit and the Two Sources from which it Spring: The Propensity to Save and the Propensity to Consume - A Treatise on Gold, Interest and Discount:

© 2018 Antal E. Fekete

Cover, & text editing
© Pintax cvba, Belgium

Index research and composition:
© David van der Linden

Published by Pintax cvba - February 2019

All rights reserved

No part of this publication may be reproduced, stored in a retrieval system or transmitted in any form or by any means, electronic, mechanical, photocopying, recording, scanning or otherwise, no exceptions, without written permission from the publisher. Requests to the publisher should be addressed to:

Pintax cvba
Industrial Estate C 102
Betekomsesteenweg 19
3200 Aarschot
Belgium

BE Depot Nr. D/2017/14.095/6
ISBN 13: 978-9082065565

Published by Pintax cvba Belgium - March 2019

Available in this series :

By Antal E. Fekete

Critique of Mainstream Austrian Economics In the spirit of Carl Menger (2017) ISBN 978-90820655-27

Credit Volume I : Money and Credit - The Essential (February 2019) ISBN 978-90820655-34

Credit Volume II : Money and Credit in an Unhampered Market (March-April 2019) ISBN 978-90820655-41

Credit Volume III : Money and Credit in a Mixed Economy (March-April 2019) ISBN 978-90820655-58

Credit Volume IV : Money and Credit - Reconstruction (March-April 2019) ISBN 978-90820655-65

By Peter. M. Van Coppenolle

The Austrian Business Cycle Revisited(2012) ISBN 5800094365307

De Oorsprong van Geld (Carl Menger) translated to Dutch (2015) ISBN 978-90820655-10

In Search of Order - History of (Junk) Ideologies (target date April 2020)

By Rudy Fritsch

Beyond Mises - bases on the work of Antal E. Fekete (2010) ISBN 978 -06153734-09

By Darryl Schoon

Time of The Vulture (2012) ISBN 978-0615677088

Online video resources that belong to the Money & Credit Series:
–https://www.youtube.com/channel/UCnz5gMwVp6VVTuxbHjZaB7Q
Advanced Research Topics
– https://purelytheoreticalresearch.com
Applied Investment Strategies by NASOE members
– https://bullionplay.com
– https://lbnow.co.nz
– https://drschoon.com
– https://monetary-metals.com
– https://goldstandardinstitute.us or .net
– https://survivethecrisis.com

▶ Para libros españoles sobre economía austríaca : Amazon.es | Juan Ramón Rallo & https://www.juandemariana.org

Prof. Dr. Antal E. Fekete

About The Author

Antal E. Fekete, Professor, Memorial University of Newfoundland, was born in Budapest, Hungary, in 1932. He graduated from the Loránt Eötvös University of Budapest in mathematics in 1955. He left Hungary in the wake of the 1956 anti-Communist uprising that was brutally put down by the occupying Soviet troops. He immigrated to Canada in the following year and was appointed Assistant Professor at the Memorial University of Newfoundland in 1958. In 1993, after 35 years' of service he retired with the rank of Full Professor. During this period he also had tours of duty as visiting professor at Columbia University in the City of New York (1961), Trinity College, Dublin, Ireland (1964), Acadia University, Wolfville, Nova Scotia (1970), Princeton University, Princeton, New Jersey (1974). Since 2005 he has been Professor at Large of Intermountain Institute for Science and Applied Mathematics (IISAM), Missoula, Montana.

Professor Fekete is an autodidactic expert on monetary economics. During his associations with various universities and institutions he has done research and lectured on economics. On one such occasion, in 1974, he gave a talk on gold in the seminar of Paul Volcker, then Senior Fellow at Princeton University, soon to be named as President of the Federal Reserve Bank of New York and, later, as Chairman of the Federal Reserve Board.

In 1984 Professor Fekete was invited by the American Institute for Economic Research in Great Barrington, Massachusetts, to spend a year there as Visiting Fellow. He served as Editor of the Monograph Series of the Committee for Monetary Research and Education, then headquartered in Greenwich, Connecticut, while contributing several monographs to the Series, reproduced on his website. He also acted as Senior Editor for the American Economic Foundation in Cleveland, Ohio, and produced the popular pamphlet series *Ten Pillars of Sound Money*, also reproduced in Volume I of this series. When in 1984 South Africa celebrated the 100th anniversary of discovering gold in the Witwatersrand, at the conference Gold 100 commemorating that event in Johannesburg, Professor Fekete delivered the keynote address entitled Gold in the International Monetary System, also reproduced on his website.

In 1985 Congressman William E. Dannemeyer of Fullerton, California, invited Professor Fekete to join his staff in Washington, D.C., to work on fiscal and monetary reform. While on this assignment, lasting for five years, he gave numerous lectures on Capitol Hill as well as in California. Ultimately the proposals hammered out in Congressional offices under his chairmanship were taken to the White House by a delegation of ten Republican Congressmen led by Congressman Dannemeyer. According to these proposals the runaway government deficit could be reined in by refinancing the entire U.S. government debt through issuing gold bonds. The historic meeting took place in the Oval Office in October, 1989, and was duly reported by The New York Times. Having listened attentively to the presentation of Mr. Dannemeyer, President George Bush, Sr., instructed his Treasury Secretary, also present at the meeting, to let the Congressional and Treasury staff meet and put forward a joint proposal. This initiative came to nought as the Treasury deliberately derailed negotiations through procrastination.

—◊—

Contents

List of Figures

List of Abbreviations

BIS   : Bank for International Settlements
FED   : Federal Reserve Bank (System)
GFC   : Global Financial Crisis
GNP   : Gross National Product
GDP   : Gross Domestic Product
IMF   : International Monetary Fund
NPV   : Net Present Value of a cash flow
OECD : Organisation for Economic Cooperation and Development
PV   : Present Value
QE   : Quantitative Easing
QTM   : Quantity Theory of Money
RBD   : Real Bills Doctrine
SCC   : Social Circulating Capital
WACC : Weighted Average Cost of Capital
ZIRP   : Zero Interest Rate Policy

VOLUME IV

Money And Credit – Reconstruction

Introduction

Money and Credit's first volume functions as an extended introduction to the other three. You are holding volume IV, the final volume. The sorting of subjects into coherent volumes inevitable leads to overlap. I have tried to avoid the latter, although I am sure some overlap exists. Volume I contains all essential elements to reconstruct an unadulterated gold standard. The most ancient philosophical texts known to mankind, the Rig-Veda's of ancient India circulated both horizontally in space and forward in time, by way of oral tradition from one generation to the next. Originally conceived to educate the young, the Vedas used the oral tradition in story format – some call it myth – and its makers set it in rhyme for easy absorbtion. They ancient Indians were not the only ones following this recipe. Antal Fekete choose to emulate the old way by using the story form for his message to the next generations as much as possible, so that the memory can easily absorb its contents. Pity about the rhyme. Antal Fekete did not plan to write a new Vedas though, yet the contents of Credit may nevertheless turn out important enough for generations to come. Time will tell. The effort to convert content into story form will not have been in vain, if it can help put the science of economics back on track as a human science.

In Volume II economic theory of an unadulterated gold standard, (not the one professed by its promotors some hundred and fifty years ago) has been worked out. Forty years of research and thinking finally resulted in the formulation of theorems based on consulting the older texts. The more recent economic text books may be safely ignored for they contain no science and certainly no solutions to the problems we have to surmount today. Rather, today's economic problems seem to have been caused by disarding ancient wisdoms and adopting modern ideology instead. Modern economics is a contributary cause of our problems, not a solution. The contents of Fekete's approach to economics – based on the sober Austrian economist Carl Menger – will doubtlessly baffle the contemporaneous economics student; he will not encounter anything he recognises and unfortunately, the modern student needs to *detoxify* his mind first form all modern ideologues. So his task is harder. Antal Fekete, being a professional mathematician, has the habit of keeping what must surely come across as a rather stiff pace and high level in his texts. Yet, people with less or no exposure to modern economics indoctrination, provided they grasp some financial algebra, will find their way rather quickly. To overcome the usual confusion in people's minds that may hinder comprehension, I have added a glossary in Volume. And because life is not meant to be taken all that serious, lot's of it is deliberately rather tongue-in-cheek. The end of Volume II doubles as an first introduction to the modern problems completely engineered by what is known today as fiat money, treated in Volume III. The last chapter in Volume II treats the formation of capital markets, not under a gold standard, but under a fiat money standard.

Volume III concerns the results of estrangement from reality in economic science, brought about by this fiat money standard. I called it the lunatic asylum of irredeemable currency. The derailment of economic science becomes luminous as one progresses through this volume. I would not have dared to speak of the 'derailment of economic science' as a young student of 18 years. However, I am unable to suppress my scholarly nature, however dificient. I indulged myself for long enough in this matter of the taboo subject called the gold standard, I have now zero doubt in my mind about the parasitic nature of whatever took its place. Antal Fekete cannot treat insults to humanity with any dignity. Nevertheless, his disparaging language and tone concerning the replacement of the gold standard needs no change in my considered opinion. Volume III exposes the deluded derangements of late 19th and early 20th century *ersatz* economic science. For reasons of political expediency such nonsense holds an entire scientific profession in its grip. Today's economic situation shares all of the hallmarks treated by George Orwell's 1984, socialist and communist utopia's or national socialism better known as Nazism. Would you treat Nazi or communists crimes with any respect?

In Volume IV, if you have made it this far, some more advanced and deeper insights provide the basis for further research. Here too you will find what cannot be found in any standard mainstream economics textbooks: concepts such as *contango, backwardation, basis trading* and the *economics of mining*. But not before we clean the Augean stables and re-theorise the lot. Mainstream economic textbooks show conceptually no difference with revolutionary manuals on how to advance a cause and make the community pay for pet political projects. In case you think I am pretty much off the wall, consider Chapter 48, entitled *Deconstructing Ideologies*. Better yet, study E. Voegelin's *New Science of Politics, An Introduction*, (1958) before taking on contemporary mainstream studies in economic science. Lest any of our readers think these volumes are some madcap conspiracy theory, we can state it formally: conspiracy is hard to prove, short of a confession. However, in a lunatic asylum, contagious madness amongst its occupants acting in unison for no good reason, goes a long way, especially because the protagonists deny being lunatics. If that does not convince you, consider Richard Hooker, late medieval Anglican thinker, who surgically dissects Puritan madmen and analyses their demonic practises to justify murder in the name of religion. To be sure, we can think of others to accuse likewise, but the point is Hooker constructed a precision dissection tool to diagnose what Voegelin has named the 'pneumopathology of gnosticism.' Don Hugo Salinas already provided a glimpse in Volume I's introduction to this important affliction – not of the mind, but of the soul. You may want to pay heed to the symptoms before the contagion spreads to you or your children! One way this estrangment from reality spreads, is by obtaining a platform in television and public schooling, by making tax payers foot the bill. ... Like influenza, I guess we'll never get rid of it.

Voegelin, a contemporary of von Mises, shocked the philosophical world, especially because his diagnosis proved immensely incisive, penetrating and universally applicable in the detection of ideological pathologies. It exposed how widespread and deep the contagion had progressed and that it needed to be barred at all costs from all science, including and especially from philosophy. Voegelin himself granted his choice of terminology could come across a little unfair towards the pre-Christian gnostics. I have chosen nevertheless to go with Voegelin's vocabulary, for he never recanted and had good reasons not to. Doubtlessly, new terminology is badly needed in this unexplored field – even Voegelin admitted. And the field of philosophy (and sociology and economics, ...) needs to develop better languange to describe the realities of life, which have been barred from these fields. I have added the 'dualist' aspect to the list of diagnostic tools – a crippling adjective, denoting amongst other things, a penchant for double standards. Perhaps it helps in clearing the confusion with ancient gnostics, who *rejected* the world, instead of wanting to *transform* its nature, magically. Modern gnostics aim for the latter. Of course, changing something's or someone's nature cannot happen without destroying the object or person. Beware of activists hellbent on 'changing the world'...!

Voegelin not only diagnosed the presence of the contagious affliction, he also formulated a proposal for a cure. Recognising the omnipresence of this worrisome pneumopathology in large groups of people, the healthy realist will refrain nevertheless from engaging in violent activism, lest (s)he stands accused of utilising the same antics as the one (s)he disagrees with. Frustrating as this may be for the energetic defender of civilisation, there is a better way to confront the opposition. We may take an example in the person of Karl Kraus, contemporary of Menger and Voegelin; his famous publication of *Die Dritte*

Walpurgisnacht (a ridicule of Hitler's *Dritte Reich*) may guide us in resisting the modern forms of derailment – derailments such as Nazism, Communism, Maoism, Pol Pot, Scientologists, Branch Davidians, Aum Shinrikyo, Ku Klux Klan and what have you...

Modern derailed gnostics, having been exposed and publicly humiliated, dropped the 'National' in their creed for a new ideological cover called the 'Welfare State', a German invention of the 1870s. Like Carl Menger's contribution to the *Methodenstreit*, all dissenters of the modern welfare state, which is the same *Methodenstreit* under a new name, may expose this new outbreak of the same old disease by poking fun at it!

Caustic satire never was a monopoly of bards or court jesters. Cartoonists lampoon everyone worthy of attention. After all, studying philosophy will inform anybody who cares to respect life and expose stupidity – with respect and caring love for the human nature of the *person* nevertheless. Hating *people* makes for bad karma. Denouncing unacceptable parasitic *behaviour* of people does not fall in the same category, though.

Nevertheless we conclude volume IV with a forward peek into the future and finally, as a closing chapter, we poke some fun at the 'lunatics' in the asylum with an anthology of monetary cranks.

PETER VAN COPPENOLLE

Belgium

PART 8

CLEANING THE AUGEAN STABLES

I. Reconstruction Of Money

⚜ Chapter 38 ⚜

Unadulterated Money

The gold standard is a monetary system which, unlike the regime of irredeemable currency, is free of coercion. Its main significance is not to be found in the stabilisation of prices, which is neither possible nor desirable, but in the stabilisation of interest rates.

A gold standard is established when the unit of currency, or standard of value, is defined by the Constitution as a definite weight of gold of definite fineness. All other forms of currency are then redeemable in gold on demand at the statutory rate. To be effective, a gold standard must have some paraphernalia such as (1) a standardised gold coin, (2) minted free of charge (exclusive of the cost of refining) at the Mint (3) in unlimited quantities on the account of anyone tendering the metal. Furthermore, (4) owners of the gold coins of the realm may hoard them, (5) melt them, (6) export them freely without penalty or the threat thereof. This right is part and parcel of ordinary ownership title which cannot be curtailed, abrogated, or summarily suspended without due processes of law. It should be noted that, although the right of owning property in general may be subject to limitations and could be suspended temporarily in case of extreme emergency (a typical example is the ownership of grain in a town under enemy siege), gold is explicitly exempted from this provision. A shortage of gold, unlike a shortage of grain, never gives rise to an emergency. The consumption of gold is mostly in the arts and jewellery and is never for the satisfaction of the most urgent needs of society. A shortage of gold is always a symptom of mismanagement of the credit system by the banks, usually under the auspices – even sponsorship – of the government. If gold is in short supply, it simply means that individual citizens and creditors of the government are dissatisfied with credit policy. Hoarding gold is the only way they can protest effectively. They will release gold in their control as soon as they have been persuaded that the banks and the government mend their ways and they will keep their promises to pay. They will keep their sight liabilities within the limits of their quick assets. They will create no debts without seeing clearly how these debts can be paid. A shortage of gold, therefore, is not a real shortage and can be ended quickly through corrective measures in bank and government credit policies. The Constitution and the legal system should recognise this by specifically exempting gold from arbitrary seizure under sections of the legal code governing eminent domain.

The gold standard has been criticised for reasons of variation in the exchange value of gold. Critics have charged that gold is not sufficiently stable to serve as the standard of value. (see Part 10 Chrysophobia) To assess this charge we must observe that variations in the exchange value of gold during the past 500 years were the result of the over-issue of fiduciary media redeemable in gold. In the absence of this abuse the exchange value of gold would have conformed to its 'intrinsic' value governed by gold's marginal utility. Gold was promoted to the status of a monetary metal by the markets over thousands of years of evolution that has made the marginal utility of gold as nearly constant as possible (while the marginal utility of other goods is subject to steep decline, more or less. No other commodity would be more stable when used as money. Least stable is the irredeemable currency based on debt. We may therefore, conclude that if the exchange value of gold appears undermined, the culprit is to be found in the unwarranted issue of fiduciary media by the banks under the sponsorship of the government. Moreover, this abuse takes the form of illicit interest arbitrage as elaborated in volume III. The criticism must be re-directed from gold to the legal system of the country, which has failed to outlaw illicit interest arbitrage and borrowing short to lend long.[1]

> There is, therefore, need to re-define a gold standard in such a way that these credit abuses by the banks under the protection of the government are eliminated.

In particular, the exemption of banks from the full penalty under contract law for breach of contract (including the right of creditors to sue for liquidation) and the double standards aiding and abetting banks guilty of understating liabilities and overstating assets, must be abolished. The definition of the unadulterated gold standard must stipulate the removal of all special privileges for the banks. It was these privileges that allowed banks to carry on business as usual after they have defaulted on their promises to pay gold to their depositors. It was these privileges that have let banks borrow short to lend long. It was these privileges that made it possible for them to milk society through the practice of illicit interest arbitrage. The very idea that banks may be allowed to suspend payments in gold coin and continue in business is preposterous. The gold coin is there, in the first place, to protect the bank's creditors against unsound credit practices. Legalising suspension is tantamount to condoning the practice of declaring bankruptcy fraudulently and to confirming the thief in possession of stolen goods. At any rate, legal protection of banks against the legitimate claims of creditors rewards incompetence and fraudulent behaviour while penalising competence and integrity. With such a code, problems will never be solved, only compounded.

Arbitrage Versus Speculation

Critics who argue that the gold standard is inherently unstable confuse the stability of a metallic monetary standard with the instability of the credit of government. They also betray their ignorance of the difference between arbitrage and speculation. No government *per se* can keep the value of the currency stable, except by the good offices of the arbitrageur. If he is persuaded about the good faith behind the promises of the government, then he will step in every time there is a deviation between the nominal and the market value of paper currency in order to restore parity. It is well-understood by students of metallic monetary standards that arbitrage is the catalyst whereby the value of paper currencies is *maintained*. But the arbitrageur will carry on his beneficial activities only if he is fully convinced of the good faith of the government. He will support the value of the government's promise only if it is worth supporting, the judgment being based on past performance, present policy and future intentions. A government that has a record of periodic lapses into bad faith, that makes promises frivolously, that has inclination to declare bankruptcy fraudulently (more commonly known as devaluation) is inviting the arbitrageur to stop supporting its currency.

> In actual fact, conditions influencing the credit of government can be even more precarious. Not only may arbitrageurs, whose support alone maintains the value of government paper, withdraw their services *en masse* and without notice. Worse yet, speculators would be happy to step into the shoes abandoned by the arbitrageurs and cause massive harm to the credit of the government.

The behaviour of the speculators is as different from that of the arbitrageurs as night is different from day. The speculators are specialists in making a market in paper of dubious or uncertain value. They make it their business to study which currency is the weakest and is most likely to fall next. They are totally immune to double talk and the siren song appealing to 'patriotism'. Speculators treat paper currency most disrespectfully. They sell it short. They buy it only at a deep discount.

They are very strong: they can make governments eat their words. They know exactly how to respond to the government's loud declaration that 'the national currency will never ever be devalued'. In this cat-and-mouse game, the role of the *mouse* appears to have been assigned to the *government*.

Currency speculation, just as bond speculation, was virtually unknown under the gold standard. [2] There was only beneficial arbitrage. The sycophant chorus of financial writers and economics professors has never been able to grasp this fundamental fact governing the gold standard. The strength of the gold standard is not grounded in mythology. It is grounded in the superb confidence that arbitrageurs have in the government's promises to pay gold. Once the government destroys the basis for this confidence, arbitrageurs vacate the field which is subsequently occupied by a new breed, the currency and bond speculators. With arbitrage gone, speculators have a field day. They dictate currency values unopposed. They ratchet down the value of all irredeemable currencies, one after another, going after the weakest first. This may make the false impression that the strongest currency is indeed a strong currency. Well, it is not. In no way is it strong in the absolute sense of the word. One can only talk about relative strength: even the strongest currency is losing its value over time, albeit more slowly than the others, but losing it nevertheless.

The Tyranny of Gold

Things are very different under a circulating gold coin standard. If the government has a record of performing punctiliously on its promises to pay gold, if there is no reason to question its good faith, if it has a policy to balance its budget and it can show the revenue that will retire its outstanding debt, then gold comes out of hiding and will flow to government coffers in exchange for paper promises to pay gold. The only competitor gold money may have and that is a formidable competitor indeed, is the promise of the government to pay gold. If the promise can be trusted, then the value of paper will be kept on a par by the arbitrageurs through thin and thick. Here is what Benjamin M. Anderson had to say about the tyranny of gold.

> "*Gold is an unimaginative taskmaster. It demands that men, banks and the government be honest. It demands that they create no debt without seeing clearly how these debts can be paid. If a country will do these things, gold will stay with it and come to it from other countries. But when a country creates debt light-heartedly, when a central bank*

*makes interest rates low and buys government securities to feed its
money market and permits an extension of credit that goes into slow and
illiquid assets, then gold grows nervous. There comes a flight of capital
out of the country. Foreigners withdraw their funds from it and its own
citizens send their liquid funds away for safety.'*

(Op.cit., Chapter 64.)

Legal Tender

Under a gold standard the gold coin is the only legal tender. This
means that only the gold coin is acceptable in unlimited quantities in
discharge of debt, not by coercion but by the free choice of the contracting parties. Other means of payments are acceptable within legal
limits or at the risk (and humiliation) of the receiver. It is important
to realise that the original concept of legal tender has nothing to do
with coercion as it does today. It is a corollary of the principle of the
sanctity of contracts. A search of financial annals fails to reveal an instance of a creditor ever protesting payment in gold coin as contracted.
Originally, legal tender legislation referred to tolerance standards of
circulating coins. Commerce is greatly facilitated if gold coins circulate by tale rather than by weight, thus, bypassing the cumbersome
and time-consuming process of weighing. But then a practical problem arises: creditors may refuse to accept at face value coins that are
worn more or less, thus, undermining the efficiency of the gold standard. The problem is solved by introducing legal tolerance standards
regulating the minimum weight of a gold coin that is still allowed to
circulate by tale, while making substandard coins circulate by weight.
There is no coercion involved. Creditors are not coerced into accepting at face value gold coins with impaired weight. Legal tender legislation, as conceived originally, obliges the government to cover losses
caused by wear and tear of coins in circulation. The Mint will accept
at face value worn gold coins within the limits of tolerance and will
replace them with newly minted ones. The government absorbs the
loss. This is comparable to its function of maintaining public roads in
good repair. This wise provision is enacted to facilitate commerce. It is
unfortunate that the meaning and purpose of legal tender legislation
was later distorted and made an instrument of coercion. Today legal
tender laws are a travesty of justice. They pretend to protect the public;
in actual fact, they protect special interests. Today legal tender means
that creditors are coerced into accepting dishonoured promises to pay
in final discharge of debt and no amount of sophistry can change that

fact. Everybody who accepts and holds an irredeemable bank note is a **creditor** of the government holding evidence of indebtedness (i.e. the government owes the holder)that cannot be validated as a consequence of legal tender legislation. The general public stands to be **victimised** by this piece of chicanery changing the original meaning of the term legal tender, as the 90 percent loss in the purchasing power of the dollar during the 1970s has forcefully demonstrated.

Unadulterated Gold Standard

Under a 'mixed' gold standard the stock of circulating medium has three components:

(1) the gold component,
(2) the clearing component and
(3) the fiduciary component.

The *gold component* consists of the gold coins of the realm in the hand of the general public plus that part of bank notes and deposits which are covered by reserves in the form of gold.

The *clearing component* consists of maturing (gold)bills of exchange in the hands of the public plus that part of bank notes and deposits which are covered on simple demand by assets consisting of such (gold)bills.

The *fiduciary component* consists of that part of bank notes and deposits which belong neither to the gold nor to the clearing component.

The gold standard is called **unadulterated** if the stock of circulating medium has **NO fiduciary component**.

> ▷ This means that the banks issue no bank notes and create no bank deposits except when buying gold or discounting a bill of exchange.
> ▷ Bills of exchange eligible for discounting are strictly limited to those drawn on merchandise in high demand on its way to the final cash-paying consumer, with maturity no longer than 91 days.
> ▷ In particular, the banks are not in the business of discounting finance bills, anticipation and accommodation bills, treasury bills and they buy no stocks, no bonds, nor any mortgages in excess of their liabilities on capital account.

The Haberler-Pigou Effect

The most important consequence of establishing an unadulterated gold standard is that an across-the-board increase in the prices of consumer goods is no longer possible. Such an increase would immediately trigger the Haberler-Pigou effect as follows.

> The consumer controlling the gold coin could effectively resist higher prices by delaying his purchases, buying alternative products, or by patronising outlets selling at the old price. This consumer action would roll prices back, should an across-the-board increase in prices ever occur.

The fact is that such an increase would inflict capital losses on the consumer, which would show up in the consolidated balance sheet of the nation. He would have to recoup the loss by restraining consumption. This restraint is the driving force behind the roll-back of prices.

> Note, however, that the Haberler-Pigou effect **does not operate on the fiduciary component** of the stock of circulating media. To the extent that fiduciary media are in circulation, the effectiveness of the protection that the gold coin provides to the consumers is undermined.

The consumers may, if they care, try to combat higher prices by delaying or limiting purchases or by shifting custom. It is still true that they have suffered a capital loss but, because they are creditors to the extent of their holdings of fiduciary media, another group of people 'their debtors' will experience capital gains equal to the creditors capital losses. The effect of the stepped-up spending of the latter offsets that of the spending restraint of the former, thus, validating the price advances.

The consolidated balance sheet of the nation shows no change, Hence, individual resistance to higher prices remains ineffective.

The price level under the adulterated gold standard and, for the stronger reason, under the regime of irredeemable currency, is no longer stable. If a country wants a **stable price level** for consumer goods, it will have to adopt the **unadulterated gold standard**.[3]

The Quantity Theory Of Money

Detractors of the gold standard argue that fluctuations in gold production influence the price level adversely. In particular, a decline in gold production causes deflation, economic contraction and unemployment. This is false. Our argumentation can be found in volumes II and III.

Moreover, in deflation prices fall and in response marginal gold mines go into production. The quantity theory is a very crude device which would be valid only in the antiseptic world where credit is non-existent and all payments for consumer goods are made in gold coin, where merchandise is always consumed upon purchase and never re-sold. In reality, a large part of payments in a modern economy are for future delivery, often for products not yet in existence. Even if payments are for immediate delivery, the goods can be sold and re-sold several times before they disappear into consumption. As we have seen, the theory of social circulating capital is the *exact opposite* of the quantity theory. It demonstrates that the supply of consumer goods is determined by demand. Moreover, the mechanism that makes the adjustment of supply to demand operates, not on prices, but on the discount rate.

A second, even more serious objection to the quantity theory of money is that, as its name suggests, it is completely blind to the quality of circulating media, the stock of which has many components each of different quality. This is especially important in the case of components consisting of credit instruments. The government can, of course, make the quality of purchasing media uniform by centralising credit. However, this can never improve the quality of the currency, but can make it deteriorate. It is well-known that credit instruments of inferior quality go to a discount in the markets. It is disingenuous to explain away currency depreciation by quantitative arguments. First, there are obvious examples showing that credit instruments of inferior quality can lose all their market value even if their quantity is constant or decreasing. Second, even if it were true that historically all currencies losing their purchasing power showed a simultaneous increases in their quantity, this would not establish a causality relation between the quantity and the purchasing power of money. The chain of causation may well run in the opposite direction. Several qualified observers noted that in hyperinflation an acute shortage of the circulating medium develops owing to the accelerating decline in the purchasing power of the monetary unit and the central bank is under pressure to put more bank notes into circulation than originally intended, in order to alleviate the shortage.

This means that in fact there is no unambiguous causality relation between the quantity and the purchasing power of the circulating medium. The only way to get to the crux of the matter is to study the quality of the circulating media or, if they have been made homogeneous by the centralisation of credit, then to analyse the history and the marketability of the assets on the books of the monetary authority balancing its note and deposit liabilities. Several authors argue that the quality of credit is of no significance because, thanks to legal tender legislation, creditors are obliged to accept irredeemable currency in discharge of debt in any amount without demur. This is a shallow, not to say cynical, answer to a problem that deserves a deeper and more earnest analysis.

Basically there are two sides to the problem: the behaviour of domestic and foreign creditors. As the writ of the government stops at the border, the latter are not bound by legal tender legislation. Foreign creditors are not in the habit of giving advance notice of their intention to dump the paper of a government to which they owe no allegiance. This shows that the quantity theory puts the country's resources embodied in its foreign credit into jeopardy. This is a very serious matter even if the country in question is self-sufficient in essential raw materials.

Considering the behaviour of domestic creditors, the problem boils down to the question whether the producers of goods and services will indefinitely keep exchanging real goods and services for irredeemable promises to pay which, by their very nature, constantly depreciate in value. If history is any guide, then these merchants and workers will not allow the government to victimise them indefinitely. They can do something about it. They could re-introduce bill-circulation.

The World Without Banks

People who handle the social circulating capital have, without realising it, a most potent instrument in their hand, namely, the bills they still keep drawing on one another. Presently the movement of goods to the consumer is financed by bank credit of questionable quality. However, banks are progressively discrediting themselves in the eyes of the population.

> When the payment system breaks down, there will be starvation amidst plenty and, rightly or wrongly, the banks will be made scapegoats.

At that point bills drawn on merchandise in urgent demand will start to circulate, replacing irredeemable paper issued by the government.

It is futile to speculate about the future course that history may take. But it appears that the rise of an international bill market on merchandise in most urgent demand is ultimately inevitable, if an all-out trade war is to be averted. Such a bill market would be the most potent force in the preservation of international division of labour. It would be a precision-instrument activating instant changes in the direction, size and composition of the flow of short-term capital to countries that need it most urgently. No time would be lost in negotiating government credits, doing legal work and other formalities. Moreover, short-term capital would be dispatched to the country in need in the form of consumer goods which were in most urgent demand. If the discount rate in a country rose above the level prevailing elsewhere in the world, consumer goods would be dispatched on the same day to that country, since it was a good place on which to draw bills. It would be the discount rate that would direct the flow of short-term capital world wide, rather than political considerations. The nimbleness of the discount rate and the instantaneous response to its changes by drawers and acceptors of bills, would be the guarantee of each and every country adhering to the international gold standard that the full complement of international division of labour stood by in the hour of its need to help solve its problems quickly and efficiently. Far more quickly and efficiently than autarky or politically motivated inter-governmental assistance ever could.

The Mistake of Sound-Money Advocates

This marvellous instrument, the bill market based on the international gold standard, was the first casualty of the guns of August in 1914. The governments of the garrison states that emerged after the cessation of hostilities did not allow the bill market to make a come-back. There has been no bill-trading on a world-scale for the past eighty-eight years. In spite of prodigious increases in world trade, it took eighty years to surpass the volume prevailing in 1913. Today foreign trade and relief is the business of the governments (i.e., none of your business). The direction, the size and composition of foreign trade is determined by political considerations, rather than by need. People who control liquid funds are intimidated. If they send their funds abroad in search of better returns, those funds may be frozen by foreign exchange controls and may be subject to capital losses due to currency devaluation. Foreign trade is at the pleasure of the governments which could slam on tariffs, quotas, or punitive embargo without notice. Even in countries that tolerate import and export on private account, trade is subject to lengthy licensing procedures and other government controls. By the time the permit is issued, the opportunity to import or export profitably may well be lost.

> Profits are impossible to calculate due to the daily (or hourly) variation in foreign exchange rates. International division of labour and individual self-reliance are reduced to insignificance,

while everybody is made utterly dependent on government largesse and ukase.

Advocates of sound money made a grave mistake at the end of hostilities in 1918 when, in demanding a return to the gold standard, they failed to call for a full rehabilitation of the international bill market. They allowed the banks to hijack the social circulating capital, thereby disenfranchising the producers and the savers. Instead of an unadulterated gold standard, the politicians set up an international gold standard of a most adulterated kind: the *gold bullion* and the *gold exchange* standard. In the 1920s there was much talk about the shortage of gold. In actual fact the shortage was caused by the deliberate policy to withdraw gold coins from circulation and to replace them with bank notes of small denomination. When people see that the government is out to grab the gold coin, their natural reaction is to clutch theirs ever so tightly. The correct policy should have been to place gold coins in the hand of the consumers and trade should have been financed by bill circulation. The gold shortage would have disappeared as if by magic, facilitating reconstruction. Instead, an orgy of debt pyramiding, commodity, real estate and stock market speculation followed. The debt pyramid collapsed at the end of the 'Roaring Twenties' giving way the Great Depression. Ever since the international monetary system is 'on a 24-hour basis', meaning that it is a non-system based on constant government meddling. The gold standard was doomed, as it was no longer reinforced by a bill market linking the flow and ebb of circulating media to the flow and ebb of newly emerging merchandise in the markets.

These mistakes must not be repeated now. The Mint should be opened to gold at once. If the U.S. government refuses to do that, it will run the risk that the regime of the irredeemable dollar will collapse, causing enormous economic pain to the American people, similar to the pain the people of Argentina or Venezuela are now put through. As a solution to the problem, gold coins should be placed directly in the hand of the consumers and trade should be financed by bill circulation. There is no need to give blood transfusion to the banks.
Let them die in peace.

The Relevance of the Gold Standard to Capitalism

Let us raise the question: what is capitalism?
In its simplest form capitalism is an economic system which is based on the concept that individuals should and would produce as generously as possible and live on something less than they produce, in order

that they may posses a residue in the form of legally (socially) protect-ed property to insure the education of their young, the support of their elderly and other future projects of theirs. However, in order to achieve these ends we must have a facility to exchange income for wealth and wealth for income. Interest, in this view, is not a premium on present goods as opposed to future goods, but the indicator of the efficiency of converting wealth into income and income into wealth. In particular, zero interest marks the least efficient way of converting, namely, the conversion of income into wealth by hoarding gold and of wealth into income by dishoarding it.

Capitalism is an economic system that makes the spontaneous capi-talisation of incomes possible. In more details, capitalism means unob-structed and uninhibited capital formation through the voluntary part-nership of the annuitant (typically, an elderly man drawing an annuity) and the entrepreneur (who pays the annuity income from the return to capital put at his disposal in the form of wealth of the annuitant). (See Vol. II) Capitalism means a gold bond market where the residual savings of the people are pooled, parcelled and allocated. In the gold bond market the marginal producer is free to perform his function as arbitrageur between two types of earning assets: capital goods and gold bonds. It is this arbitrage that validates the marginal productivity of capital in fixing the ceiling for the rate of interest. Capitalism means a gold standard without which the marginal bondholder would be unable to perform his function as arbitrageur between present goods (gold) and future goods (the gold bond). It is this arbitrage that validates the marginal time preference of the saving public in fixing the floor for the rate of interest. Capitalism means a bill market where the marginal shopkeeper is free to perform his function as arbitrageur between the two forms of social circulating capital: fast-moving merchandise and bills drawn on them. It is this particular arbitrage that validates the marginal productivity of the social circulating capital, in determining the discount rate.

Insofar as gold is the indispensable catalyst of spontaneous capitali-sation of incomes, the government's deliberate destruction of the gold standard is to be considered a major step towards the destruction of capitalism. Government intervention in the bill and bond markets may bring no possible benefit to society and is likely to make conditions for human welfare worse. Intervention in the bill market falsifies the discount rate and intervention in the bond market falsifies the inter-est rate. The falsification of these important indicators causes serious misallocation of resources and paralyses the regenerative faculty of the economy. It will, little-by-little, destroy our distinctively human symbiosis: the peaceful and voluntary cooperation of individuals under the system of international division of labour. This symbiosis was the vision of the greatest practitioners of our science: Adam Smith, Carl Menger and others. The invisible hand of the market, through the signal function of prices, discount and interest rates, guides the 'selfish' pursuits of individuals and harnesses their efforts for the greater benefit of the commonweal.

In the words of the Bard: *'One for all, all for one we gage.'*
And this shall remain the best hope for mankind.

Endnotes to Chapter 38

[1] The legal system is usually a positive law system and once again, positivism would have to be carefully examined in law, especially in a constitution. E. Voegelin fell out with his mentor Kelsen - a known constitutional positivist- about this very subject and his criticism can be found in Voegelin's work.

[2] It would be non-existent under an unadulterated gold standard, for one cannot speculate against oneself.

[3] This then, is the simple task of central issuing banks (but also FED, ECB, BoE, BoJ,...) which they neither can nor ever will implement as its official raison d'être cuts perpendicular to its instrumentation.

Dismantle the central banks, BIS, World Bank, IMF, etc... and reopen the Mints. Let's not kid ourselves. What started out as a harebrained scheme, grew into a massive abuse, attracting the psychopaths of the world driven by their *libido dominandi*. Removing these people and preventing them from hijacking the institutions of the people like the Mint, or genuine government will prove a Herculean task. But allowing them to continue will come at the price of losing our entire civilisational achievements.

～ Chapter 39 ～

Resurrect the Latin Monetary Union

The sovereign debt problem, especially as it threatens Greece, Italy, Spain and through them the entire European Monetary System, is like the Gordian knot. Moreover, the solution is similar to that of Alexander the Great. He thought of doing something nobody before him did and nobody after him could: he drew his sword and cut the knot. The solution of the Gordian knot of the European Monetary System is very similar, except there is a little extra secret. It would not work unless the sword was made of gold.

During the recent protracted debate about raising the debt-ceiling in the United States not once was the word 'gold' uttered. That is an indication of the I.Q. of American politicians. Are their European counterparts any better? Possibly. They at least understand that gold and debt go hand in hand. Debt within reason, that is.

A proper diagnosis of the debt crisis reveals that the world's payments system as it is presently constituted lacks an ultimate extinguisher of debt. The pipe dream that the fiat dollar or the fiat Euro could serve as such was shattered as the Great Financial Crisis unfolded. When paying debt with dollars, the debt is not extinguished. It is merely transferred from the debtor to the U.S. Treasury. Transferring debt is not the same as extinguishing it. There is a saturation point which, when reached, will cause the welcome-mat for the dollar withdrawn. This is nothing new: the world was treated to the dress rehearsal already forty years ago: in 1971. [See Exhibit A] At that time finance ministers and central bankers succeeded in convincing people that the secret of turning the dollar into an ultimate extinguisher of debt is Milton Friedman's formula: the stock of dollars must not be increased faster than the cabalistic rate of 3% per annum.

Then they did some fancy footwork in redefining money supply to make 7% look more like 3%. When that did not work, they tried heroically to push interest rates down all the way to 0, following the script of John M. Keynes. That worked for a while, until it bankrupted weaker countries such as Portugal, Ireland, Italy, Greece and Spain that could no longer sell their debt in competition to U.S. Treasury debt the value of which has been increasing for the past 30 years.

No matter how you look at it: there is only one ultimate extinguisher of debt that always works, rain or shine, war or peace and that is gold.

But gold could not perform its ordained function of discharging debt if it is locked up in central bank vaults, while debt keeps piling up in the world economy in want of an ultimate extinguisher. What's going on? Well, doctrinaire economists prevent gold from entering the monetary bloodstream. Governments are brow-beaten if they as much as uttered the word 'gold'. Their knee-jerk reaction is to follow the Keynesian-Friedmanite script.

Greece, Italy and Spain are great nations. They have talented and hard-working people, first-rate institutions, they have some exquisite natural resources, including sunshine and the best tourist-destinations in the world. They've also got gold. What they don't have is a gold income – but that's their own fault.

My message to them is: don't let doctrinaires blind your vision and steer you away from your unique opportunity to save and restore the credit of your nation. You can do it in two easy steps, neither of which involves bailouts. Both of them involve your great European traditions, such as the Latin Monetary Union and its great gold and silver coinage.

Step One: Gold Income For the Government [1]

The credit of a government depends, for the most part, on its ability to secure a gold income. In order to have one, the government must open the Mint to gold and keep it open to the unlimited coinage of gold and silver for the account of anyone bringing the metal for coining. It will not be free, but a seigniorage charge as low at 5 percent applies. It will be a monopoly income initially. As your monopoly erodes because other countries will play copycat, it will get smaller. But you have made a head-start. Further gold and silver income could be derived from custom duties, excise and real estate taxes. We have an historical example showing how that works in practice. In 1862 during the American Civil War the North introduced irredeemable currency, endearingly called 'greenbacks'. The Union did not close the Mint to gold and silver; nor did it make the greenback unlimited legal tender. Certain taxes such as custom duties and excise taxes continued to be payable in gold coin. The Union did have a gold income.

To this you could add real estate taxes payable in silver. The gold revenue of your country could be used to eliminate government debt in irredeemable Euros, as will be discussed below. The silver revenue from real estate taxes should be collected by local governments and it could be used to finance public works. That would extend the employment base locally. Unemployment insurance, so called, ought to be abolished altogether. In this world you get what you pay for. You get unemployment if that's what you pay for. But you get clean streets, pleasant public parks, great infrastructure and happily employed people if you pay those who are willing to work and, if necessary, relocate away from big cities.

Mintage could start with the two great standard coins of the now defunct Latin Monetary Union – to which all three countries used to belong : the standard 20-franc gold piece and the standard silver piece formerly called 5 franc but now has to be renamed since the tie between the values of the gold franc and the silver franc has been cut. Let's call the former 5-franc silver piece Thaler. Fractional gold and silver coins would also be struck in order to facilitate the payment of these levies. There must be no rigid ratio set between the value of the 20-franc gold cold coin and the silver Thaler. Neither must the Euro 'price' of gold and the Euro price of silver, nor must their ratio be fixed: they must all be determined by the market.

Please note that what I recommend here is not a metallic monetary standard. That would be far too controversial and it would put the success of the reform in jeopardy. The Euro bank notes and coins would continue to circulate as before, except they would no longer be legal tender for the payment of certain taxes. What I describe here is a scheme to mobilise gold and silver to help finance government.

Step Two: Refinancing Government Debt With Gold Bonds & Sinking Fund.

The governments of Greece, Italy and Spain should offer 30-year **gold** bonds and 10-year **silver** bonds in exchange for their outstanding Euro-bond obligations. This would be the first gold bond issue in the world since 1935. There is a great pent-up demand in the world for gold bonds. In taking the initiative and making them available once more, Greece, Italy and Spain would show the way for the United States and other European countries how to harness gold-bond financing to avoid bankruptcy. All the over-indebted country needs to do is to mobilise its gold reserves. [2]

Why Does Gold-Financing of Government Work?

It adds new resources, heretofore idle, namely, government-owned gold, to the liquid wealth of the nation. Privately owned gold may be coaxed out of hiding, further increasing the liquid wealth of the nation. One ounce of gold 'on the go' is worth ten ounces idled, just like one acre of cultivated land is worth ten acres left fallow.

Circulating gold inspires confidence; gold kept under lock indicates lack of confidence.

Gold is a great stabiliser. Fiat money has never succeeded in stabilising foreign exchange rates; gold is doing it routinely if given the chance.

Fiat money has never succeeded in stabilising interest rates. Gold can do it. Stabilisation of interest rates is extremely important: volatile interest rates spell capital erosion or even destruction. Stabilisation of prices is neither possible, nor desirable. Variation of prices is a market signal that could be suppressed only at your peril. Stabilisation of interest rates is both possible and desirable.

Gold has always been used as money directly or indirectly throughout history, for thousands of years. In 1971 gold was forcibly removed from the monetary system and was replaced by 'synthetic credit'. The result was: disaster. Now, a mere forty years later, we are facing a complete credit collapse, due to the Debt Tower ready to topple. The conceit of the managers of the international monetary system exceeds the conceit of the builders of the biblical Tower of Babel.

Under an irredeemable currency system bonds are irredeemable as well. This removes the logical basis supporting lending, including lending to the government.

One day the world will wake up and realise that the enormous paper wealth it thought it had has just disappeared. The shock and the suffering that is bound to follow would be devastating. Yet no one can say that it came unexpected. Tried innumerable times, experiments with irredeemable currency have always ended in disaster.[3]

A gold bond promises to pay interest and principal in standard gold francs; a silver bond, in standard silver thalers. This promise should be stated on the face of the bond, together with a declaration that the country issuing the bond considers repudiation unconstitutional, immoral and reprehensible and would not allow to happen again.

The coupon rate on the gold bonds should be fixed at fifty basis points above the one-year gold lease rate and the coupon rate on the silver bonds at five basis points above the one-year silver lease rate, both averaged for the past ten-year period.

Three *sinking funds* should be maintained by these countries: the first to keep the value of the gold bond on a par, the second to keep the value of the silver bond on a par; and a third one, a Euro-fund, to support the price of the country's outstanding Euro-bonds, should it be necessary. The expectation is that the market will have a preference for the gold and silver bonds. Therefore, these countries will be able to retire the outstanding public debt on favourable terms over a ten-year period. A residual gold-bonded and silver-bonded debt would remain.

However, these are needed in order to support the operation of insurance companies, pension funds and other financial institutions.

The gold and silver bonds would be highly liquid in view of the sinking-fund protection. The interest rate on them could be used as the benchmark in bank lending and in issuing corporate bonds, gold backed.

The plan to mobilise the gold resources of Greece, Italy and Spain, if adopted, will stabilise government finances in these countries. The rate of interest on gold and silver bonds is the lowest possible. These countries will refinance their public debt in making them gold-bonded or silver-bonded. The sword of Damocles, the threat of a violent increase of the rate of interest on the public debt, needlessly haunting a lot of countries under the regime of irredeemable currency, will be permanently removed.

The example of these pioneer countries will probably be contagious. If adopted world-wide, the system of financing government through gold and silver would inject new liquidity into the international monetary system sufficient not only to fend off a threatening world depression, but also to imbue the domestic and world economy with great optimism concerning future prosperity. Domestic economies, as well as the world economy would start growing again.

There could be no better way to pay homage to the ancient Greeks and Romans to whom we owe most of the values of our civilisation than letting these three countries: Greece, Italy and Spain lead the world back to monetary and fiscal rectitude.

Side Notes On The Latin Monetary Union [4]

By a convention dated December 23, 1865, four charter members: France, Belgium, Italy and Switzerland formed the Latin Monetary Union (LMU). They adopted a common bimetallic currency, in France, Belgium and Switzerland called the franc, in Italy (inclusive of the Vatican state) called the lira, defined as 4.5 grams of silver or 0.290322 gram of gold, 900 fine (a bimetallic ratio of 15½ :1). The design, although not the size, of coins minted by different countries were different. The idea was to facilitate trade between different countries by making their coins perfectly *interchangeable*.

The agreement came into force on August 1, 1866. The four nations were joined by Greece with its drachma and Spain with its peseta in 1868. In 1889 four more European and a South American country,

Venezuela (the only fully-fledged non-European member in the history of the LMU) with its bolivar joined.

The basic cause of failure of the LMU was its adherence to bimetallism, in spite of evidence that it was not a stable monetary system. It pretended that the gold/silver market price ratio was constant when, in fact, it was variable. Sometimes the market undervalued gold at the Mint, at other times it undervalued silver. As a consequence, bimetallism was in reality a flip-flop between silver monometallism (when the market ratio undervalued gold at the Mint) and gold monometallism (when the market ratio undervalued silver). This had the wasteful consequence that silver and gold were flowing back-and-forth between the Mint and the refinery. When gold was undervalued at the Mint, gold coins moved to the refinery to be melted down; when silver was undervalued at the Mint, silver coins moved to the refinery to be melted down. In either case, the other metal was moving to the Mint to be coined. This arbitrage meant risk free profits for the arbitrageur at the expense of the Treasury. The solution to the problem would have been a dual monetary system using both gold and silver coins, but without a fixed official bimetallic ratio. It is most unfortunate that the LMU did not make a recommendation along these lines. Bimetallism consequently 'self-destructed', as it were. Germany made a fateful step in demonetising silver and making gold monometallism official, at the same time selling very large quantities of silver from melted coins in the world market. The world price of silver went into a tailspin, taking the gold/silver price ratio from a low of 15 ½ :1 in 1874 to a high of 85:1 in 1932. [5] The LMU closed its Mints to silver in 1878; to gold, in 1936. Subsidiary silver coins made according to the standards of the LMU were discontinued in member countries other than Switzerland during World War I.[6] In Switzerland they continued until well after World War II; the last ones were made in 1967. Having lost its purpose, the LMU disbanded in 1927.

The resurrection of the LMU would add a great deal of liquid wealth to the world's financial resources. I have admitted above that a rapid change back to the gold standard at this juncture is not feasible or, at least, is not realistic. On the other hand it appears insane to quarantine monetary gold for no better reason than that it offers an unwelcome competition to the regime of irredeemable currency, when there is such a great need for it in order to stabilise debt in the world economy. Thus, the resurrection of the LMU may be the happy compromise, bringing about a hybrid monetary system in the world, paper and metallic, with a variable exchange rate between them. 'Let the people choose.'

Central bankers of the world show themselves superbly confident that with their expertise and skills the regime of irredeemable currency can be made a durable and stable monetary system. Whatever one may think about their self-confidence, it might take a revolution to remove central bankers from power in spite of the fact that their hold on power is apparently getting ever wobblier as time goes on. The reason for this is the fast breeder of debt that irredeemable currency set into motion and the lack of an ultimate extinguisher of debt that could stabilise the system.

But to have an open mind about it, let us not exclude the possibility that the hybrid monetary system may work. The resurrection of LMU would solve the problem of runaway debt, since the mobilisation of monetary gold in the European economy could make an orderly debt-reduction possible. This seems to be the only chance for the regime of irredeemable currency to 'save its hide.' Central bankers may see the writing on the wall. Be that as it may, it is up to the central bankers to prove that the monetary system they manage is able to compete with gold and silver.

In closing I shall answer the question: where will people get the gold and silver to be able to pay the taxes that will give the gold and silver income to the government? I admit that this question goes to the heart of the matter. Some retrenching on the part of consumers may be necessary. Let me look at two typical cases.

Some cutback in imports may be necessary because a part of the final price paid at the cashier includes gold taxes that not everybody may be prepared to pay. Fine, so domestic industry has to reinvent itself to satisfy the demand of those who opt out of paying the import duties. This in itself may be a good thing, as it will contribute to 'job creation'. But obviously there will be enough people who want the imported goods, do have the gold and are willing to pay it out in the form of custom duty and excise tax to have them. Their spending 'will prime the pump' and put gold coins into circulation.

Some cutback in owner-occupied housing may be necessary because not every home-owner has the silver to pay the real estate taxes involved in home-ownership.

Fine, so the rental-property industry has to reinvent itself and satisfy the demand for housing of those who want to opt out paying the real estate tax. This in itself may be a good thing because not every bread-winner is able to handle the financing of such a major purchase as a home. But obviously there will be enough people who want to own their home, do have the silver and are willing to pay it out in the form of real estate taxes to have it. Their spending, again, 'will prime the pump' and put silver coins into circulation. In this way, starting with the purchases of luxury and big-ticket items, the purchasers will have to dig into their gold or silver hoard and take their metals to the Mint for coining. As we have seen, this in itself will have help easing the debt problem of the government and start the process of 'dishoarding' the monetary metals, gold and silver.

So whatever people decide to do, whether to pay the gold and silver taxes or not, some benefits will accrue to society and that's the way it should be.

***

The resurrection of the Latin Monetary Union will, of course, be a challenge to central bankers. They may not like the idea of having to compete with gold and silver coins. For this reason, there is a conflict of interest which dictates that the Mint must be completely independent of the Central Bank.

It would be wonderful if Greece, Italy and Spain turned defeat into victory and resurrected the Latin Monetary Union with a new series of silver and gold coins that would actually circulate domestically and across national boundaries. While the exchange rate between domestic paper money and the gold and silver coins would fluctuate, foreign exchange (consisting of gold and silver coins) rates within the LMU would not. And that would be a great blessing to the world economy, facilitating an increase in world trade, ultimately benefiting everybody.

Endnotes to Chapter 39

[1] An honest government may be a stretch at any time ...See Plato's *Republic* and make sure you either read the original Greek or obtain a good , i.e. ideologically neutral translation.

[2] It is not all, there is more : they would necessarily have to break their IMF and World Bank and OECD treaties, to whom these countries are parties. Several of its senior civil servants have strong positions, commitments and promises for career advancement within these parasitical organisations. It would be tantamount to and much bigger than another Brexit showdown. This is how strong the self-destructive parasite is that holds civilisations in its deadly iron grip.

[3] See Ralph T Nelson, *ibid*.

[4] The Latin Monetary Union is the complete antithesis of the World Bank, OECD and IMF treaties. Civil servants losing their careers in the IMF or World Bank may not necessarily be transplanted to the new LMU. They have diametrically opposed ends.

[5] At the time of writing the silver to gold ratio has been fluctuating from 40:1 and about 80:1

[6] Preparations to introduce enforced checking accounts were made in 1909 through social laws in France and Germany.

II. Reconstruction Of Credit

Ꙩ Chapter 40 Ꙩ

Spontaneous Bill Circulation

In the words of the Old Testament 'the use of false weights and measures is the greatest abomination in the eyes of the Lord'. (King James Version, Wycliffe translation, Proverbs, XX1 0.)
The Great Coin Melt of 1933 by Franklin D. Roosevelt certainly, answers the description 'greatest abomination'. He confiscated the gold coins of the American people; he melted them down and wrote up the value of the proceeds. He pretended to have compensated people for their stolen gold by giving them Federal Reserve notes in exchange. The historical record shows that these notes have, by 1971, in hardly more than a generation, lost 98 percent of their purchasing power. Then, to crown a great job done, Roosevelt by Executive Order [1] closed the U.S. Mint to gold in order to prevent succeeding generations from undoing the damage. They were condemned never to be able to recover their honest weights and measures: Along with their gold coins of the realm they have also been deprived of their Mint where new ones could have been struck.

The question that arises from all this is as follows: has Roosevelt succeeded in mesmerising all people of the world, present, past and future in making them believe that the broken promises of the U.S.government can be used as a true measure of value? – With unlimited debt-extinguishing power to boot, in order to match that of the gold coins? Shall the remonetisation of gold really be impossible forever and ever? – as the 'Amen' choruses of Keynesians and Friedmanites shout from their rooftops? – Or, perhaps, after all, the human race is not condemned to worshipping the 'paper calf' of irredeemable currency in perpetuity, since the shock of the Great Coin Melt, has cured it of the disease called by Virgil in the Aeneid *Auri sacra fames* (the accursed hunger for gold). – as imputed by Keynes.

Relief is coming from the free market in the form of a substitute in the form of a universally acceptable means of payments the stock of which no central bank but the people themselves directly regulates – as indeed ordained by the U.S. Constitution.

Now, for the first time, we are getting the answers these questions.

Like it or not, we see that the stupidity of the monetary scientists, (so-called), of the 20th century yields to the enlightenment of the 21st. The ingenuity of people (under pressure but still in a relatively free market) has come up with a synthetic substitute for a new metamorphosis of gold. Roosevelt's closing of the U.S. Mint is getting overruled. It consists in converting twenty-five kinebars into one octandor, a new universally acceptable unit of value (see the glossary in this text, below), the stock of which is regulated directly by all people willing and able to obtain them rather than an unconstitutionally established central bank.

Introduction

Falling prices and vanishing world trade in the wake of devastating currency wars with no winners but with lots of losers are a clear indication of our deflation morphing into a depression. The international monetary system based on the irredeemable dollar is in its death-throes. What kind of monetary regime will follow it?
The foolhardy insists that whatever it will be, under no circumstances will it be the gold standard:
> *'You cannot put spent toothpaste back into the tube!'*
> *'You must not resurrect the extinct barbarous relic!'*
What kind of currency will the 'wave of the future' bring? Why, it will bring the defaulting banker's dishonoured promises, naturally. Similar propaganda was spread in past centuries every time an influential banker defaulted on his promises to pay. It is true that the latest episode in the saga of turning the *lowest kind of money* (namely, fraudulent promises) into the *highest* (namely, high-powered central bank credit) has been the longest. But it does not follow that 'this time it's different'.

The exiled sovereign, gold, is being reinstated on its throne before our very eyes through reinventing Carl Menger's 'most marketable good' through spontaneous market processes – never mind the wishes of the government or others. Profit seeking business is also reinventing Adam Smith's real bill maturing into the unit of value of the realm.

The Resurrection of the Real Bill

What is more important still, circulation of real bills subject to discount turns gold into an earning asset. Once again, gold is able to return an income in gold through the mechanism of discounting – exactly as it has been the case before World War I. To understand the significance

CREDIT AND ITS TWO SOURCES – VOLUME IV

of this development we have to go back and retrace history to see how the gold standard was sabotaged after hostilities ended in November, 1918.

The victorious Entente Powers had to lift their sea blockade of Germany pursuant to the Armistice agreement. In their wisdom, policymakers decided to keep blocking the circulation of gold bills financing Germany's foreign trade. They thought it was a smart move to replace the blockade with the blocking of the bill market. They failed to see that this was tantamount to castrating the international gold standard by removing its clearing house, the London bill market. The policymakers wanted to blunt the efficiency of German industry, [2] even at the cost of forcing inefficient bilateral trade (a liars barter) on the world replacing the much more efficient multilateral trade under the international gold standard.

The measure boomeranged. The destruction of the London bill market also meant the destruction of the Wage Fund (See Rittershausen, supra Volume II) out of which the wages of workers producing merchandise were paid, up to 91 days before the merchandise was paid for in cash by the consumers themselves. There was a hiatus of 91 days in paying the wage-bill. There was no one to advance the funds. Workers had to be laid off. The result was a hideous worldwide unemployment.

> Policymakers who were responsible for the disaster in the first place were quick to blame it on the whipping boy, the 'contractionist' gold standard.

But truth must ultimately be told. The unprecedented tsunami of unemployment was not a failure of the gold standard. On the contrary, it was the consequence of blocking the circulation of gold bills by the victorious Entente Powers. It was the direct consequence of their malicious trade policy wanting to cripple Germany's foreign trade after lifting the wartime blockade, by other means.

Now, for the first time since November, 1918, gold bills are getting ready to circulate once more, whether the British and the U.S. government, the chief culprits of sabotaging the gold standard like it or not. This will change the nature of gold hoarding. People will scramble to exchange their gold bullion for gold bills. They want to take the opportunity to earn an income in gold by reinvesting the proceeds from maturing gold bills into fresh gold bills.

Earning an income in gold is vastly different from earning an income in irredeemable dollars. Hoarding dollars has by now lost all its roots in logic. If the dollar were able to retain its value as long as the depreciation cycle was completed, it did make sense to build dollar reserves for the purpose of replacing physical capital after its value was eroded through natural wear and tear. But the point where the dollar could no longer do this is long since passed. As a result of deliberate debasement the dollar is losing its value so fast that less is left after the completion of the depreciation cycle than what is needed to defray the cost of buying new capital goods. The acceleration has by now reached the level that the dollar is useless for the purpose of serving as catalyst to replace capital eroding through wear and tear. You might as well save in a substance that evaporates before you can catch enough of it.

As people switch from hoarding gold to generating a gold income a point must be reached where as much gold is released from hoards as it takes to finance the production and distribution of foodstuff in most urgent demand. Anything less means world-famine in the midst of plenty (echoing the famine during the Great Depression of the 1930s). Thus, then, gold bills will take over the financing of trade in a world increasingly reluctant to accept the irredeemable dollar (or, for that matter, any other irredeemable currency) in exchange for real goods and real services.

The solution for the problem of replacing the dishonoured dollar as a reserve currency lies not in the inventing of yet another Esperanto currency, be it called euro, asio, africo, amero or australo. The solution lies in reinventing Adam Smith's real bill that has served the world well for many a century. I shall now explain this transition that is destined to save the world from famine – and civilisation from turning itself into barbarism.

Glossary

Kinebar is the name of a 5 gram, 9999 fine gold wafer produced and stamped by the State Mint of Austria with a serial number. The obverse of the kinebar is stamped with a hologram depicting a rider of the Spanish Riding School of Vienna in action. The movements of horse and rider explain how the kinebar earns its name. The production of kinebars was suspended in 2014. Equivalent 5gram 9999 fine gold wafers continue to be manufactured by the Austrian State Mint. We shall refer to these wafers in the sequel as 'kinebars'.

Octandor (rhymes with 'octane door') is the name of a composite gold bar, resembling a bar of chocolate, made up of twenty-five kinebars. The total weight of an octandor is 125 grams or slightly over 4 Troy ounces. This makes it equally marketable in Europe and America. 'Octandor' is abridgement for 'one eighth of one kilogram of gold'. This explains how the octandor earns its name. Octandors can be exchanged at the rate of one hundred to one for international good delivery gold bars weighing 400 ounces or 12 ½ kilograms (more or less).

Octandors are designed to compete with gold coins. [3] They are 9999 fine, as compared with the gold coin's usual fineness of only 8350.[4] Moreover, gold coins fail to be divisible. At any rate, if broken up into smaller pieces, a gold coin ceases to be negotiable – except after costly assaying. By contrast, octandors enjoy divisibility into kinebars without any loss of value. What is more, they can be individually identified through serial numbers with which the component kinebars are stamped – which gold coins can't. Thus, octandors, unlike gold coins, are suitable for purposes of making allocated deposits at depository institutions.

To recapitulate, octandors represent a significant improvement in marketability over that of traditional gold coins.

Matador is the suggested name of a firm whose business is the manufacture of octandors. In more details, the process involves sandwiching kinebars between two transparent plexiglass covers. Matador imparts added value to kinebars through metamorphosis, as it were. In putting the component kinebars together, Matador creates a gold bar, the octandor, possessing increased marketability, equally recognisable in Europe and in America. (This is a consequence of the incidental fact that 125 grams is only slightly greater than 4 Troy ounces.)

Bancor is the suggested name of a firm whose business is to act as a marketmaker for octandor bars as well as for bills of exchange (called octandor bills) maturing into octandor bars in 91 days, the estimated time it takes to manufacture and distribute octandor bars (including delays due to congestion at Matador).

In more details, Bancor posts its asked and bid prices at which it is prepared to sell and buy octandors, as well as octandor bills, in unlimited quantities.

Curaçao is a small island country belonging to the Kingdom of Netherland in the Caribbean (located just north of the Venezuelan coast; its capital city: Willemstad). It has virtually unrestricted sovereignty. Its self governance is more complete than that of the similar small island colonies of the U.K. such as Gibraltar, Bermuda or the Cayman Islands. Curaçao has recently attracted international limelight after it introduced a new tax code for internet companies registered in its territory and for ecommerce initiated by them. They are taxed at the flat rate of 2 percent. Both Matador and Bancor are internet companies and may choose to register and be taxed in Curaçao. They finance ecommerce by raising credit in octandor bills that mature in octandors. [5]

The Metamorphosis of Gold

The metamorphosis of the kinebar into the more marketable octandor at the hands of Mondor is akin to that occurring at the Mint as the blank ingot is being stamped and turned into the coin of the realm, of greater marketability than that of the blank ingot. Economists have neglected to study the ability of the Mint to impart marketability to the blank ingot higher than justified by its meltdown value (the value it enjoyed before being stamped). The word 'metamorphosis' aptly describes this almost miraculous transition. As a result of this neglect F.D.R. and other policymakers deprived the world of a great resource, the gold standard and the metamorphosis of gold it makes possible. One hundred years ago, they had to decide how to finance World War I. The choice was: either to finance it through the metamorphosis of gold at the minting press, or the metamorphosis of paper at the printing press.

To the world's great misfortune they chose the latter. Had they chosen the former, the conflict could have been resolved much earlier, saving life and treasure, changing the course of history in the process. But they were mesmerised by miracle of the metamorphosis of paper and they were only too happy to sacrifice the gold standard.

One could put the similarity between the Mint and Matador into high relief by suggesting that both are in the business of manufacturing the measuring rod of value. The difference is that while the Mint is a government agency and its stamp constitutes an official guarantee of weight and fineness, Matador is a private firm and the manufacture of octandors need imply no such guarantee. (The increase in value is 'in the eyes of the beholder'. Happy are those who have eyes to see.)

It is next to impossible to exaggerate the importance of the rediscovery of the metamorphosis of gold. For the first time ever, the government Mint is rendered superfluous. No longer is it a sine qua non for the metamorphosis of gold. The same effect can be produced by profitseeking private enterprise, while still benefiting people at large. Consider two cases:

(1) Suppose Bancor receives an order from a third party wanting to buy x octandors. Bancor buys 25x kinebars at the asked price of the Austrian State Mint or at the open market asked price, whichever is smaller and delivers them to Matador while drawing a bill with face value of x octandors on the latter. That there may be a problem with completing this transaction become clear when considering the size of x. If it is of routine size, no further consequences need to

be considered. But if it is of extraordinary size, then Bancor may be put on alert. Next time it may not accept the same discount rate but will push for an increase. It wants to protect its flanks against the contingency that the asked price for kinebars in irredeemable currency is going up.

(2) Conversely, suppose Bancor receives an order from a third party wanting to sell x´ octandor bills at the market. Bancor makes the sale at its posted bid price and will replace the octandors spent by buying octandor bills. If this turns out to be difficult, then Bancor will lower its bid price for octandor bills. Note that the bills Bancor just acquired mature into an octandors in 91 days' time. The asked price quoted in octandor bill units includes a markup representing the profit margin of Bancor, equivalent to seigniorage imposed by monarchs of a bygone era. They earned it by allowing their effigy to be stamped on the gold coins.

Why the Closing of the Mint to Gold Was a World-Class Disaster

But why should anyone be willing to pay a markup in buying an octandor bill? Well, for the same reason third party buyers were willing to pay a markup for real bills as predicted by Adam Smith's Real Bills Doctrine. They wanted to capture a gold income on funds that otherwise would lay idle.

The Mint was formally closed to gold in 1931 when Britain, followed by the U.S. in 1933, defaulted on their gold obligations. While the default caused some indignation at the time, the closing of the Mint was hardly newsworthy. Yet the event destroyed an all-important Constitutional right of the people, as I will now show.

Trying to Legislate For the 'Benefit' Of All Future Generations By Trampling on the Constitution

I have dwelt on the metamorphosis of gold at some length because we are witnessing a historically unprecedented phenomenon: the ingenuity of private enterprise making government certification of weight and fineness of gold superfluous. Up to now it was thought that the opening of the Mint to gold within a sovereign jurisdiction was a necessary condition for the monetisation of gold. Without this condition being satisfied there was no guaranteed future conversion of gold bullion into gold coins. In more detail, the gold coin of the realm could go to a premium relative gold bullion. Governments could limit the quantity of the coin of the realm in existence by closing the Mint to gold. This would make the coin of the realm scarce, hurting all businessmen who have outstanding contracts payable in these coins. Naturally, they would be reluctant to accede to contracts the monetary value of which was not properly fixed therein.

Thus, then, we can see why the closing of the Mint to gold was far more than a mere 'housekeeping change' as pretended by historians. If the U.S. government could close the Mint to gold, then it could also change the unit of value unilaterally, by keeping the Mint closed. Incidentally, this was the very reason why the Founding Fathers insisted that the U.S. Constitution mandate the the opening of the U.S. Mint to minting silver and gold free of seigniorage charges.1 The closing of the Mint is an example of a misguided attempt 'trying to legislate for the benefit of all future generations by trampling on the Constitution'. At any rate, this is how mainstream economists would rationalise the unconstitutional measure of closing the Mint.

Throwing Souvenir Gold Coins into the Eyes of the People

Please do not let yourself be misled by the red herring of minting souvenir gold pieces in limited numbers on Treasury account. Minting gold coins on Treasury account is as different from minting them on private accounts as night is different from day. When the U.S. Treasury started minting souvenir gold coins in the last decades of the 20th century, it did so in order to throw dust into the eyes of the public. 'See? We have reopened the Mint to gold and nothing happened. Certainly, the new coins failed to go into circulation! Here is your proof, if proof is needed, that gold is finished as money for good! Nothing can replace the dollar as money that can circulate hand to hand!'

Divisibility and Restorability

In addition, to divisibility the octandor also has the property of restorability. Suppose we break off a kinebar from it. Later we can restore the integrity of the octandor by replacing the missing piece at no extra cost.

Haircut, 1935 Style

Yet minting gold coins on private account remains a matter of Constitutional rights. Only an amendment to the U.S. Constitution could take that right away; presidential proclamations and acts of the Congress could not. That right still exists today as it existed before 1933.

The fact that it has been usurped by the U.S. Treasury for the past 82 years has no legal effect. It has turned out that the ingenuity of private enterprise could outsmart the U.S. Treasury. The opening of the Mint to gold is no longer a sine qua non for turning gold bullion into the gold coin of the realm (i.e., for remonetizing gold). Bancor could perform the metamorphosis of gold without government license, simply by ordering a consignment of octandors from Matador to be manufactured for its own account. Why is this important? Well, we have to go back to the Great Coin Melt of 1933 for an answer. The first proclamation of Franklin D. Roosevelt after his inauguration on March 4, 1933, as president of the United States was the closing of the U.S. Mint to the free and unlimited coinage of gold – along with the arbitrary closing of banks under the jurisdiction of the U.S. government. The circulating gold coins of the U.S. were summarily confiscated and melted down. Irredeemable Federal Reserve notes were paid out in compensation.

Pretence was maintained that this was a just and full compensation. It wasn't, justification for the highway robbery offered two years later notwithstanding. According to the decision of the U.S Supreme Court, handed down in 1935, 'the domestic debt-discharging power of the Federal Reserve notes was not abridged'. Well, if it wasn't, that was due to the unconstitutional decision of the same High Court in upholding legal tender laws to protect the value of the irredeemable Federal Reserve notes. Absent that decision, the domestic value of the Federal Reserve notes would have suffered the same fate as their international value did: It would have undergone a 'haircut' to the tune of some 56%. (The clever simile of a haircut, designed to mitigate the harsher language of 'highway robbery', had not yet gained currency in 1935.)

Here we see the reason why establishment economists hate the Constitutional gold coin with exceptional vehemence: In contrast with government promises, they cannot be subjected to arbitrary haircuts.

The U.S. Supreme Court derelicted its duties when it handed down its decision that allowed legislation granting legal tender protection to F. R. notes to stand.

Due Processes of Lawlessness

This was just the first of a series of several episodes in which the Supreme Court of the United States of America stooped to the level of a kangaroo-court. No greater lie was ever spread than that suggesting that 'property has never been taken from an American citizen except in consequence of due processes of law'. The fact remains that in 1935 the High Court took the property of American citizens held in the form of gold certificates issued by the U.S. Treasury. If 'due processes of law' means anything, it must mean that each case must be adjudicated separately, on its own merit. The Supreme Court's handing down a single decision to the effect that in all cases where a citizen is found in possession of a gold certificate the Constitution is automatically suspended, is a shameless instance of exceeding the powers granted to the judiciary branch!

Pyrrhic Victory

Curiously, the High Court did say that the federal government had no power to alter its contracts unilaterally. In doing so it apparently did try to protect the property rights of those Americans who owned bonds with a gold-clause protection issued by the U.S. Treasury. Seigniorage was increased from 0% to 100% by a stroke of the pen. Apart from a few Constitutional experts and monetary scientists, no one recognised the chicanery involved. By now this shameful episode of retroactive legislation and rights-mutilation is conveniently forgotten through the rewriting of history.

Global Irredeemable Currency

The international implications of the usurpation of Constitutional rights were even more ominous. Prior to 1933, all attempts to introduce irredeemable currency on a global scale failed ignominiously everywhere. Countries that resisted the trend and stayed on the gold standard were able to help their weaker brethren to return to monetary rectitude. But after 1933 all countries, including France and Switzerland to mention but two examples, were forced to follow the American lead. In 1936 the French and Swiss franc were also devalued in terms of gold. For all intents and purposes they have also become an irredeemable currency and the international monetary system was converted into a club of countries inflicting the curse of irredeemable currency on their citizens and trading partners. Redeemable currencies have been wiped off the face of earth. The fast-breeding of debt could now start in earnest, with unforeseeable catastrophic consequences.

He Laughs Best Who Laughs Last

This was the end of honest dealings between the government and its subjects and, hence, the end of honest dealings between private individuals. Honest weights and measures were effectively outlawed. According to the Old Testament such abuse of government power 'was the greatest abomination in the eyes of the Lord'. Having closed their Mint to gold, governments thought they could keep them closed as long as they wanted (that is to say, forever). In this way they could prevent future generations from returning to a system of honest weights and measures by reopening the Mint to gold.

However, as the saying goes, he laughs best who laughs last. Governments have left the ingenuity of private enterprise out of calculation. Here is how government dishonesty is rendered ineffective by the ingenuity of private enterprise. Bancor (the drawer) delivers 25 kinebars while drawing an octandor bill on Matador (the acceptor). The octandor bill, duly accepted (endorsed), is returned to the drawer.

Having two good signatures (those of the drawer and the acceptor), the octandor bill is enabled to circulate through endorsement and discounting. The discount is proportional to the number of days remaining till maturity. The proportionality factor is the gold discount rate. It depends on the supply of and demand for octandor bills. The octandor bill is a gold device uniquely capable of yielding a return on gold in gold, the gold discount rate marking the yield. As the demand for octandor bills is virtually unlimited, the discount rate is positive. The amount of newly mined gold going into hiding is no longer 100% as it was under Z.I.R.P.

Octandor bills have no competition. Nor could such a competition arise after 1931 and 1933 when the gold standard fell victim to British-American sabotage. [6] We are, here and now, witnessing the remonetisation of gold by market forces – apparently against the wishes of the governments of the U.K. and the U.S. that have never lived down the ignominy of defaulting on their gold obligations over eighty-two years ago.

The 'Wave of the Future'

Once octandor bills arise through the manufacture of octandors, they go into spontaneous circulation. There is unlimited international demand for them as the following example of financing world trade demonstrates. Assume that Saudi Arabia wants to buy wheat to be delivered in 91 days. Russia will have the wheat by then and is well able to fill the order. The trouble is that Russia is not interested in payment in irredeemable dollars. 'Once discredited, always discredited!' Russia insists on getting paid in gold or in gold devices. Saudi Arabia, if it wants wheat badly enough, has to go into the bill market to buy gold bills maturing in 91 days. Alternatively it can use gold from its foreign exchange reserves to pay for the purchase of octandor bills.

Naturally, Saudi Arabia will not pay the face value of the gold bill. As a result of a bargain with Bancor, Saudi Arabia will buy octandor bills at a discount. Russia is glad to accept octandor bills from Saudi Arabia in exchange for wheat futures contracts. They mature into octandors in 91 days' time, while the alternative, dollar credits will remain as irredeemable as a doornail even after 91 days.

This example shows how the circulation of octandor bills is capable of revitalising vanishing world trade in a world increasingly reluctant to accept irredeemable dollars (or any other irredeemable currency subject to unlimited augmentation, a.k.a. Q.E. in exchange for real goods and real services such as wheat or crude oil and the wages of workers who are working in constructing pipelines.

Note that gold is indispensable for the reviving and revitalising vanishing world trade. This also means that the rehabilitation of the bill market through the circulation of gold devices such as octandor bills will eliminate the threat of unemployment, as far as employment of those eager to work for wages is concerned.

The gold discount rate, unlike the rate of interest can be serially halved any number of times without any untoward consequences for the national economy. In this way the capital requirement for business that move merchandise from producers to the ultimate consumer will be reduced.

Therefore, the solution to the problem of replacing dishonoured and discredited dollar lies, not in inventing yet another irredeemable currency. It lies in putting gold bills maturing in 91 days into circulation. These bills represent the 'wave of future'. They are the best earning assets commercial banks can have. They are the best monetary reserve to hold against a maturing bond issue, or against a real estate deal to be closed out in the future, or against just any contingency monetary liability, such as the import bill in case of an unexpected earthquake, flood or tsunami. Far better than the irredeemable debt of a default-happy government which, to boot, is also the greatest debtor on record, with its debt increasing at an alarming rate, with no visible sources from which to reduce its debt ever.

Notice further that the octandor bill is the perfect antidote against deflation. If there are not enough of them in circulation, then their asked price will rise and the gold discount rate will have a tendency to fall. The incentive for exchanging gold for octandor bills will be high. But the octandor bill is also the perfect antidote against inflation. If there are too many of them in circulation, then their bid price will fall and the gold discount rate will have a tendency to rise. The incentive for exchanging gold for octandor bills will be low.

Central banks will be put under pressure to compete with octandor bills when it comes to financing trade in merchandise commanding the highest consumer demand. Bank notes redeemable only in unpaid and unpayable debt have no chance facing competition from devices maturing into gold.

Nor will they have a chance to compete against devices maturing into gold when it comes to serving as reserve in the Wage Fund. Irredeemable currency will fall by the wayside, by virtue of the sheer logic that creditors need meaningful collateral, rather than relics from distant past (such as the pound sterling and the dollar.) when upright countries used to have redeemable currencies. If central banks want to survive, then the credit they issue must be based on short-maturity real bills payable in gold at maturity – exactly as they did prior to 1914. The argument that no such bills presently exists is no longer valid. They do exist, for example, the octandor bills. We can take it for granted that there will be no shortage of imitators once the concept is understood by the general public. Incidentally, this brings out the tragic failure of economists through the whole spectrum from Keynesians on the left, through Friedmanites in the middle and postMises Austrians on the right, who all failed to distinguish between the rate of interest as it is regulated by the propensity to save and the discount rate as it is regulated by the propensity to consume.

Conclusion

It used to be axiomatic that the remonetisation of gold could only come about through the decision of a sovereign jurisdiction to open the Mint to the unlimited coinage of gold on private account free of seigniorage charges.. This meant the granting of the right to private individuals and firms the right to bring gold bullion to the Mint in unlimited quantities and exchange it for freshly minted gold coins of the realm ounce for ounce.

This has now changed. There is a new, synthetic way of remonetizing gold that needs no government Mint, nor government and legislation asserting individual rights.

Here is how the synthetic way of gold remonetisation works. Individuals or firms that have gold bullion to sell can offer it to Bancor for sale against octandors or octandor bills. Bancor stands ready to buy unlimited quantities at its posted bid price. As it does, the gold bullion so sold, has been remonetized.

I have studied the question of gold remonetisation in all its pertinent details in partnership with my mentor the late Ferdinand Lips. I stake my professional reputation on the thesis that profitseeking private enterprise will find a way to remonetize gold, thus, coaxing gold that had gone into hiding during the long inept campaign of the U.S. government to drive the rate of interest to zero.

Endnotes to Chapter 40

[1] Executive Order Nr. 6102 of 1933 is linked to the Trading With the Enemy Act (TWEA). The TWEA is still operational. Technically, the USA is under martial law.

[2] We admit that before WW I, during the reign of Bismarck and the Kaiser, the unification of Germany had some side effects socially and economically, which we may call a society in the hands of an economic élite that also partook in government. This situation is known as fascism, politically, but economically, German industry ran like clockwork, in a *laissez-faire* environment with a handful of very rich industrialists that were truly globalist. General Electric (GE) in the USA was in the same hands as *Allgemeine Elektrizität-Gesellschaft* or AEG. General Steel in the US and Germany were in fact one and the same. To improve agriculture, Germany needed fertiliser, which used to come from guano excrement, until chemical giant *IG Farben* provided alternatives and it even had patents and cooperations worldwide to provide oil-additives for rubber and petrol industries thanks to Rockefeller's Standard Oil. Short: Germany was an industrial spider, a *giant* one.

[3] To be sure: if the Mints do not open or will not accept gold for coining or are not cooperative for some reason, the octandor is an alternative and it does not involve the Mint's cooperation.

[4] We admit that the octandor, being pure 9999 is less resistant to bending and plying, unlike the stronger coins.

[5] But basing companies in exotic islands is no prerequisite for doing any manufacturing or trading. It can be done anywhere in the world. Besides fiscal situations tend to flucuate with the wind.

[6] See the great coin meltdown by Rooselvelt.

~~~ Chapter 41 ~~~

Recapitalise the Pension Funds with Gold

Privatising Profits, Socialising Losses

The 0.7 trillion dollar bailout plan of Treasury Secretary Paulson must be seen for what it is: a scheme to privatise profits while socialising losses. The scare tactics with which he was trying to railroad it through Congress has failed and the world is better for it. The malady has to be diagnosed properly. I summarise the popular diagnosis in five points.

(1) The bursting of the housing bubble has led to a surge of defaults and foreclosures which has, in turn, led to a plunge in the value of mortgage-backed securities – assets which are in effect capitalised mortgage payments. [1]

(2) These losses have left many banks short on capital account. Their problems were compounded by the fact that as their capital ratios were shrinking, rather than reducing their debt exposure they aggressively increased it.

(3) 'Leveraging' is the word to describe the deliberate shrinking of capital ratios, i.e., making smaller capital support a larger amount of risks. Aggressive leveraging was characteristic of the pre-crisis boom.

(4) When they recovered after the dizzying ride, banks needed a microscope to read their capital ratios and they reacted in a predictable way. They were unwilling (unable?) to fulfil their mission to provide the credit that the national economy needs for its day-to-day operation.

(5) As a defensive measure financial institutions have been belatedly trying to pay down their debt by selling assets, including mortgage-backed securities, but as they were doing it simultaneously, they drove down asset prices. This has damaged their balance sheets even more. A vicious circle is engaged that some call the 'paradox of de-leveraging.'

Capital Destruction

I should hasten to say that I disagree with this popular diagnosis which puts the cart before the horse. My diagnosis, described in the first part of this article, identifies the destruction of capital as the *cause* and the credit crisis as the *effect*.

The problem goes back to the U.S. government foolish decision to destabilise the interest-rate structure (and, hence, bond prices) in 1971. As a consequence, long-term interest rates shot up to 16 percent per annum by the early 1980s, from where they started their long descent that still continues.

Falling interest rates destroy capital as they raise the liquidation value of debt contracted earlier at higher rates. By 'liquidation value' is meant the sum that will liquidate the debt, should it be necessary to pay it off before maturity. In a falling interest-rate environment it will take a larger sum to retire the same debt. Why? Because the scheduled stream of interest payments is now capitalised at a lower rate of interest and, therefore, it falls short in liquidating the debt.

This means that, paradoxically, falling interest rates do not *alleviate* but *aggravate* the burden of debt. All observers miss this point as they blithely assume that debt is automatically refinanced at the lower rate. It is not. Falling interest rates create a deficiency on capital account since it takes a bigger bite to service existing debt than originally provided for and the deficit is made up at the expense of capital. (see volume III and inserts there) Over-leveraging is not the **cause**; it is the **effect**. What it shows is that the banks do not pay heed; they persist in error. They simply ignore shrinking capital ratios. This ultimately causes wholesale bankruptcies, leading to the vicious downwards spiral.

The banks should have made provision to compensate for eroding capital as interest rates were *falling*. None of them did.[2] None of them understood the insidious process of capital erosion [3] in the wake of declining interest rates. They reported losses as profits. Then they were hit by the negative feedback: capital eroded further. When the truth dawned upon them, it was already too late.

Interest rates have been falling for the past 28 years. The *liquidation value* of outstanding debt has been *increasing* by leaps and bounds. It reached the tipping point in February, 2007 as indicated by the unprecedented jump in the price of credit-default swaps. It revealed that any further decline in the rate of interest would plunge bank capital into negative territory. At this point capital dissipation stops: there is nothing more left to dissipate. For the banks, this is sudden death.

No commentator could explain why banks have all run out of capital *at the same time*, while making obscene profits.(Paper capital gains.) My explanation is simple. There have been no profits, obscene or otherwise. The banks were paying out *phantom profits* in the belief that their capital accounts were in good shape. They weren't. The banks were unaware that the falling interest rate structure has been making inroads on their capital. Since all banks have been working with microscopic capital ratios as a result of 28 years of capital erosion, the failure of one single bank would trigger the 'domino-effect' on the rest. [4]

Why Gold?

This puts the role of gold into high relief.

Had gold been retained as a component of bank capital, credit-default swaps would have never been invented.

Gold is unique among financial assets in that it has no corresponding liability in the balance sheet of others. Gold is the only financial asset that will survive any consolidation of bank balance sheets, in contrast with paper assets that are subject to annihilation (e.g., when the bank is consolidated with its counter-party holding the liability side of that asset).

Suppose we consolidate the balance sheets of the global banking system. Then all assets will be crossed out out with the sole exception of gold.[5]

But since the global banking system as it is presently constituted has no gold assets, under any consolidation the banks will be denuded of assets while note and deposit liabilities to the public remain. This is why the regime of irredeemable currency is susceptible to collapse that could be violent, taking place with lightening speed.

It can also be seen that trying to save banks from collapsing through consolidation, mergers, takeovers and shotgun marriages is pouring oil on the fire: it accelerates the meltdown of bank capital, rather than retarding it.

Implosion of the Derivatives Monster

My thesis also explains the explosive growth of the derivatives markets. First round insurance against decline in the value of bonds in the banks' portfolio can be had by selling bond futures. Those writing first-round insurance need to cover their assumed risk in the form of second-round insurance, they do so by selling call or buying put options on bond futures. But those writing second-round insurance also need to cover their risk: they do it in the derivatives market by purchasing credit-default swaps. The point is that an infinite chain of credit-default swaps is being built on every bond in the banks' portfolio, as shown by the derivatives monster's more than doubling in size every other year, already having reached the size of one half quadrillion dollars and still counting.

Why is the derivative monster so dangerous? Because it is subject to implosion that could destroy an inordinate amount of bank assets. If the derivatives tower is consolidated, then its value collapses to zero as claims are wiped out by counter-claims. It is possible that this implosion has already started, but the banks (and their supervisory agencies) keep the lid on this information to avoid a world-wide panic. The earth quakes badly under the foundations of the Derivatives Tower of Babel. Its toppling may be imminent. If gold had been retained as a component of the bank capital structure, then there would have been no derivatives monster to fret about.

Those who explain the proliferation of derivatives by the popularity of 'dry swaps', that is to say, swaps created for the sole purpose of speculative profits they promise in view of their ultra-low price-to-reward ratio, are wrong. All those credit-default swaps were purchased by actual insurers insuring actual risks going with bond ownership, in trying to hedge their own risks.

Recapitalising Banks [6] With Gold

The credit crisis could be solved through the recapitalisation of banks with gold. The Treasury should pledge to match subscriptions of new private capital, in gold, at the ratio of two to one. This means that two gold shares of capital stock subscribed by the private sector (individuals, firms and institutions) shall invite one share of capital stock subscribed by the Treasury. Gold subscribed by the private sector should be constitutionally guaranteed against capital levy and confiscation. [7]

There is no better use to which Treasury gold can be put which has been foolishly idled for the past 36 years. What is needed is the mobilisation of gold hoarded by the Treasury and by the private sector. The trouble is that much of the privately owned gold is in hiding and won't surface for reasons of *lack of confidence* in the monetary system. But as soon as there is a market for the shares of the recapitalised banks, private gold can be coaxed out of hiding and made to participate actively in the great task of rebuilding world credit.

Capital stock of the recapitalised banks would pay dividend, in gold, at the rate of one tenth of one percent per annum to stockholders, exempt of all taxes. This would make it possible, even for people of modest means, to acquire gold earning a safe return in gold.

The maliciously false propaganda of the past decades that gold is a sterile asset in that it earns no interest is easy to refute. Gold has been lent and borrowed at interest (facetiously called the 'lease rate') without interruption, in spite of its so-called 'demonetisation' by the government. In fact, the gold rate of interest is the benchmark on which all other interest rates are still based, after adding a risk-premium reflecting the risk that the monetary unit may lose its gold exchange value.

The tax-exempt feature of dividends has great merits to recommend it, especially if no other exemptions across the economic landscape are granted. You could look at it as society's protection of widows and orphans and other members of society who are unable to fend for themselves in a competitive environment, to live in dignity away from the hurly-burly of the investment world.

What is the use of recapitalising banks with irredeemable promises to pay? It has been tried for the past 45 years; it doesn't work.

No Chain Is Stronger Than Its Weakest Link

The newly recapitalised banks must offer their old assets for sale to the public, in exchange for the gold shares of capital stock, through competitive auctions. In this way the true value of the old paper assets can be determined and whatever can be salvaged will be salvaged. The market for bank assets, presently frozen, would be made liquid once more. If a bank wants to retain a part of its old assets in the balance sheet, it must bid for it in the same way as if it were buying from another bank through competitive auction. If an asset cannot be disposed of in this way, then it must be written off. Any delay in validating bank assets through the sieve of competitive auction will only prolong and deepen the crisis.

The 'securitisation' of bank assets was an idiotic strategy motivated by the fraudulent idea that in lumping sub-prime assets together with valid assets would somehow impart value to the former and the marketability of the product would be enhanced. This, of course, is just a ploy to cheat the buyer. [8] It is like trying to make a chain containing a weak link stronger by adding any number of strong links. The weak link must be replaced with a strong one. No chain can be stronger than its weakest link.

The re-liquefying of bank assets is a first order of business in the present runaway global credit crisis. We are past the point that the wild-fire can be localised. Mobilisation of gold is the only way.

Save the Pension Funds!

This crisis is a warning, possibly the last one, that the recapitalisation of banks with gold cannot be further postponed without risking the total collapse of the financial system. If there was some hope that the Treasury might have a contingency plan to mobilise gold in case of a crisis such as this, the Paulson bailout plan has dispelled it. When the moment for the 'break-the-glass' rescue plan has arrived, what did we find behind the broken glass? More irredeemable promises to pay, to augment bank capital. All chaff, no grain.

Global credit collapse would bring enormous hardship in its train for ordinary people who have worked hard and saved hard through a lifetime only to see the fruits of their efforts going up in smoke. The result could be total social chaos and lawlessness. At risk are all the insurance companies, pension funds, money market funds. Also at risk is the taxing power of the government, as a prostrate economy won't be able to bear the tax burden, but will spawn a grey economy that finds ways to evade taxes. The rejection by the U.S. House of Representatives of Paulson's bailout plan can be viewed as a taxpayer revolt. Is it the first, with more to come?

Close Of Keynes' And Friedman's System

Understandably, it will be hard for policy-makers, academia and media and the accountants' profession to admit that they have been wrong all along about gold and its essential role in the economic bloodstream and in accounting. They have fallen victim to the charm of John Maynard Keynes, the prankster who invented the idea that gold was a barbarous relic and the gold standard was a 'contractionist fetter' upon the world economy. Now we have proof that the blame for the contraction should be assigned, not to the use but to the misuse of gold. The debt collapse is the burial ground for Keynesianism.

After Keynes was gone, policy-makers, academia and media and the accountants' profession fell under the spell of another visionary and adventurer talking with a forked tongue, Milton Friedman. He was fond of posing as a free-market man, but in promoting irredeemable currency he did more than anybody, save Keynes, to destroy the free market. Friedman promoted the spurious idea that gold is superfluous in the international monetary system as floating foreign exchanges rates can mimic the operation of the gold standard and will balance the trade accounts. But as the record shows, Friedmanite nostrums have ruined the dollar, as well as the once flourishing and peerless American productive apparatus.

Politicians, academia and media and the accountants' profession must swallow their pride and get the confession off their chests that their prognostication, policies and advice about gold have been in error. If they fail to do this and continue to block the way of gold to make a return to the economic bloodstream, then their responsibility for the suffering caused by the credit collapse in this country and in the world will be total. They will be shown as doctrinaire wreckers of human cooperation under the system of division of labour, who muzzled their critics and usurped unlimited power, while paving the way to a world disaster akin to that of the Bolshevik revolution.

After the close of Marx' system, the close of Keynes' and Friedman's system is inevitable. But the wounds they have caused would take a long, long time to heal.

Endnotes to Chapter 41

[1] capitalised mortgage payments that were tokenised

[2] Although the capital gains were definitely thrown in their lap, at the expense of the public.

[3] Capital erosion is only possible under fiat, not under an unadulterated, circulating gold coin standard.

[4] Prof. Fekete in fact points a finger at bank actuaries, being fast asleep at the job. And the same reasoning applies to any business: all of them ought to make really large provision to replenish capital, not at the nominal value, but at its purchasing power value. Better yet, why not keep books in gold accounts? Not that the taxation authorities will go along with your reasoning. At any rate, the largest burden of taxation is borne by indirect social taxation such as pension or medicare contributions, which have their own problems. There are nevertheless a host of hurdles in the form of taxation-by-any-name.

[5] You would need a bit a of applied economics in the form of advanced accounting (consolidation). If not, it suffices to grasp the principle that during consolidation, all balance sheets, assets and liabilities, unify into one.

[6] Of the type of cooperatives and mutuals., not the type of banks we have today.

[7] But a society not open to reason, will not guarantee the constitutional guarantees either. The gnostic warriors will gladly overturn the constitution. It is incumbent, therefore, to keep our societies politically sane too. It can only be achieved by proper education, not the kind of serf-training our children are subjected to today.

[8] In legal terms: fraud or *'fraus omnia corrumpit'*.

III. Re-Theorise Economic Science

≈ Chapter 42 ≈

On the Pension Funds

Marginal Productivity of Labour

In Human Action Mises does not treat marginal productivity. There is one sentence on the marginal productivity of labour in the essay Planning for Freedom. I have quoted that sentence above. More can be found on this subject in his *The Anti-Capitalistic Mentality* (see References).

Following Mises I define the marginal productivity of labour to be the change in net output upon the elimination of the marginal worker from the labour force. A worker is marginal if his contribution to net output is smaller (at any rate, no greater) than that of any other worker. It is that worker whose job has become redundant, is no longer justified on grounds of productivity and will be terminated by the producer at the first opportunity. (In his original definition Mises did not qualify the noun 'worker' with the adjective 'marginal'. This would appear to leave the concept of marginal productivity of labour ambiguous.)

It is important to distinguish between two distinct possibilities of increasing marginal productivity of labour and to analyse the difference. Marginal productivity may increase when workers reaching retirement age are replaced by newly trained workers aided by newer, better tools. The new marginal worker produces more than the recently retired marginal worker. The marginal productivity of labour has increased. Mark that total output and possibly employment has also increased. We may call this the case of a progressive increase in the marginal productivity of labour.

The other possibility is very different. Here the marginal worker has been laid off without replacement. The next more productive worker at the lower end of the productivity spectrum, who is in employment already, is promoted to the position of being the marginal worker. There is no improvement in tools and production methods, only a shift of the margin from less to more productive labour. As a result, both output and employment shrink. We may call this the case of a retrogressive increase in the marginal productivity of labour. As an example to show how this might happen, consider an increase in the rate of interest. It will turn marginal workers into submarginal ones, earmarking them for layoff, thereby increasing marginal productivity but decreasing total output and employment.

The difference between the progressive and retrogressive increase in the marginal productivity of labour can also be seen in relation to capital. In the progressive case there is capital accumulation. Newly perfected tools or production methods are introduced as freshly trained workers are employed. This is a dynamic change that cannot help but increase total output and possibly employment, too. In the retrogressive case the change has increased marginal productivity at the expense of employment and, more seriously, there is capital decumulation. Material factors, still serviceable, are phased out of production along with the elimination of marginal workers. No new factors of production are introduced, only the attrition of workers and their obsolescent tools is stepped up.

Marginal Productivity of Capital

Apparently nowhere in his published works did Mises define the concept of marginal productivity of capital formally (although he refers to it in *Human Action* and also in *The Anti-Capitalistic Mentality*). Presumably he shied away from developing this aspect of the theory because it would quickly reveal that a position according to which productivity has nothing to do with the rate of interest is untenable.

> I define the marginal productivity of capital as the change in net output which occurs when a unit value (say, $10,000 worth) of marginal material factor is withdrawn from production. A material factor of production is marginal if its contribution to net output is smaller (at any rate, no greater) than that of any other of the same value. It is that piece of equipment or plant that the producer will discard or have idled first – because it is insufficiently productive – at which time another piece of equipment or plant with a higher productivity takes its place (quite possibly at another firm).

Again, it is important to distinguish between two distinct scenarios in which the marginal productivity of capital can increase and to analyse the difference. In the first scenario the producer plays an active role. In making investments to improve tools and methods of production he aims at producing a greater amount and better quality of goods than before. There is a dynamic shift from the less to the more productive through reshuffling workers and tools. Whether the removal of a marginal piece of equipment or plant simply means reassigning it to a new task, or whether it means scrapping and replacing it with brand new material factors, makes no difference. In neither case is there a contraction of output or employment; there might well be an increase. We may call this the case of a progressive increase in the marginal productivity of capital.

The other scenario is again very different. Here the producer plays a passive role. He responds to forces outside of his control. He leaves marginal material factors of production idle. He lays off workers who have been operating the now-idled tools in the now-idled plants. Marginal productivity increases solely on the strength of a shift to another marginal material factor that is already in service. There is no improvement in tools and production methods per se. As a result of the shift of the margin from the less to the more productive, marginal tools and plants are rendered submarginal. Both output and employment shrink. We may call this the case of a retrogressive increase in the marginal productivity of capital. Typically, it occurs whenever the rate of interest rises.

It is important to look at the reaction of the marginal producer in response to an increase in the rate of interest. He will sell his idle equipment or plant (or at least will stop maintaining them) and buys bonds with the proceeds. This will allow him to participate in the earnings of other producers whose material factors produce at a higher rate of productivity than that of his own. When the rate of interest subsequently declines, the marginal entrepreneur will sell his bonds. Indeed, he has an incentive to do so: he can sell them at a profit and he can now redeploy his capital more profitably if he buys new material factors with the proceeds. As the rate of interest has come down, he can now successfully compete with other producers.

This is arbitrage between the capital goods market and the bond market. It reveals that marginal productivity of capital sets the ceiling to the range within which the rate of interest may vary. The arbitrage of the marginal producer between the market for material factors of production and the bond market is a most important instance of human action, one that promotes not only the stability of interest rates, but also helps renew society's park of capital goods. Along with the analogous arbitrage of the marginal bondholder between the bond market and the gold market, these two instances of human action are indispensable for the understanding of the market process responsible for the formation of the rate of interest. It goes without saying that both have a bearing upon the pension problem.

Relation Between the Marginal Productivity of Capital And Labour

The first interesting question that arises in connection with the pension problem is the relation between the two marginal productivities: that of capital and labour. The observation, made by Mises, that improvement in the marginal productivity of capital must precede and exceed that of labour, is justified by the necessity to create the funds needed to improve the quality of life of working people. This is why the health of the pension plans has such an utmost importance. The first impetus in the long chain of improvements from the marginal productivity of capital, through the marginal productivity of labour, through the improvement in wages to the improvement of pensions must come from the pension funds themselves. If they are healthy (meaning fully funded), then they will serve as the source from which the capitalist borrows the funds lending them to the entrepreneur, who will invest them either in more tools, or in research leading to new production methods.

The second question is how to allocate the available new capital between simply purchasing more tools, or investing it in research and development (R&D) to devise improved production methods. Further analysis will show how the allocation problem is solved by the market. Clearly, it cannot be solved at the level of the shop-floor, nor even at the level of the executive board-room. The decision must be made at the *level of the pension funds* themselves, taking into account demographic movements such as net changes in the number of pensioners relative to the number of workers contributing to pension plans. In other words, we must compare the number of old workers entering the rank of pensioners, who stop contributing to pension funds and start drawing pensions, to the number of new workers entering the labour force and start contributing to pension funds.

I have treated this allocation problem at length in my other writings, through graduating from a simple diagonal model of the capital market involving two participants (the supplier and the user of capital, a model I consider hopelessly inadequate) to what I call the square, pentagonal and hexagonal models of the capital market in Volume II. I shall not pause here to repeat the evolution of these models. Let it suffice to look at the hexagonal model of the market for capital goods involving six participants: the annuitant, the annuitand, the entrepreneur, the inventor, the capitalist and, finally, the investment banker (see Volume II).

If the balance between the annuitands and annuitants changes in favour of the latter (otherwise expressed, there is a demographic shift increasing the number of pensioners relative to the number of new entrants to the labour force, decreasing the demand for pension rights), then *more* funds will be allocated to entrepreneurs to acquire more or better tools and *less* to the inventors working on improved production methods. This is so because production of consumer goods must increase immediately to cover the needs of the increasing retired population, *while the increase in the marginal productivity of capital can wait.*

Conversely, if the balance between the annuitands and annuitants changes in favour of the former (there is a demographic shift increasing the number of new entrants to the labour force relative to the number of new pensioners, increasing the demand for pension rights), then more funds will be allocated to inventors to work on improvements of production methods and less to entrepreneurs to upgrade their park of material factors of production. This is so because the *priority now is to prepare for a future increase in the marginal productivity of capital.* The future pension payouts to workers who are just entering the labour force must be met when they will be ready to take retirement. There is no pressing problem to increase the production of consumer goods immediately, because the younger workers will tend to save more in the form of pension contributions or otherwise and, accordingly, will have less free-spending cash available.

The point is that the distributed wisdom from the pension fund management (the market, if you so desire) will always find the 'optimal mix' of allocating funds between entrepreneurial and R&D capital to fit the given demographic data, provided that it can operate freely and the central bank is constitutionally barred from 'regulating' the rate of interest and the government refrains from setting up compulsory 'pay-as-you-go' pension schemes. The optimal solution of society's pension problem furnishes the strongest arguments against the so-called welfare state and the so-called compensatory monetary and fiscal policy of the government.

Reconstruction Of Accounting Standards

They May Be Insensitive To Capital Destruction

The accounting principle, the Law of Liabilities, asserts that a firm must carry its liabilities in the balance sheet at its value upon maturity, or at liquidation value, whichever is higher. This Law is universally ignored by present accounting standards, which threatens the economy with massive deflation through the destruction of capital, in view of the persistent fall of interest rates for the past 25 years, as it keeps increasing the liquidation value of debt.

The Book-keeper's Dilemma

One of the plays of George Bernard Shaw branded 'unpleasant' by the playwright himself is entitled *The Doctor's Dilemma*. The protagonist is a physician who comes into conflict with the Oath of Hippocrates (c. 460-377 B.C.) He has developed a new treatment for a fatal disease, but the number of volunteers for the test-run exceeds the number of beds in his clinic. Unwittingly, the doctor finds himself in the role of playing God as he decides who shall live and who shall die.

By the same token Shaw could have written another 'most unpleasant' play entitled *The Book-keeper's Dilemma*. The protagonist, a chartered accountant, finds himself in conflict with the letter and spirit of book-keeping set out by Luca Pacioli (c. 1450-1509). As a result of compromising the high standards of the accounting profession, the book-keeper becomes the destroyer of Western Civilisation.

Finest Product Of The Human Brain

Luca Pacioli taught mathematics at all the well-known universities of Quattrocento Italy including that of Perugia, Napoli, Milan, Florence, Rome and Venice. In 1494 he published his *Summa Arithmetica, Tractatus 11*, which is a textbook on book-keeping. The author shows that the assets and liabilities of a firm do balance out at all times, provided that we introduce a new item in the liability column that has been variously called by subsequent authors 'net worth', 'goodwill' and 'capital'.

This innovation makes it easy to check the ledger for accuracy by finding that, at the close of every business day, assets minus liabilities is equal to zero. If not, there must be a mistake in the calculation.

But what Pacioli discovered was something far more significant than a method of finding errors in the arithmetic. It was the invention of what we today call double-entry book-keeping and what Goethe called 'the finest product of the human brain' (Wilhelm Meister's Apprenticeship.)

Why was this discovery so important in the history of Western Civilisation? Because, for the first time ever, it was now possible to calculate and monitor *shareholder equity* with precision. This is indispensable in starting and running a joint-stock company. Without it new shareholders could not get aboard and old ones could not disembark safely. There would be no stock markets. The national economy would be a conglomeration of cottage industries, unable to undertake any large-scale project such as the construction of a transcontinental railroad, or the launching of an intercontinental shipping line.

The invention of the balance sheet did to the art of management what the invention of the compass did to the art of navigation. Seafarers no longer had to rely on clear skies in order to keep the right direction. The compass made it possible to sail under cloudy skies with equal confidence. Likewise, managers no longer have to depend on risk-free opportunities to keep their enterprise profitable. The balance sheet tells them which risks they may take and which ones they must avoid. It is no exaggeration to say that the present industrial might of Western Civilisation rests upon the corner-stone of double-entry book-keeping. Oriental (Chinese) and Middle-Eastern (Arabic) civilisations would have outstripped ours if they had chanced upon the discovery of the balance sheet first. By the same token, the continuing leadership of the West depends on keeping accounting standards high and isolated from political influences.

Barbarous Relic Or Accounting Tool?

There is cause for concern in this regard. For the past 75 years the West has been fed the propaganda line, attributed to John Maynard Keynes, that the gold standard is a 'barbarous relic', ripe to be discarded. The unpleasant truth, one that propagandists have 'forgotten' to consider, is that the gold standard is merely a proxy for sound accounting and, yes, for sound moral principles.

It is an early warning system to indicate erosion of capital. It was not the gold standard per se that politicians and adventurers wanted to overthrow. They wanted to get rid of certain accounting and moral principles, especially as they apply to banking, that had become an intolerable fetter upon their ambition for aggrandisement and perpetuation of power. Historically, accounting and moral principles had been singled out for discard before the gold standard was given the coup de grâce.

The attack on accounting standards and on the gold standard was heralded by the establishment in 1913 of the Federal Reserve System (the Fed) in the United States, the chief engine of monetising government debt. Just how the monetisation of government bonds has led to a hitherto unprecedented, even unthinkable, corruption of accounting standards – this is a question that has never been addressed by impartial scholarship before.

Bonds And The Wealth Of The Nation

In order to see the connection we must recall that any durable change of interest rates has a direct and immediate effect on the value of financial assets. Rising interest rates make the value of bonds fall and falling rates make it rise. As a result of this inverse relationship the Wealth of the Nation flows and ebbs together with the variation of the rate of interest. Benefits and penalties are distributed capriciously and indiscriminately, without regard to merit.

This was hardly disturbing under the gold standard, as the rate of interest was remarkably stable and the corresponding changes in the Wealth of the Nation were negligible. A lasting increase in the rate of interest could only occur in the wake of a national disaster such as an earthquake, flood, or war. In all these cases a higher rate of interest was beneficial.

It had the effect of *spreading the loss* of wealth due to the destruction of property more widely, easing the burden on individuals. Those segments of society that were lucky enough to escape physical destruction had to share in the loss through the increased cost of servicing capital due to higher interest rates. Everyone was prompted to work and save harder in order that the damage might be repaired quickly and expeditiously. As the rate of interest gradually returned to its lower level, the Wealth of the Nation expanded. Once again, everybody shared equally, as the lower interest rate benefited all, through the reduction in the cost of servicing capital.

> It is not widely recognised that the chief eminence of the gold standard is not to be found in stabilising the price structure

(which is neither desirable nor possible). It is to be found in stabilising the interest-rate structure. By ruling out capricious and
disturbing swings, the Wealth of the Nation is maximised.

The gold standard ruled supreme before World War I. It was put into
jeopardy when general mobilisation was ordered in 1914 by the manner in which belligerent governments set out to finance the war effort. Governments wanted to perpetuate the myth that the war was
popular and there was no opposition to the senseless bloodshed and
destruction of property that could have been avoided through better
diplomacy. The option of financing the war through taxes was ruled
out as it might make the war unpopular. The war was to be financed
through credits. In more details, war bonds were sold in unprecedented
amounts, subsequently monetised by the banking system. Naturally,
these bonds could not possibly be sold without a substantial advance
in the rate of interest. Accordingly, the Wealth of Nations shrank even
before a single shot was fired or a single bomb dropped.

Under the gold standard bondholders are protected against a permanent rise in the rate of interest (which in the absence of protection
would decimate bond values) by the provision of a *sinking fund*. In case
of a fall in the value of the bond the sinking fund manager would enter
the bond market and would keep buying the bond until it was once
more quoted at par value. Every self-respecting firm issuing bonds
would offer sinking-fund protection.

Even though governments did not offer it, it was understood and,
in the case of Scandinavian governments explicitly stated, that the entire bonded debt of the government would be refinanced at the higher
rate, should a permanent rise in the rate of interest occur. Bondholders
who have put their faith in the government would not be allowed to
suffer losses. The banks, guardians of the people's money, could regard
government bonds as their most trusted earning asset. They were solid
like the rock of Gibraltar. Such faith, at least in Scandinavian government obligations, was justified. The risk of a collapse in their value
was removed. Governments, at least those in Scandinavia, occupied
the moral high ground. The money they borrowed belonged, in part,
to widows and orphans. They took to heart the admonition and did
not want to bring upon themselves the Biblical curse pronounced on
tormentors of widows and orphans.

Law Of Assets

However, there was a problem with war bonds issued by belligerent
governments. They were quickly monetised by the banking system

making the refinancing of bonded debt impossible. This created a dilemma for the accounting profession. According to an old book-keeping rule going back to Luca Pacioli that we shall refer to here as the Law of Assets, an asset must be carried in the balance sheet at acquisition value, or at market value, whichever is lower. In a rising interest-rate environment the value of bonds and fixed-income obligations are falling and this fall must be faithfully recorded in the balance sheet of the bondholder.

There are excellent reasons for this Law. In the first place it is designed to prevent credit abuse by the banks and other lending institutions. In the absence of this Law banks would overstate their assets that could be an invitation to credit abuses to the detriment of shareholders and depositors. If the abuse went on for a considerable period of time, then it could lead to the downfall of the bank. In an extreme case, when all banks disregarded the Law of Assets, the banking system could be operating on the strength of phantom capital and the collapse of the national economy might be the ultimate result. For non-banking firms the danger of overstating asset values also exists and can serve as an invitation to reckless financial adventures. Even if we assume that upright managers would always resist the temptation and stay away from dubious adventures, in the absence of the Law of Assets the balance sheet would be an unreliable compass to guide the firm through turbulence, materially increasing the chance of making an error. Managerial errors could compound and the result could again be bankruptcy.

Economists of a statist persuasion would argue that an exception to the Law of Assets could be safely made in case of government bonds. The government's credit, like Caesar's wife, is above suspicion. The government will never go bankrupt. Its ability to retire debt at maturity cannot be doubted. As a guarantee these economists point to the government's power to tax. However, the problem is not with paying the nominal value of the bond at maturity, but with the purchasing power of the proceeds. Currency depreciation is a subtler and, hence, more treacherous form of default. Governments, However, powerful, cannot create something out of nothing any more than individuals can. They cannot give to Peter unless they have taken it from Paul first. Nor is the taxing power of governments absolute. Financial annals abound in cases where taxpayers have revolted against high or unreasonable taxes, sometimes overthrowing the government in the process. If the taxing power of governments had been absolute, then they could have financed World War I out of taxes. Bondholders would have suffered no loss of purchasing power as a result of debt-monetisation, at least on the victors' side. It is true that governments as a rule do not go bankrupt, but this could be a disadvantage. Putting a value on bonds higher than what they would fetch in the market is a fool's paradise. Governments could use methods, fair or foul, to stave off ill effects of their own profligacy. Awakening could be postponed, but it would be made that much ruder.

A strict application of the Law of Assets would have made most banks and financial institutions in the belligerent countries insolvent. The dilemma facing the accounting profession was this. If book-keepers insisted that the Law be enforced, they would be called 'unpatriotic' and be made a scapegoat held responsible for the weakening financial system. Demagogues would charge that the accountants were undermining the war effort. On the other hand, if they allowed banks to carry government bonds in the asset column at acquisition rather than at the lower market value, then they would compromise the time-tested standards of accounting and expose the firm and ultimately the national economy, to all the dangers that follow from this, not to mention the fact that they would also draw the credibility of the accounting profession into question.

Illiquid Or Insolvent?

The story of how the accounting profession solved the dilemma has never been told. It may be a safe assumption that the dilemma was solved for it by the belligerent governments in prohibiting the public disclosure of the banks' true financial condition. In the meantime a new accounting code was created, far more lenient in adjudicating insolvency. The Law of Assets was thrown to the winds and was replaced with a more relaxed one allowing the banks to carry government bonds at face value, regardless of true market value, as if they were a cash item. A new term was introduced to describe the financial condition of a bank with a hole in the balance sheet punctured by government bonds. Such a bank was henceforth considered 'illiquid', but still solvent. Never mind that the practice of allowing the illiquid bank to keep its door open is a dangerous course to follow. It has far-reaching consequences, including the threat to the very foundations of Western Civilisation. The scandals involving Enron and Bear-Sterns may be only the beginning of the unraveling of the financial system. It is clear that the recent 'sub-prime crisis' is a delayed effect of the unwarranted relaxation of accounting standards back in 1914.

While I cannot prove that a secret gag-rule was imposed on the accounting profession, I am at a loss to find an explanation why an open debate of the wisdom of changing time-honoured accounting principles has never taken place. [1] Apparently there were no defections from the rank and file of the accountants denouncing the new regime as unethical and dangerous. The underhanded changes in accounting practice have opened the primrose path to self-destruction.

The dominant role of the West in the world was due to the moral high ground staked out by the giants of the Renaissance, among them Luca Pacioli. As this high ground was gradually given up and the commanding post was moved to shifting quicksand, rock-solid principles gave way to opportunistic guidelines. Western Civilisation has been losing its claim to leadership in the world. It comes as no surprise that this leadership is now facing its most serious challenge ever.

The chickens came home to roost as early as 1921 when panic swept through the U.S. government bond market. Financial annals fail to deal with this crisis (exception: B. M. Anderson's *Financial and Economic History of the United States, 1914-1946*, posthumously published in 1949).[2] Nor was it given the coverage it deserved in the financial press. Information was confined to banking circles. An historic opportunity was missed to mend the ways of the world gone astray in 1914. It was the last chance to avert the Great Depression, already in the making.

Law Of Liabilities

Purely by using a symmetry argument we may formulate another fundamental principle of accounting: the Law of Liabilities. It asserts that a liability must be carried in the balance sheet at its value at maturity, or at liquidation value, whichever is higher. Since liquidation would have to take place *at the current rate of interest*, in a falling interest-rate environment the liabilities of all firms are rising. This spells a great danger to the national economy, one that has been completely disregarded by the economists' profession, as it also has by the accountants' profession.

Economists have failed to raise their voice against the folly of allowing the interest-rate structure to fluctuate for reasons of political expediency, implicit in the application of both Keynesian and Friedmanite nostrums. It is possible that the reason for this failure was the fatal blind spot that economists appear to have in regard to the danger of overestimating national income in a falling interest-rate environment.

The proposition that a firm must report liabilities at a value higher than that due at maturity whenever the rate of interest falls is, of course, controversial. Let us review the reasons for this crucial requirement. If the firm is to be liquidated, then all liabilities become due at once. Sound accounting principles demand that sufficient capital be maintained at all times to make liquidation without losses possible. If the rate of interest were to fall, then, clearly, earlier liabilities had been incurred at a rate higher than necessary. For example, if an investment had been financed through a bond issue or fixed-rate loan, then better terms could have been secured by postponing it. A managerial error in timing the investment had been made. This is a world of crime and punishment where even the slightest error brings with it a penalty in its train. Marking the liability in the balance sheet to market is penalty for poor timing. If the investment had been financed out of internal resources, penalty is still justified. Alternative uses for the resource would have generated better financial results.

Even if we assume that the investment was absolutely essential at the time it was made and we absolve management of all responsibility in this regard, the case for an increase in liability still stands. After all has been said and done, there is a loss that must not be swept under the rug. If the balance sheet is to reflect the true financial position, then the loss ought to be realised. Any other course of action would create a fool's paradise. To see this clearly, consider losses due to an accidental fire destroying physical capital uncovered by insurance. The loss must be realised as it is absolutely necessary that the balance sheet reflect the changed financial picture caused by the fire. That's just what the balance sheet is for. The proper way to go about it is a three-step adjustment as follows:

(1) Create an entry in the asset column called 'fund to cover fire loss'.
(2) Create an equivalent entry in the liability column.
(3) Amortise the liability through a stream of payments out of future income.

It is clear that if the accountant failed to do this, then he would falsify future income statements. As a result phantom profits would be paid out and losses would be reported as profits. Not only would this weaken the financial condition of the firm, but it would also render the balance sheet meaningless, which may compound the error further.

Exactly the same holds if the loss was due not to accidental fire but to a fall in the rate of interest. The way to realise the loss is analogous. A new entry in the asset column must be created under the heading 'fund to cover overpayment in servicing capital, due to a fall in the interest rate', against an equivalent entry in the liability column, to be amortised through a stream of payments out of future income. This is not an exercise in pedantry. It is the only proper way to realise a loss that has been incurred as a result of the inescapable increase in the cost of servicing productive capital already deployed, in the wake of a fall in the rate of interest. Ignoring that loss would by no means erase it. It may well compound it.

Historic Failure To Recognise The Law Of Liabilities

I anticipate a torrent of criticism asserting that there is no such a thing as the Law of Liabilities in accounting theory or practice. I submit that I have no formal training in accounting, or in the theory and history of accounting. Nor do I recall having seen the Law of Liabilities in any of the textbooks on book-keeping that I have perused (although I have seen the Law of Assets in older textbooks that have long since been discarded by professors of accounting as obsolete). But I shall argue that either Law follows the spirit if not the letter of Luca Pacioli. Affirming one Law while denying the other makes no sense. Every argument that supports one necessarily supports the other. The Law of Liabilities is a mirror image of the Law of Assets, arising out of the perfect logical symmetry between assets and liabilities.

Ignoring either Law is a serious breach of sound accounting principles, possibly with grave consequences. Consider the example of Japan, allowing the rate of interest to fall practically all the way to zero during a fifteen-year period. Present (in my opinion deeply flawed) accounting rules allowed companies and banks in Japan (including those banks that not so many years ago were among the world's ten largest) to understate their liabilities. Hence, they showed profits, whilst they actually had losses, because provisions were made or adjustments booked to compensate for the variations in the interest rate. Wholesale capital consumption and destruction was the result, without anybody realising what was going on. Japan now has to live with a brain-dead banking system operating on phantom capital.[3]

Banks and producing firms would operate on the strength of phantom capital and would ultimately collapse. This could bring the national economy to its knees, spelling deflation, depression, or worse (as it seems to be occurring in Japan right now). This depression appears to be metastasising across the Pacific to the United States through the yen-carry trade, foolishly encouraged by both central banks concerned.

Even if the fact were established that the Law of Liabilities has never been spelled out in any accounting code going back all the way to Luca Pacioli, we should still not jump to the conclusion that there is no justification for it. A convincing argument can be made explaining why the Law of Liabilities has escaped the notice of upright and knowledgeable accountants in the past with the consequence that it has never been codified. Since time immemorial the powers-that-be have shown a persistent bias favouring debtors against creditors, as demonstrated by their desire to suppress the rate of interest by hook or crook. However, this effort has remained counter-productive before the advent of central bank open market operations in the 1920s championed by the Fed. Indeed, the usuriously high rates charged on loans in pre-capitalistic times were not due to an alleged greed of the usurers. They were due to the usury laws themselves. Charging and paying interest had been outlawed, but the result was not zero interest on loans as the authors of the usury laws had foolishly anticipated. On the contrary, the result was rates higher than what the free market would have charged, representing compensation for risks involved in doing an extra-legal business transaction. For these and other reasons the problem, traditionally, was not falling but rising rates. In such an environment the Law of Liabilities remains inoperative and is easily overlooked. It is hard to discover a law that has been inoperative through all previous history.

The situation changed drastically when the Federal Reserve started its illegal open market operations. (The practice was later legalised through retroactive legislation.) Speculators were happy to jump on the bandwagon of risk-free profits. They could easily preempt the Fed by purchasing the bonds beforehand. After the Fed has bought its quota, speculators dumped the bonds and pocketed the profits. The net result was a falling interest rate structure.

In fact, the opportunity for risk-free profits from bond speculation due to the introduction of open market operations was a major cause of the Great Depression. Yet to this day textbooks on economics hail open market operations as a refined tool in the hands of monetary authorities 'to keep the economy on an even keel'. Only one other mistake economists have made surpasses this one in enormity. Textbooks blame the Great Depression on the 'contractionist bias' of the gold standard. This is just the opposite of the truth. The Great Depression was largely caused by the governments sabotaging the gold standard in preparation for its overthrow, as I shall now show. The persistent fall of interest rates in the 1930s has never been properly explained. What happened was that the only competition for government bonds, gold, has been knocked out through confiscation and other measures of intimidation. Freed from competition, the value of government bonds started to rise, making interest rates fall, causing prices to fall, too. The Great Depression was self-inflicted. Governments in their zeal removed the gold standard, the policeman cordoning off the black hole of zero interest to prevent interest rates from falling in. Speculators were quick to understand that this also meant the removal of a ceiling on bond prices. For the first time ever, there was an opportunity to bid bond prices sky-high. Speculators abandoned the high-risk commodity markets in droves and flocked to the bond market to reap risk-free profits made available by the regime of open market operations. You cannot understand the Great Depression without understanding how speculators reacted to the removal of competition for government bonds. Only by searching for the consequences of the forcible removal of gold from the system can the unprecedented fall in interest rates and the Great Depression be explained.

Threat Of A New Depression

Superficial thinking may suggest that if the rise of interest rates is bad, then their fall is good for the economy. Not so. A falling rate is even more damaging than a rising one. I am aware that my thesis is highly counter-intuitive. I have been challenged by many other economists who deny the validity of my contention. They argue that if the present value of future income is lower when discounted at a higher rate, then it must be higher when discounted at a lower rate of interest. We may admit that this statement is true. However, obviously, the firm has to be around to collect the higher income. [If interest rates fall, income falls, due to increased competition with better financing rates.] Many of them won't be, as they succumb to capital squeeze caused by falling rates.[The persistent falling of interest rates demands an increased capital base to sustain the present income flows, hence, if it does not increase sufficiently and promptly, it will be squeezed]

My critics hold that falling rates are always beneficial to business and it is preposterous to suggest that they aggravate deflation. These critics confuse a falling structure of interest rates with a low structure. While the latter is beneficial, the former is lethal to producers. When interest rates are falling, the low rates of today will look like high rates tomorrow. A prolonged fall creates a permanently high interest-rate environment. This paradox explains the reluctance of the mind to admit that falling rates spell deflation and, in an acute case, depression.

Falling rates mean that businesses have been financed at rates *far too high.* This fact ought to be registered as a loss in the balance sheet and be compensated for by an injection of new capital. If businesses choose to ignore the loss and they merrily go on paying out phantom profits in the form of dividends and executive compensation, then they will further weaken capital structure. When they finally plunge into bankruptcy, they wonder what has hit them. They don't understand that they have failed to augment their capital in the face of falling interest rates. Their downfall is due to insufficient capital. In a falling interest rate environment all producers are affected by the elusive process of capital destruction. This was true in the 1930s; it is still true today. Incidentally, this also explains why American producers have been going out of business in droves since the mid-1980s, resulting in the export of the best-paying industrial jobs to Asian countries such as China and India where labour costs were lower.

The U.S. government may be unconcerned about the fact that the liquidation value of its debt is escalating by several orders of magnitude due to falling interest rates. After all, the Fed has the printing presses to create dollars with which any liability can be liquidated, However, large. American producers are not so fortunate. They have to produce more and sell more if they don't want to sink deeper in debt. But selling more may not be possible in a falling interest-rate environment, except at fire-sale prices. What this shows is that the cause of deflation is not falling prices: it is falling interest rates. As they fall, a vicious circle is set in motion. Bond speculators take advantage of the opportunity created by the central bank's open market operations. They forestall central bank buying of government bonds. The resulting fall in interest rates bankrupt productive enterprise that could not extricate itself from the clutches of debt contracted earlier at higher rates. The debt becomes ever more onerous as its liquidation value escalates past the ability to carry it. The squeeze on capital causes wholesale bankruptcies among the producers.

Central bankers never consider that, while they have the power to put unlimited amounts of irredeemable currency into circulation, they lack the power to make it flow in the 'approved' direction. Money, like water, refuses to flow uphill. In a deflation it will not flow to the commodity market to bid up commodity prices as central bankers have hoped. Rather, it will flow downhill, to the bond market, where the fun is bidding up bond prices. As the central bank has made bond speculation risk free, the bond market will act as a *gigantic vacuum cleaner* sucking up dollars from every nook and cranny of the economy. A sense of scarcity of money will become pervasive. In feeding ever more irredeemable currency to the markets the central bank cuts the figure of a cat chasing his own tail. More fiat money pushes interest rates lower; falling interest rates squeeze producers more. They cut prices in desperation and cry out for the creation of still more fiat money, completing the vicious circle. The interest rate structure and the price level are linked. Subject to leads and lags, they keep moving together in the same direction. The Fed through its open market operations generates a deflationary spiral that may ultimately bankrupt the entire producing sector. Like the Sorcerer's Apprentice, the Fed can start the march to the black hole of zero interest, but hasn't got a clue how to stop it when the pull of the black hole becomes irresistible. At that point the deflationary spiral gets out of control.

Stop The March To The Black Hole Of Zero Interest!

Restoring sound accounting standards is imperative if we want to avoid the pending disaster. We must stop turning a blind eye to the deleterious effect of a falling interest rate environment on capital deployed in support of production. Open market operations of the Fed, the chief cause of deflation as demonstrated by the pull of the black hole of zero interest, must be outlawed. Only the gold standard can effectively cordon off the black hole of zero interest. By opening the Mint to gold, the U.S. government must restore the gold standard.

Endnotes to Chapter 43

[1] We are at a loss of an explanation, short of concluding that a taboo issued by the Gnostic Warriors is in place, which means that they have been able to reach critical mass, sufficient for self-censure in the sense described in chapter 49, 'Deconstructing Ideologies.'

[2] Benjamin M. Anderson, *Economics and the Public Welfare, A Financial and Economic History of the United States, 1914-1946*, D. Van Nostrand, 1949, New York.

[3] Accounting is one of the few disciplines that is largely unified worldwide. One key pre-requisite in accounting is the demand that the books reflect a true and fair state of the business. It is a key principle in accounting. From this principle flows the obligation of performing a periodic valuation of assets and liabilities. There is the chance to apply the law of liabilities, even if it is not directly mandated in specific legal scriptures. Arithmetic is what it is, not even the government can change that. Why is it not applied? Why are no provisions booked every time the interest rate varies? Why is capital not increased adequately?

~~~ Chapter 44 ~~~

Reconstructing Mining Economics

Introduction

W hile doing research in the Library of the University of Chicago in the early 1980s I came across the unfinished manuscript of a book with the title: *The Dollar: An Agonising
Reappraisal*. It was written in the year 1965. It was never published
(although it received private circulation). The author, monetary scientist Melchior Palyi, a native of Hungary, died before he could finish it.
Monetary events started to spin out of control in 1965, culminating in
the default on the international gold obligations of the United States of
America six years later in August,1971. Palyi had correctly prophesied
that event which occurred after he died. He had also correctly diagnosed the malady and prescribed the remedy that could have arrested
the train of events that would in all likelihood cause a crash further
down the road. As part of the offering of the Gold Standard University,
I have published the manuscript serially in the form of excerpts, along
with with my commentary, concentrating on parts that are still timely.
Here the manuscript is republished in its entirety.

Biographical remark. Melchior Palyi (1892-1970), the internationally recognised educator, author and economist was born and got his early education in Hungary. He was Professor Emeritus of the University
of Berlin and also taught at the Universities of Munich, Göttingen and
Kiel. He was the chief economist of the Deutsche Bank of Berlin, the
largest on the European continent at the time and was adviser to the
Reichsbank, the central bank of Germany, from 1931 to 1933. He was
then guest of the Midland Bank, Ltd., in London and visiting lecturer
of the University College of Oxford.

Palyi moved to the United States in 1933. He was visiting professor
and research economist at the University of Chicago, Northwestern
University, the University of Wisconsin and the University of Southern
California. He was involved in broad literary and lecture platform activ-
ities. The bibliography of his literary output is extensive; let it suffice to
mention the titles of some of his books: *Compulsory Medical Care and the
Welfare State* (1949). He is credited with the saying 'where the Welfare
State is on the march, the Police State is not far behind'.[1] *Managed*

Money at the Crossroads (1958), *A Lesson in French: Inflation* (1959) and his swan song: *The Twilight of Gold* (1970).

The Gold Paradox

Nineteen sixty five will be remembered in the modern history of money. For the first time, private buyers absorbed almost the entire supply of new gold coming on the market. 'Newly mined gold plus Russian sales amounted to approximately $1.9 billion', reported the First National City Bank of New York, but 'only some $250 million worth is believed to have reached officially recorded monetary stocks' (all quantities are stated in gold dollars, reckoned at the gold 'price' of $35 per Troy oz.) And none whatsoever accrued to U.S. monetary reserves – which has actually declined by a near record amount of $1.66 billion.

What is happening to all that disappearing gold? Why does it refuse to go to official gold reserves? Why, in particular, is the U.S. Treasury on the losing side year after year, with no sign of terminating this process? And, above all, what does it say about the stability of the dollar, the economic health of the nation and the future prospects of the Western World?

The central problem is the actual maintenance of the parity. The U.S. Treasury is under obligation, in effect, to assure that on the world's markets 35 dollar means the same value as one ounce of gold. Thereby the value of the dollar is anchored to the solid rock of a fixed quantity of gold. As long as this external convertibility of the dollar appears to be guaranteed, world public opinion will not question the equivalence between the currency unit and a set amount of the yellow metal. That is why to the world at large the dollar is 'as good as gold'. In the words of President J. F. Kennedy, speaking in September, 1963: 'We are determined... to maintain the firm relationship of gold and the dollar at the present price of $35 an ounce and I can assure you we will do just that.'

Gold Vanishing Into Private Hoards

1950 is the watershed year marking the start of a new era in the relationship between gold and paper money. In the twelve year period ending in 1964 the Western World's gold mines and Russian gold sales (about $1 billion in 1963-64) combined, produced $16 billion worth of gold, but official gold reserves have grown only by $7 billion. More than 50 percent, on average, of the new gold bypassed official reserves and vanished in private hoards. On the top of that the prime reserve currency, the U.S. dollar (that is backing many other currencies) had lost close to one-half of its gold reserves. By the end of 1965 our reserves have declined from a peak of $24.7 billion in September, 1949, to less than $14 billion – of which $835 million is a sight deposit of the International Monetary Fund. Not only has the richest country failed to attract any part of the new gold supply; it has actually lost more than $10 billion's worth. If continued, this process would herald the breakdown of the entire gold-based monetary setup of the West, with incalculable consequences.

To have some idea of the order of magnitude of gold vanishing into private hoards during the period 1950 and 2007, let us look at the following table .

Gold Vanishing Into Private Hoards

(approximate quantities by source, in gold dollars at $35/oz)

Period	New production	Russian sales
1950-1951	2.000 US$ m	
1952-1965	16.600 US$ m	4.500 US$m
1966-1968	3.400 US$m	
1969-2007	77.400 US$ m	

As is clear from the table, gold absorption into private hoards for the 15-year period from 1950 through 1965 was of the same order of magnitude as the U.S. gold reserve at its peak in 1949, the largest gold concentration ever in history, just short of $25 billion. This private absorption of gold is unprecedented, both as to its magnitude and to its speed. The total amount of gold absorption for the entire 57-year period 1950-2007 was approximately $......., an amount greater than all the gold produced in history before 1950. Clearly, something ominous is happening to the dollar. Vanishing gold is trying to tell us something, that is, if we have ears for hearing.

More remarkable still than these extraordinary quantities of wealth shifted out of paper assets into physical gold, worth about $ ... trillion at today's gold 'price', a process that is still continuing at an accelerating rate, is the fact that mainstream economists and their paymasters in government are not asking questions about, nor offering explanations for this incredible movement of wealth going into hiding. The apparent lack of interest about the identity and intentions of the owners of this wealth on the part of the economists profession is in itself a worthy subject to investigate.

Put it differently, paper wealth in the world is being destroyed at the rate of the annual gold production, approx. $2.8 billion gold dollars (equivalent to $55 billion paper dollars at today's gold 'price'), but this earthquake-style destruction is allowed to go unnoticed by academia and the financial media. They are satisfied that paper wealth so destroyed will not be missed. The U.S. Federal Reserve banks are dutifully replacing these real assets and more, by printing paper assets. 'See no evil, hear no evil.' 'What you can't see won't hurt you.'

Nobody asks whether the large quantities of gold vanishing into private hoards could cause a crisis when its size reaches critical mass. Be that as it may, thinking people ought to realise that, the official 'propaganda of silence' notwithstanding, the disappearance of such inordinate quantities of gold cannot help but, in the fullness of time, have an untoward effect on their lives and on their children's lives.

Fifty percent of all gold in existence has been produced since 1960. The same fifty percent has been withdrawn during the same period of time from the public domain and disappeared in private hoards. There is no way to account for this gold. We do not know the location, the identity of owners, nor their intentions what they wanted to do with it. This is a sea change portending a still greater sea change to come. This is a situation comparable to the disappearance of the gold and silver coinage of ancient Rome portending the fall of the Empire. For this sea change the public is totally unprepared. It is left in complete ignorance, due to the deep silence of the media.

'The Most Uneconomical Medium Of Circulation'

At this point the reader may raise some pertinent questions. Why is gold essential for the monetary system? Why should anyone want to hoard it? Is it not a useless gadget, good only for jewellery and dentistry? Why base the currency on such an odd commodity, or on any commodity for that matter? We have eliminated gold from hand-to-hand circulation; why not finish the job and dethrone the 'barbarous relic', as Lord Keynes called it?

Indeed, we seem to be on the way to wipe all traces of gold out of the monetary system. The first (1915) Annual Report of the New York Federal Reserve Bank argued that 'gold is the most uneconomical medium of hand-to-hand circulation since, when held in bank reserves, it will support a volume of credit equal to four or five times its own volume'. (That was an unintended admission of the inflationary bias indigenous to American money-management.)

Twenty years later, in 1934, we proceeded to 'demonetise' gold, forcibly taking it out of circulation. This was followed, in 1945, by the reduction of the Federal Reserve banks' gold reserve requirements to 25 percent of total liabilities. By 1965 we had abolished gold as a mandatory backing of the deposit liabilities of the Federal Reserve banks altogether.

The Rationale Of Gold

The first thing to know about gold is that there is no alternative to it. Gold is the one and only commodity that has no marketing problem. There is no sales resistance and no competition to overcome. A gold reserve is as important for the nation as a bank account for the firm or individual. You keep part of your funds in idle bank balances in order to be 'liquid' – to be able to pay your bills. Gold is the ultimate and unquestioned world-wide 'liquidity'. It is accepted in payment of claims. Hence, it is imperative that a country should possess gold, or to have access to gold, in order to take care of an unfavourable balance of foreign payments that arises when it has to purchase abroad more goods, services and assets than other countries buy from it. This has been the chronic case for the United States in the post-World War II era, resulting in gold losses and in a huge volume of short-term debt to foreigners.

The gold reserve inspires confidence in the currency at home and abroad. 'Even the most prejudiced managed-money advocate cannot deny that no form of paper or arrangement can ever command the confidence and trust inspired by gold, a store of value in itself' (The Statist, London, December 25, 1964.)

In addition, to the monetary there is also a non-monetary demand for gold. The very promising metallurgical and medical applications of gold are still in their infancy. Its use in the arts is ancient history. In any case, the non-monetary demand provides a substantial part of the value of the yellow metal and is the root-cause of its use as the Number One store of value. This function loses its importance when the national currency is safely anchored in gold. But it is promptly revived and expanded whenever convertibility comes under a cloud.

Paper money can be multiplied sine fine, virtually at no cost. Gold is available only in limited quantity and at a substantial cost of production. This fact is not a negative but a highly positive factor for determining gold's monetary fitness. Gold derives further strength from another circumstance. The annual new production is a very small part of the accumulated total supply, hardly ever more than 3 percent at any given time. In 1965, for example, the $1.9 billion new gold reaching the market was less than 3 percent of the total supply of over $60 billion accumulated in the central banks of the West and in private hoards. (The latter has been 'guesstimated' at $17 billion.)

No commodity known to man combines as gold does the qualities of durability, unlimited marketability, portability, homogeneity, steady demand, stability of supply growth, fitness for being stored, low cost of storage per unit of value and, last but not least, independence from authoritarian manipulation of the total supply. This is why totalitarians (and their dedicated or subconscious fellow-travellers) are violently opposed to its private ownership that provides the citizen with a large measure of freedom. By having gold he can hedge against arbitrary policies of the Omnipotent State, or even slip out from its clutches.

Explanation Of The Gold Paradox

The paradox of a chronic flight into gold and out of the U.S. dollar which is tied to gold, is the outstanding symptom of a critical situation. The pat explanation for the paradox is to blame the recurrent runs on the 'speculators'. This is a characteristic throwback to medieval economics, confusing symptom and cause. In truth, responsibility belongs to the authorities who create opportunities to induce speculators to go short on the dollar or to buy gold on margin. A far more important factor may be the manoeuvring of the cautious who do the exact opposite of 'speculating': they are trying to protect their assets and incomes by hedging against a possible devaluation...

Another pat explanation relegates the problem to the fringes of the global economy. In areas where political, legal, or monetary insecurity prevails, there is a compulsive instinct to seek security in hoarding gold. No country can beat India in this regard. The hidden gold of her population has been estimated by India's Reserve Bank at some $6.4 billion (!), built up over a period of 100 years or longer.

But the less developed economies are altogether too poor to absorb each year the huge amount of vanishing gold. And why would they not hoard convertible currencies instead of gold, as they did in the past? Actually, an appreciable fraction of foreign aid dollars has been used by the recipients to acquire gold – another vote of no-confidence for the dollar, as well as for the respective local governments.

Even more significant is the fact that leading European central banks display definite signs of impatience with the dollar. Given the $13.7 billion holdings of dollar claims by monetary authorities, not counting some $6 billion held by international organisations, the danger this implies for the American gold reserve and the maintenance of the dollar's convertibility can scarcely be overestimated.

It is more than a problem in monetary management. Our very prosperity and the integrity of our economic system is at stake!

Explanation, Forty Years Later

In the following parts of this series I shall take the analysis of the gold paradox beyond the point to which Palyi has taken it. I shall ask the question who the hoarders are and what motivates their gold hoarding. My thesis is that gold hoarding is a win-win strategy, the only valid one as such. (All other win-win strategies are Ponzi schemes.) However, there is a strict condition, one that most would-be beneficiaries are unable to meet. The gold hoarder must be mentally capable of using gold exclusively as his *numéraire* in calculating asset values as well as profit and loss. He must understand that profit/loss accounting in terms of the paper dollar is tantamount to trying to measure length with an elastic measuring-tape. The obvious result is a cover-up for the deficiency of length, akin to the cover-up for the deficiency of wealth and to making losses parade as profit. Watch for the day when people wake up from their delusion.

Admittedly, very few people are able to adapt their thinking to the requirement of discarding the dollar (or any other fiat) as *numéraire* of wealth. The dollar is far too deeply ingrained in their psyche, unfortunately. As a result, very few people see the fragility of wealth under the regime of an irredeemable currency. [2] Those who can are not tempted by the 'spectacular' profit opportunities in stock, bond and real estate speculation. They know full well that yielding to the temptation would be tantamount to sitting in a crowded auditorium just before the fire alarm was ready to sound. Their chance to reach the fire exit alive would be practically nil.

This also explains the little guy's agonising watch on a hesitant gold 'price' to go up. He is conditioned by a host of cheerleaders of get-rich-quick schemes. The more enlightened hoarders of gold (whom I have called elsewhere 'bulls in bearskin') – a tiny minority – are in no hurry to see the dollar to bite the dust, or the 'price' of gold to go to outer space. They do have the philosopher's stone, gold, well in hand. More importantly, they also have the matching wisdom without which gold is just another dead asset. They know that the most productive use of gold is not sitting on it, waiting for the miracle of a gold 'price' in five digits to spring upon the world. They want to derive maximum advantage from their possession of the metal. In particular, they know how to make gold yield an income in gold, something even Aristotle believed was impossible.[3] Most importantly, they need not release control over their gold while deriving an income from it. Mark that in all other cases deriving an income from an asset involves putting the asset to risk. The fact that gold income is an exception to that rule in that it can be harvested risk free even while the gold is locked up in one's own vault, is due to the idiosyncrasies of irredeemable currency.

The 'enlightened hoarders of gold' prefer the security of a gold income, that they can enjoy in relative peace, to the insecurity of an exploding gold 'price'. They understand that they could not enjoy their exploding wealth once the gold 'price' escaped from the earth's gravitation, because of the blood that would be flowing in the streets where the have-nots did battle with the haves over the bone of contention: gold.

The common perception is that commercial traders are selling gold short *naked* in order to drive *down* the gold 'price' where they can cover their short positions at a huge profit. Thus, the bears are sucking the blood of the bulls. This is a myth. Commercial traders are mere agents. If they trade for their own account, the amounts are paltry in comparison. Commercial traders act on behalf of principals who do hold the gold and want to derive an income from their holdings. It is understandable that the principals wish to stay anonymous and, in an unexpected reversal of Andersen's tale, *The Emperor's Clothes*, they foster the misperception that they are naked!

Historical Precedence: Vanishing Gold In Ancient Rome

The last time in history when huge amounts of gold were going into hiding occurred during the twilight of the Roman Empire. It was an ominous portent of bad tidings. People were withdrawing gold coins from circulation. They declined to spend them hoping that saner and safer times would come. As a rule people do not spend their gold coins unless they see that they will be able to get them back on the same terms. As saner and safer times did never come, these ancient hoards were forgotten and remained buried in the ground throughout the Dark Ages. Present day archeologists still keep finding them fifteen hundred years later.

Owners of those ancient gold hoards were helpless. They could not enjoy their gold as they were unable to retard the coming of the evil day when the Roman monetary unit would become worthless and the Empire would fall. In this respect latter day gold hoarders are better off. They seem to be able to retard the fall of the dollar towards worthlessness and, in the meantime, they could enjoy a gold income in relative security. Of course, this will not fend off the ultimate collapse of the American Empire, although it may materially postpone it. The fortunes of empires tend to coincide with the fortunes of their currencies.

The present episode of gold vanishing into private hoards is no less ominous than the previous one that was followed by the collapse of the Roman Empire and the onset of night in the civilised world.

As this 'agonising reappraisal' shows, the days of the dollar are numbered. Regardless whether it be a large number or small, the next Dark Age looms large on the horizon.

Maximise Life, Not Profits!

We often hear the term 'Peak Oil', but there are probably some pretty good arguments against being able to predict when the 'peak' date will arrive. Certainly, no oil company has put out a prediction of peak production, much less one predicting that oil output will drop by 10 to 15% within a decade.'

I wish to provide a definitive answer to Tom Szabo's question: yes, we are approaching 'Peak Gold' if we have not already passed it. The last twenty-five years in the history of gold mining has been a gross aberration during which gold was mined as if it were a base metal, namely, at the top grade of ore reserves (that is, most recklessly).

> This is in the sharpest contrast with how gold has been mined traditionally as dictated by the economics of gold mining, namely, at the marginal grade of ore reserves (that is, most conservatively).

The world is witnessing a sea change: gold, having been mined as a base metal, is once more being mined as a monetary metal.

By marginal grade of ore is meant that grade which can still yield a profit (i.e., is payable), however, any lower grade is already submarginal (i.e., is non-payable). Clearly, marginal grade varies inversely with price: it goes higher as the price goes down and vice versa. Gold mining used to be the very opposite of base metal mining which must, of necessity, maximise profits, just like any other enterprise. Not many people realise that gold mining is the only exception to this rule. The goal of the gold miner is not to maximise profits. Far from it. His goal is to maximise the life of the gold property. There are several reasons for this, the outstanding one being that gold is the monetary metal par excellence. Whenever private enterprise rather than the government or its central bank controls its creation, new money is not railroaded (should we say air-dropped by helicopter?) into circulation. Money creation is then guided by economic rather than political considerations.

Worst Grade First, Top Grade Last

Historically, the propensity of governments is to debase the currency rather than maintaining its value. The longer gold stays underground locked up in the gold-bearing ore, the longer it stays outside of the government's reach. We must remember that gold in the ground can still be an efficient store of value. The aberration of the last twenty-five years of mining gold at break-neck speed and selling it forward, in some case as much as fifteen years of mine production, is *ending*. All mines will realise that premature exhaustion of their gold property is suicidal. They will have to learn again the wisdom of gold miners of old: worst grade first, best grade last. Ben Franklin's dictum that 'experience runs an expensive school, but fools will learn in no other' applies here as well and, therefore, the learning process may take some time. Be that as it may, the smartest gold miner has probably shifted back to mining at the marginal grade already. He reasons as follows: 'If I can only keep my mine operational long enough, dollar debasement will catch up with my submarginal grades and will make them go through a metamorphosis. My submarginal grades of ore will become payable. My expiring gold mine will be rejuvenated and given a new lease on life, thanks to the misguided monetary policies of spendthrift governments. Ergo I had better work my mine as conservatively as possible and lengthen its working life by all available means'. This line of thinking is well summarised by the adage: 'in and out of ground gold teaches man husbandry'.

Barrick Bringing Good Tidings For Gold Bugs

The present negative roller coaster ride for monetary metals is leading to an increase in absolute terms of the price, which appears unstoppable. (Negative, because an ordinary roller coaster ride ends at the lowest, not the highest, level.) The latest confirmation has come from a most unexpected source. Barrick, the gold miner held in contempt by most gold bugs (for its presumed activities in trying to cap the gold 'price', nay, to club it down) is now saying that the 'price' of gold will rise during the next five to seven years because supplies from the mines will drop more than anyone in the market can anticipate. This is an extraordinary statement coming, as it is, from a gold producer with a millstone-size and weight of a hedge-book around its neck.

As Dorothy Kosich reports on Mineweb in her article 'Barrick Opines on Gold Supply and Price' (Aug. 3, 2007), during a conference call Barrick delved into its future prospects including gold 'prices'. President and CEO Greg Wilkins and Executive Vice President and CFO Jamie Sokalsky revealed that Barrick has been 'digging in very deeply on the supply side of the business' working with a research firm to uncover evidence and trends increasing Barrick's optimism for the future gold 'price'. Mark the word optimism. Perhaps it should read pessimism. Barrick's hedge-book is so hopelessly under water that the company cannot afford to buy it back, as did Newmont making it the largest 'unhedged' gold mine, while the going is still good. The future gold 'price' spells disaster for Barrick that cuts the pitiable figure of a moose standing on the train track fixated on the headlights of the fast approaching train.

'Timeo Danaos Et Dona Ferentes'

Barrick is still studying the research reports, but Sokalsky already told analysts that 'our initial analysis shows the buy side (sic) is likely to drop a lot quicker and more than most in the market are anticipating.' While he insisted that 'it is still too early to talk about any specific numbers', Barrick's research has uncovered much that 'should be a lot more positive for the gold 'price''. Sokalsky has divulged that a 10 to 15% drop should occur in overall mine supply of gold within the next five to seven years. That's a *volte-face* if there ever was one. Gold was fetching $300 an ounce around the year 2000 and Sokalsky boasted that if *horribile dictu* the gold 'price' went to $600, Barrick would still be O.K. It could not get a margin call on its gold leases for fifteen years. It need not sell into its hedge-book at a loss. It could always sell its output in the open market at a profit. 'Barrick would make every cent of that increase'.

Every cent? The gold 'price' presently is well over $600 and the same Sokalsky is talking about much higher gold 'price's for the next five to seven years. He must have Santa Claus for bullion banker who carries Barrick's short position most cheerfully, regardless of staggering losses.

Since we have it from reliable sources that Santa Claus does not exist, not in the gold mining business anyway, the bullion banks have barred Barrick from speculating in the bond market with the proceeds from the sale of leased gold. Moreover, they took away Barrick's freedom to sell its output in the open market without putting a prescribed amount of gold into the hedge-book. *In effect, Barrick's gold production is in escrow.*

In all but name the company is foreclosed on its gold leases.

The 15-year moratorium on margin calls is a myth that has been exploded by the market. Tom Szabo seems a bit skeptical about Barrick being the first to report the bad news – bad, that is, from the point of view of those who have endeavoured to cap the 'price' of gold during the last decade of the last century. Who knows, maybe research shows an even bigger than 15% decline in output, but Barrick has opted to tamper with the data in order to show a smaller anticipated decline in gold production than justified by the research, as part of its unending quest to keep the lid on the gold 'price'. Tom Szabo adds that, joking aside, these projections are incredibly bullish for the long-term gold 'price'. What Barrick implies, in effect, is that despite billions of dollars thrown at exploration during the past 2 or 3 years, there are not enough new projects even in the early discovery stage (much less in the late development stage) to maintain the current level of output, as production at the existing sites will start to decline in the next few years.

I myself am also skeptical. '*Timeo Danaos et dona ferentes*' [4] (I fear the Greeks especially when they bear gifts). President Wilkins is on record that, while reducing its hedge-book somewhat, Barrick will retain its hedge plan as an 'essential risk-management tool' and a means of 'stabilising revenues'. It gives Barrick 'needed flexibility' and, Barrick's creditors, necessary collateral. I think Wilkins should have come clean during the conference call. The talk about 'risk-management' and 'stabilising revenues' is for the birds. Wilkins should repudiate the hedge plan in no uncertain terms and put the whole unpleasant affair behind him for once and all. Barrick and its creditors need the so-called hedge plan as they need pain in the neck. Unless... unless... there are yet more skeletons in Barrick's cupboard?

Logic would dictate that Barrick lift its short hedges first and release the research report afterwards. Doing it in the wrong order could cost a pretty penny. Barrick brings the dictum of Cicero to mind:

Mendaci neque quum vera dicit, creditur.

(a liar is not to be believed even when he speaks the truth).

Ruthless Exploitation

During the past twenty-five years gold has been mined following the worst traditions of ruthless exploitation of a resource. Barrick served both as brain-trust and ring-leader, by mining gold at the top grade of ore defying the tradition and economics of gold mining and by promoting a thoroughly mendacious, false and self-defeating forward sales program under the banner of 'hedging'. At one point during the past fifteen years Barrick had to close down operations at no fewer than ten of its gold producing sites as a result of exploitation, because ore reserves became submarginal in the wake of the falling gold 'price'. For years, Barrick has been selling gold forward with wild abandon at ridiculously low prices, in effect blocking its own escape route to short covering should the need arise. It is hard to imagine a gold mine managed more incompetently from a global point of view. Of course, Barrick's highly touted 'hedges' are no hedges at all. In so far as they mature over one year and their volume exceeds one year's mine output, they are naked forward sales misrepresented as hedges. The whole scheme has been a mindless and extravagant exploitation of a world resource.

In all likelihood it has also been a 'gold laundering' scheme. I have coined this expression to describe clandestine transfer of shareholder equity, either to management (a.k.a. embezzlement), or to an unnamed third party (a.k.a. *defalcation*). [5] We do not know whether Barrick is guilty of embezzlement, defalcation, or both and perhaps never will.

Forewarned But Not Forearmed

We need not keep guessing. I submit that Barrick has been put on notice that its so-called hedge plan would invite charges of unfaithful steward-ship as soon as the bear market in gold is over. I warned Sokalsky in person ten years ago at Barrick's headquarters. The meeting took place at the suggestion of Chairman Peter Munk with whom I exchanged letters on the matter. Sokalsky and I discussed Barrick's hedge plan for an hour and a half. I can testify that he understood my point very well. At the end of our meeting I presented to him a 50-page document entitled *Gold Mining and Hedging: Will Hedging Kill the Goose To Lay the Golden Egg?* which treated this issue exhaustively. He promised to read it and to pass his comments on to me within a month. I have never heard from him again.

In my document the process whereby a rising gold 'price' inevitably makes world gold output shrink (in terms of tonnes) is very clearly demonstrated. To explain this, I have to discuss another remarkable difference first between the ways gold and base metals are traditionally mined. This is the deliberate variation of the rate at which mill capacity is being utilised:

> ▷ The base metal miner is under constraint to mine at the

top grade of ore. But he is *free to vary the rate of mill capacity utilisation* in response to changing market conditions. Accordingly, he will increase it if he has to increase output and vice versa.

▷ Not so the gold miner, who is under constraint to run his mill full time, as close to capacity as practicable. But he is *free to vary the grade of ore* at the mill in response to changing market conditions.

Whenever the 'price' of gold rises he decreases and and when it falls he increases the grade.

He does this because the marginal grade of ore varies inversely with the gold 'price'. If he is to run his mine economically, the gold miner is compelled to go after the marginal grade of ore and leave the better grades alone. **He knows that premature exhaustion of his gold mine means dissipating shareholder equity and wasting capital resources.** The prematurely exhausted gold mine would have a lot of valuable ore-reserves left behind that would become payable later when the dollar is sufficiently debased. But by then it would be too late. Once the gold mine is closed down, it could be prohibitively expensive to re-open it.

Mechanism Of Peak Gold

For example, whenever the gold 'price' rises, the marginal grade of ore falls as heretofore submarginal grades become payable. Since gold mines run their mills close to capacity, output shrinks every time the gold 'price' has reached a new high plateau, provided that they are managed economically. Uneconomically managed gold mines get exhausted prematurely and fall by the wayside, as they well deserve.

Peak Gold can be confidently predicted since the increasing gold 'price' (an inevitable consequence of deliberate dollar debasement) causes a world-wide shift in the marginal grade of every gold mine. The marginal grade of ore drops.

Since the combined milling capacity of the world's gold mines is a given quantity and it can only be increased slowly, after a great capital outlay which management may well be reluctant to make (as it would eat into profits and shorten the life of the gold property to boot), the upshot is that the gold content of mill output is falling. World production of gold shrinks (in terms of tonnes) with the rise in the 'price' of gold.

But what about opening new gold mines? As Tom Szabo has hinted, the artificially induced bear market in monetary metals between 1981 and 2001 has resulted in a great reduction in prospecting, exploration of known sites and development of mines at proven sites. We must realise, however, that the whole episode of explosive increase in world gold production from 1914 through the end of the century was a great anomaly. Even though it was engineered by governments on the warpath, the feat cannot be repeated. The inflationary escapades of governments, either acting in solo or in concert will of course continue. The governments can stay on the warpath and can expand their pet welfare projects as long as they want. In vain: the nexus between the welfare-warfare state's inflationary design and the value of gold, or the tectonics of marginal gold ore underground, has decisively been broken. Governments have expanded their *ephemeral power* to work the miracle of multiplying cash gold through multiplying paper gold. Ditto, no longer can they pretend that gold locked up in ore deposits below surface is a valid substitute for cash gold. From now on it is 'cash gold on the barrel'. False carding in the gold business has been exposed and discredited.

The great increase in world gold output during the twentieth century was a non-repeatable event, largely due to the inflationary propensities of governments under the gold standard artificially suppressing, as they did, the 'fiat value' of gold. This has caused a world-wide shift in the marginal grade of ore in every gold mine. The marginal grade was boosted and, with it, the world's gold output. Such background has created Peak Gold in the first place: a reckless exploitation of a world resource whose production would have increased much more evenly in the absence of inflationary escapades.

But that is history. The present reality dictates that uneconomic increases in production and naked forward selling are over for good. On the supply side, limited and diminishing injections of newly mined gold shall replace unlimited and ever increasing dumping of paper gold. When you need gold, you demand cash gold, the supply of which from the mines is going to decrease from now on. It is satisfying to see Barrick acknowledge this first.

Hedging Proper

In the sequel I shall explain, as I did to Jamie Sokalsky years ago, the principles of proper hedging. I suggested to him that Barrick should announce a bilateral hedge plan to succeed its notorious unilateral plan. The latter involves *short hedges* (forward sales) to the exclusion of *long hedges* (forward purchases). The former involves both.

Just as its forward sales are balanced by Barrick's need to market future production, forward purchases, had they been entered, could have balanced Barrick's future need to acquire new gold properties in anticipation of the exhaustion of its ageing sites. Had Barrick listened to my advice, Peak Gold would not have been to its chagrin. Not only would profits on the long hedges have outstripped losses on the short ones; they would have covered the hefty increases in the price that Barrick has now to pay for new gold properties. Barrick could have scaled Peak Gold with the flying colours and without a penny loss on its short hedges. What is more, it could have plenty of money left on its long hedges to pay for the acquisition of fresh gold properties in preparation for a bright future bringing higher gold 'price's in its wake. Barrick would have been ready for the new bull market and could contemplate its own future with genuine optimism.

Hedging Fraudulent

In my previous papers I have explained that virtually all activities of gold mines that go under the name 'hedging' are fraudulent. To the extent hedges go out into the future more than one year, or they exceed the quantity of one year's production, they are naked forward sales, carrying unlimited risk (the risk that the gold 'price' goes to infinity, as it has in the wake of every hyperinflation).

> To understand the motivation to resort to fraud and to shoulder unlimited risk to boot, we must remember that the combined short positions in the futures and derivatives markets on gold greatly exceed monetary gold in existence.

Without compulsively selling paper gold, a short squeeze and even a corner in cash gold could develop if the longs decided to call the bluff. Thus, any exposure to the short side forces pyramiding to fend off the danger. On the other hand some shorts, especially bullion banks, have found the creation of ersatz gold a profitable business. They play a cat-and-mouse game with the longs. They have fashioned the rules of gold exchanges and ETF's in their own favour in order to make delivery a cumbersome, expensive and time-consuming procedure. As a result the 'price' of gold could be thrown into a hole so that, whenever it tried to climb out, hedgers and speculators would rush in and club it down. The shorts can get away with it because the supply of paper gold (futures and option contracts) as well as unmined gold in the ground is virtually unlimited and can be mobilised in the anti-gold campaign. It speaks volumes of the inherent strength of gold that it could still climb out of the hole in 2001 in spite of a terrible assault to push it back. The 20th century belonged to the enemies of gold. There is no need to make predictions here about the 21st .

Changing The Nature Of Gold Speculation

Significantly, the so-called hedging activity of gold mines has altered the strategic line-up in the gold market. Speculators have typically, been on the long side. They have photographic memories and recall the propensity of governments to cry down the value of the national currency in terms of gold from time to time. The opposite procedure, writing up the value of the national currency in terms of gold is virtually unknown in the annals of monetary history. Given mine hedging, so-called, speculators have changed sides and compete with the mines to sell (paper) gold at the first sign of a bullish move in the 'price'. The fraternity of speculators conceive of risk-free profits on the short side of the market as they attempt to forestall the mines. Having abandoned their traditional haunt on the long side, they are now converging on the short side of the gold market. Peak Gold is a predictable consequence. Unhedged gold mines, too, feel compelled under the threat of a falling gold 'price' to produce gold at break-neck speed while neglecting prospecting and the development of gold properties. Once the producing mines get exhausted, the supply of new gold will decline.

In summary we might say that fraudulent hedging carries with it its own punishment: Peak Gold. It leads to ruthless exploitation of gold mining resources, with no prudent provision for replenishing them through prospecting and new mine development.

'Give A Dog A Bad Name, Might As Well Shoot Him'

It is unfortunate that the perfectly honest and useful word 'hedging' has been allowed to be abused and given a completely distorted meaning. As the saying goes, 'give a dog a bad name, might as well shoot him!' It is difficult to explain the distinction between 'hedging true' and 'hedging false' when the connotation of the word 'hedging' in the minds of the people is unsavoury. It turns them off. Yet the mission of the monetary scientist obliges him to continue on the path of truth even if it is uphill all the way.

Hedging is a wide-spread practice of producers in all walks of the economy. To be valid and effective, it must be carried on at two levels: upstream and downstream. The former refers to the input, the latter to the output of production. At the input level the producer buys the

resources that go into his final product. At the output level the producer is marketing his final product. The need for hedging arises as
price fluctuations at either level, especially if they occur faster than
adjustments can be made, may cause losses. Thus, worrying about the
downstream, the producer is anxious to lock-in a favourable selling
price as it may become available for his product prior to the end of the
current production cycle. Worrying about the upstream, the hedger
aims at locking-in a favourable buying price as it may become available
for a major ingredient of his product prior to the beginning of his next
production cycle.

Upstream And Downstream Hedging

Hedging is most efficient if it is bilateral. As it has been practiced in
gold mining hedging is unilateral. It involves forward sales by way of
downstream, to the exclusion of the forward purchases by way of upstream hedging. It is a caricature of hedging. It pretends to overcome
the fluctuation of the gold 'price' as it affects the output of new gold. I
say 'caricature' because it is counter-productive.

> Rather than allowing the producer to sell high while preserving
> the value of his unmined reserves, it forces him to sell low and
> sell it fast, as the message is that the price is going to fall and any
> delay in selling will involve losses.

Yet, if done properly, either type of hedge should contribute to profitability as well as husbandry. In combination they are a legitimate form
of arbitrage, provided that the hedges are carried in the balance sheet
and profits (losses) from them are reported in the income statement.
Hedges carried off-balance-sheet are not legitimate as they conceal a
liability with the result that the income statement is falsified. Shareholders and creditors are misled. Directors and managers lock themselves into a fools' paradise. Especially dangerous are downstream
hedges carried off-balance-sheet, for reason that the short leg (forward
sale) represents an unlimited liability. [6] By contrast the long leg of an
upstream hedge (forward purchase) represents but a limited liability.
This difference is due to the fact that while the price of a commodity
can never fall below zero, there is no identifiable limit above which it
may not rise.

Another way of expressing it is to say that the downstream hedge is
subject to a squeeze and possibly to a corner. By contrast, there is no
way to squeeze or to corner a producer with an upstream hedge.

I wish to return to the question why downstream hedges must be limited in size and in volume to one year. Total net short sales must never exceed one year's output. The reason is that at the end of the fiscal year unsold output from the previous production cycle must be moved from the 'receivables' to the 'stockpiles' column and the short leg of the hedge on them must be lifted. If they weren't, then the arbitrage would be turned from hedging into outright speculation on the short side representing unlimited liability. Profits are paid out masquerading as dividends. It results in hiding paper losses. Such antics constitute a fraud.

Capital Destruction

I must confess that I cannot understand the utter lack of business acumen on the part of gold mining executives, still less on the part of investment bankers that finance their activities, in embracing such a contradictory and self-defeating strategy of marketing gold. They should be interested in maximising the price of their product. Instead, they engineer a falling price trend. They should be interested in maximising the working life of their gold producing property. Instead, their marketing policy directly contributes to the premature exhaustion of the mines. A lot of observers jump to the conclusion that the gold mines and the bullion banks, in partnership with the government, form a conspiracy to club down the gold 'price'. Theirs is a hidden agenda. The gold mine management is interested in defalcation, that is to say, to trick their stockholders out of their equity. The bullion banks think that they can harness perpetual motion in the artificially induced oscillating movement in the 'price' of gold. Governments look at the gold 'price' as a messenger with an embarrassing message about the depreciation of currency. The messenger had better be shot. Governments know that a steep increase in the gold 'price' will cause panic. Such a panic has historically served as the harbinger of hyperinflation. It must be prevented by hook or crook.

I find this reasoning unattractive. Such a conspiracy can never be proved or disproved. Governments probably use more subtle methods.[7]

Double Standard

Most 'hedged' gold mines are in violation of the important restriction that downstream hedges must not exceed one year's gold output and they must be lifted before the end of the fiscal year. Their practice transgresses not only the limits of prudence, but also the limits of upright business management. A gold mine selling forward in excess of one year's output is guilty of fraud. It is concealing a potentially unlimited liability. The accounting profession, the commodity exchanges and the government's watchdog agencies have never offered an acceptable explanation for the double standard they apply, one for the gold mining industry and another one for everyone else. While they allow gold mines to sell forward several years' production, they would immediately blow the whistle if, for example, an agricultural producer tried to do the same. It is well understood that forward sales in excess of one year's production are a predatory practice designed to hurt or destroy competition. It is also hurting other market participants downstream.

There is no justification for this double standard. It is scandalous that the government grants legal immunity to gold mines using fraudulent hedges. Worse still, the fraud is facilitated by central banks willing to lease gold which, as the bank well knows, the mine will sell for cash. Central banks are accomplices in the scheme of fraudulent hedging since they report gold that has been leased and sold as if it were still sitting in their vault. It is a form of double-counting gold by modern accounting techniques.

Selling forward more than one year's output is no hedging. It is outright speculation on the short side of the market in anticipation of a decline in the gold 'price'. Not only is such a 'naked bear speculation' illegitimate as it falsifies the balance sheet and conceals an unlimited liability, but it also makes the prospectus meaningless. There is no mention in the prospectus of any intention to indulge in short selling that inevitably results in the premature exhaustion of ore reserves and in the dissipation of the most valuable resources of the mine at artificially low prices. On this ground alone the gold mine is open to class action suit by the shareholders.

Shareholders Being Hit Three Times

Furthermore, naked bear speculation makes no economic sense for the mine. By virtue of its net short positions the gold mine assumes a vested interest in a lower and falling gold 'price' which clashes with its main mission of selling newly mined gold at the highest possible price. Such division of loyalties is inadmissible for a firm commissioned by its shareholders to convert wealth represented by ore reserves into wealth represented by bullion in a most advantageous manner. The managers of the 'hedging' gold mine have a schizophrenic stance as they are prompted to pray for a higher and a lower gold 'price' all at the same time. No enterprise with a schizophrenic management team can survive the vicissitudes of market competition and the shareholders' ire for long. Shareholders get hit three times through the schizophrenic action of the managers. First, income is shaved every time the gold 'price' is forced lower through short selling. Second, capital is being destroyed as the falling gold 'price' makes payable ore reserves to disappear (i.e., become non-payable). Third and most serious is the fact that the richest ore reserves are being frittered away for a pittance at the artificially suppressed gold 'price', thereby materially shortening the working life of the mine. Naturally, the share price will show not only the shaving of income and destruction of capital, but the premature ageing of the gold mine as well.

Paper Profit No Profit

Advocates of this senseless practice, in particular, the officers of Barrick Gold argue that these losses are more than compensated for by the extra income the firm generates from 'investments' made with the proceeds of forward sales. But insofar as this extra income is encumbered with unlimited liabilities represented by the fraudulent downstream hedge, it consists of paper profits that should not be paid out in the form of dividends. In fact, they should not be reported as profits in the first place. 'There's many a slip between cup and lip', as the proverb says. Hidden liabilities may force the firm out of business before it has a chance to realise its paper profits. The practice of window-dressing income statements using unrealised paper profits, especially as they are encumbered with unlimited liability, is blatant fraud and no amount of sophistry or government connivance will change that fact. It is the height of insolence on the part of management to treat shareholders as simpletons unable to understand the difference between paper profits on an open forward sale contract and profits that have been consummated by closing out such a contract.

Bilateral Hedging

Apologists for the practice of naked bear speculation by gold mines try to push the blame on to the banks. They point out that mines could not get financing unless they heeded the bid of banks to sell forward several years of output as collateral for the loan. Let us leave aside the fact that the banks in setting conditions involving fraud become partners in crime. It is possible that they enjoy the same immunity from criminal prosecution as the mines. Even then the argument is not persuasive. The banks are not micro-managing the mines. The responsibility for fraudulent forward sale of several years of output rests with mining management. It could have used true hedging to satisfy the banks.

In the third, concluding part of this series I shall describe in full details bilateral hedging. It is proper hedging that gold mines can practice without harming anyone. It involves upstream hedging that consist of forward purchases of gold, to compensate for the forward sales of the downstream hedging. This will reveal that the compensating long leg of Barrick's straddle is missing. Therefore, the so-called hedges of Barrick constitute no valid arbitrage. They are merely tools for illegitimate naked short speculation. They invite severe punishment in a bull market. By contrast, bilateral hedging is for all seasons. The mine prospers in a bull market as well as in a bear market.

A unilateral short hedge can always be converted into a bilateral hedge through adding a compensating unilateral long hedge. Forward sales should be matched by forward purchases. A bilateral hedge is the combination of a downstream and an upstream hedge. It is a legitimate hedge, as forward sales are compensated by forward purchases. It never gives rise to unlimited liability.

For example, an upstream hedge is created by the gold mine when a sudden fall occurs in the gold 'price'. Since management is on the look-out for new gold-bearing properties to buy, in order to replace ore reserves that are being exhausted by its mining activities, the sudden fall in the gold 'price' represents an outstanding yet ephemeral opportunity. It knocks down the value of gold-bearing properties and that of the stakes of prospectors. However, the opportunity to buy the property or the stake at such an excellent price is likely to elude the gold miner who has to go through the lengthy process of searching the title and checking the quality and quantity of gold ore in the ground. By the time this process is completed, the gold 'price' might have surged forward making the opportunity to add to ore reserves at a reasonable price disappear.

To lock in a favourable price is possible nevertheless through the forward purchase of gold. The miner creates a straddle or upstream hedge, the long leg of which is a long position in the futures market, while the short is the gold-bearing property under negotiation. Care is taken to match the value of the property with the number of futures contracts to purchase. When the deal is closed out and the property is bought, the long leg is lifted and the upstream hedge unwound. The point is that the miner is under no time pressure to close out the deal prematurely. Even if eventually he is paying more in consequence of the surging gold 'price', the miner is compensated for that by profits on the long leg of his straddle. It is true that there would be a loss on the long leg if the gold 'price' fell further. This is no problem, since the lower price paid for the gold-bearing property will take care of that loss. Adding the upstream hedge converts unilateral into bilateral hedging. It makes the illegitimate forward sale of several years' mine output legitimate. The short leg of the downstream hedge is compensated for by the long leg of the upstream hedge. The forward purchase removed the unlimited liability that was created by the forward sale of gold. The fraternity of gold speculators will return to their traditional haunt, the long side of the gold market. Gold investors are not hurt by the hedging activities of the gold mines, provided the hedges are proper.

Figuratively we may describe the proper hedges of a gold mine as a four-legged straddle. Two legs are in the upstream and the other two in the downstream market. The short leg downstream (forward sales) is counter-balanced by the long leg upstream (forward purchases) — just as the long leg downstream (gold in the ground about to be mined) counter-balances the short leg upstream (gold property about to be acquired).

Unlimited Risk Is For Real

Mr. Shedlock challenges my claim that unilateral hedging by a gold mine, in particular, the practice of selling forward longer than one year, or quantities in excess of one year's mine output is, in effect, a naked short sale, involving unlimited risk. I have suggested that unilateral hedging and forward sale of several years' output are imprudent, fraudulent and should not be allowed by the exchanges – as they certainly, are not in case of agricultural producers There is fraud involved in the practice of unlimited forward selling of gold beyond one year precisely because it may not be possible to deliver the gold as contracted. One year is the logical production cycle for gold. There is a difference between selling forward gold already in the pipelines moving towards the market and selling forward gold still locked up in ore bodies. It is safe to assume that gold already in the pipelines will make it to the market. By contrast, gold locked up in ore bodies may not. The oft-quoted dictum that 'there's many a slip between cup and lip' applies. Ore has to be extracted, pulverised, processed and refined. The company may not be there to do it if it goes bankrupt in the meantime? for example, as a result of its foolish unilateral hedging policies.

The idea of 'unlimited risk' involved in naked forward sales is real. The miner does not have the gold in hand. He has only a bird in the bush. In addition, to the risk to potential profits there is the risk that the company will be foreclosed on its naked forward sales and go into receivership. Mr. Shedlock simply ignores the dynamics of the gold market. He ignores, for example, that forward sales as practiced by Barrick rely on gold lease rates remaining stable – a fact admitted arrogantly in its last Annual Report. Perhaps Mr. Shedlock doesn't realise lease rates are nothing more than the fulcrum upon which the dollar-rate of interest and the future 'price' of gold teeter in balance.

> But what if no more gold were available for leasing, as will surely happen when the central banks finally empty their cupboards? Lease rates would explode as one piece of gold in hand would be worth several in the bush.

There is no way to hedge against this risk. The fact is that gold could go into backwardation so fast as not to allow time for the company to take defensive action. It will matter little then that Barrick claims a great deal of flexibility in its gold contracts since the very thing it has agreed to receive in exchange for gold – U.S. dollars – will have lost all of its purchasing power. Does Barrick have enough capital to deliver the 'hedged' gold for nothing and will it be given much time to do so? This is where Barrick would find that backwardation poses a serious obstacle to its survival as the value of future gold production and thus, that of a gold mine, is but a fraction of the same amount of gold when held in the hand.

Bullion bankers are, no doubt, a nice bunch of people when they coax the gold miner into the trap of unlimited risk. They will not be nearly so nice when they get ready to make their margin call and take their pound of flesh, as any Shylock worth the name would.

> Sure, profit risk runs in both directions. This is exactly why true hedging must be bilateral involving forward purchases to complement forward sales. This is exactly why unilateral hedging is false hedging. It fails to be symmetric. Bullish sentiment is nipped in the bud, while the bearish variety is cheered on. It pretends to market a product at the best price available, but all it does is ruining its own market by inviting competitive short sales from other gold mines and speculators.

Bilateral hedging works with four-legged straddles, a short and a long leg downstream, plus a long and a short leg upstream. Unilateral hedging tries to get by with one-legged straddles: the only leg being the short one downstream. [8] I ask you: which is going to win the race?

A gold mine can never be smart enough to outsmart speculators who make it their business to forestall other market participants. It is outright stupid to pursue a market strategy of long-term forward selling, given the fact that in the futures markets nimble speculators make split-second decisions to turn from a buyer into a seller. By the time the gold mine, a dinosaur in comparison, has made its long-trumpeted forward sale, the speculators have run away with the best of the pick. Unilateral long-term forward selling of gold could work, but only if governments or central banks have underwritten the losses that are almost certain to accrue.

> It is not a question of liking or not liking hedged mines. The demonstrable fact is that the leading hedger takes unfair advantage of all the other mines, hedged or unhedged, by forcing them to sell ahead of schedule at lower prices.

Unilateral long-term forward selling is a predatory practice which enables the big fish to gobble up the small. No fair play is possible as long as the practice is allowed. For this reason the suggestion that if you don't like hedged mines you should short them is puerile. Shorting a predator may be suicidal.

It is true that every production process has its production cycle. As Mr. Shedlock remarks, for agricultural commodities it is typically, from harvest to harvest, or one year. [9] Although for gold it is not so sharply delineated, it is reasonable to make the fiscal year to play that role. Once a year shareholders meet, elect new directors and there may be changes in management. Important decisions are made about acquiring new gold-bearing properties, prospecting, exploration, mine development. In this sense, yes, you plant in the first quarter to reap in the fourth, typically, the busiest season for the gold mining concern.

It is true that, as far as its fundamentals are concerned, gold production is far more stable than the production of agricultural commodities or, for that matter, the production of any other good. This is what makes gold such a superb monetary metal. It is foolish to suggest that gold, as a result of its 'demonetisation', has ceased to have stable purchasing power, a fluctuating gold 'price' notwithstanding. What the fluctuating gold 'price' shows is not the lack of stability in the purchasing power of gold; it is the lack of stability in the purchasing power of paper currencies, issued by devaluation-happy governments, in which the 'price' of gold is quoted. [10] It is certainly, not indicative of a mysterious disappearance of stability in the value of gold.

The fluctuating ''price' of gold', as well as fluctuating forex and interest rates, are not nature-given as are the fluctuating prices of agricultural products. They are man-made. They have deliberately been inflicted upon the people by governments in betrayal of their sacred mission to protect them. The fluctuating gold 'price' and gyrating bond prices are the instrument of the most vicious exploitation the world has seen since chattel slavery.

> The government in regulating futures trading has approved 'double standards' in an effort to create a practically infinite supply of *ersatz* gold, including paper gold (such as gold futures that can be sold greatly in excess of physical gold in existence) and unmined gold locked in ore bodies below ground (which can then be sold forward), in the hope of keeping the price of cash gold in perpetual check.

This is not a myth. This is a well-established fact admitted, at one time or another, by many a government in its more sober moments.

Niagara-On-Potomac

The world-wide regime of irredeemable currency would have come to a sorry end decades ago if it weren't for gambling casinos foisted upon the world by governments hell-bent to keep the game of musical chairs going non-stop. Governments, in the best tradition of casino owners, want people to gamble in gold, bond and forex futures. The futures markets in gold, bonds and forex serve a purpose and one purpose only: to provide an outlet for the Niagara-on-Potomac, money supply gushing forth from the Federal Reserve that could drown the entire world in a hyper inflationary deluge. If it hasn't, that's because excess money has been soaked up by the gambling casinos. [11] So far. People scramble for the excess because they could use them as chips at the gaming tables. But as growth in the derivatives markets (the size of which doubles every other year and by now exceeds half a quadrillion dollars or 500×10^{12} that is $500,000,000,000,000) shows, this is not a stable process secured with proper checks and balances. This is a runaway train on which the brakes (i.e., natural limitation on gold production) have been deliberately disabled. Fraudulent hedging of gold mines and double standards in regulating futures trading are part of the sabotage. This is a world disaster waiting to happen.

Hedge Fund Masquerading As A Gold Mine

Mr. Shedlock has missed my point. We may honestly disagree on the question whether long-term unilateral hedges are prudent or fraudulent. But there is no ambiguity about the fraudulent nature of a hedge fund masquerading as a gold mine. If it is the world's biggest gold mining concern, then the masquerade assumes cosmic proportions.

I repeat the verdict: the gold carry trade is criminally fraudulent. In more details: to lease gold, to sell it for cash, to invest the proceeds like a hedge fund and to report the income from these investments as profit to shareholders, as if they were profit from gold mining operations, constitutes fraud. Paper profit is no profit. It is encumbered with a contingent liability, the extent of which cannot be ascertained until the hedge is lifted and the hedge-book closed. The trouble is that by that time management will have spent the 'profit' taken out of the corporate treasury fraudulently.

The practice of window-dressing income statements using unrealised paper profits, especially as they are encumbered with unlimited liabilities, is a blatant fraud dealt with by the Criminal Code.

Are Barrick's Officers Masochistic Or Incompetent?

Previously, I mentioned that Barrick President Greg Wilkins and Executive Vice President and CFO Jamie Sokalsky announced extremely optimistic predictions about the gold 'price' for the next five to seven years in a conference call that has been widely publicised. These predictions are based on a study of gold fundamentals commissioned by Barrick. [12]

Here is my parting shot to Mr. Shedlock. He says that he disagrees with Citigroup analyst John Hill, who publicly called on Barrick to rid itself of the remaining 9.5 million ounces left on its 'project' hedgebook. According to Shedlock, Barrick should not cover those hedges now at $700. 'If it did and the 'price' of gold collapsed to $500, Barrick would be in a world of hurt... Barrick would be betting the farm that prices are heading north of $700 ... and will stay there for quite some time... Is [this contingency] really worth betting the company on?'

I ask Mr. Shedlock what makes him think that Barrick's actual bet (namely, that the 'price' of gold will collapse to $500) is a more worthwhile contingency to bet the company on? Who is Messrs. Wilkins and Sokalsky trying to fool in making prognostications potentially very damaging to the financial health of the company –in view of its hedgebook deeply under water? Are they masochistic? Do they think that they have been hired by the shareholders to run the company aground? Why did they not lift all their so-called hedges, as John Hill suggested and Newmont has done, in good time, before releasing such a devastating report putting the company in jeopardy? This is what common sense would seem to dictate, to lift the hedge first and make the announcement afterwards, is it not? If they did not have and could not raise the money to do it, at the very least they should have suppressed the optimistic prognostication on the gold 'price', in order to soften the blow to shareholders who are going to suffer one way or another the consequences of gold breaking above $700, due to Barrick's insane hedging policy.

It is understandable that Barrick's officers are reluctant to admit publicly that they have made the most colossal blunder in the history of mining, by committing their company to the policy of unilateral downstream hedging through unlimited forward sales of gold. Such an admission would be hard on the ego. They may hope against hope that their blunder will be quietly forgotten and the shareholders will buy the desperate propaganda-line that a higher gold 'price' is good for them, hedge-book or no hedge-book.

But you cannot keep kicking garbage upstairs to the attic forever, because it will keep rotting there until something gives and the accumulated garbage will come crashing down.

I have issued a public challenge to Barrick to explain why they ignored my warning ten years ago that unilateral downstream hedging is a dangerous trap they should avoid. I also pointed out to the top brass how their hedge plan could be made bilateral, a winning combination. Had they listened to my advice, they would have avoided having to carry the yoke of a millstone-size hedge-book around their neck. I take this opportunity to report that Barrick has so far ignored my challenge.

I am not sold on the conspiracy theory according to which Barrick is a front set up by governments to keep the gold 'price' in perpetual check. Not yet anyhow. But then, the other conclusion remains that the officers of Barrick are incompetent bunglers whose name will go down in ignominy in the annals of mining.

Putting The Cart Before The Horse

As discussed, a most unusual conference call took place on August 3 last. Barrick President Greg Wilkins and Executive Vice President and CFO Jamie Sokalsky officially proclaimed 'Peak Gold' by disclosing that according to research commissioned by the company world gold production has peaked and will decline from now on. They suggested that we might expect a 10 to 15% drop in overall mine supply of gold within the next five to seven years, with obvious positive implications for the gold 'price'. This was widely reported in the financial press.

What makes the announcement highly unusual, not to say suspect, is the fact that industry-leader Barrick still has 9,5 million gold ounces worth of open hedges and will suffer accordingly in the rising-price environment. It is just not logical and even appears masochistic, to make such an upbeat announcement about the gold 'price' first and lift the hedges afterwards (as it is the destiny of all hedges to be lifted ultimately).

Since the company was in possession of such an explosive information impacting the gold 'price', the logical procedure should have been to lift the hedges first and to release the report afterwards. The reverse-order procedure could hurt the company financially, hurting shareholders even more. Could it be that the top brass of the company has a hidden agenda and treats shareholders as dummies who do not understand the negative impact on the hedge-book of a positive spin on the gold 'price' by putting it even deeper under water?

Captain And Mate, First In The Life Boat

Well, we did not have to wait too long for the solution to the puzzle. On September 9 (2007) President Greg Wilkins exercised 100,000 options for company shares at $27.30 each and sold all these shares the same day at prices ranging from $38.30 to $38.80. Next day, on September 10, executive vice president and chief financial officer Jamie Sokalsky turned up and exercised 35,000 options for company shares at $23.80 each. Then, between September 10 and 14, he exercised 90,900 more options for company shares at prices ranging from $29.20 to $30.70 each. He sold all these shares the same day at prices ranging from $36.70 to $36.74, thereby reducing his total company holdings to zero. Total company holdings of president Wilkins was brought back to the original 47,500 shares – according to the Canadian newspaper National Post, September 17 and 18, 2007. After all, it is fitting that the president of a company own at least a few shares in the company, However, reluctantly.

It is hard to escape the conclusion that the captain and his mate want to be the first to claim their seats in the life boat, ahead of women and children. By releasing that most optimistic report Wilkins and Sokalsky jacked up the share price artificially so that they could exercise their options, only to sell the shares right away while selling was still good? and leave shareholders to their fate. If the share price collapses thereafter, too bad. The main thing is that captain and mate were home safe. Shareholders can be Barricked.

The sight of the captain and his mate grabbing the first seats in the escape hatch ahead of women and children is repulsive enough. But it is impossible to find the right words to express moral indignation if we consider that the mate is personally responsible for the calamity awaiting shareholders aboard the badly damaged ship, caused by the insane hedging policy of Barrick management.

As reported in this column, I have challenged Sokalsky to explain why he had failed to heed my warning ten years ago that the unilateral hedging policy of the company is not only false but extremely dangerous for a gold mining company, in view of the 100% mortality rate of irredeemable currencies. I also gave him a copy of my 50-page memorandum entitled Gold Mining and Hedging – Will Hedging Kill the Goose to Lay the Golden Egg? which spelled out that there was such a thing as bilateral hedging. It is harmless and potentially just as profitable even in a bear market as unilateral hedging, if not more profitable. Above all, it is true hedging as opposed to false hedging.

My challenge has been ignored. Now we know why. Sokalsky and his boss were busy bailing out.

Is S.S. Barrick sinking after hitting the iceberg of $700 gold? Time will tell. The ship is certainly, badly damaged by the collision. The question Barrick shareholders must ask themselves is whether it is wise to entrust their fortunes to a heavily hedged company whose chief financial officer has just reduced his own exposure as a shareholder to zero and, together with the CEO, apparently has better ideas where to park his money. The case for owning Barrick shares speaks for itself.

I have explained the extremely precarious financial position of Barrick due to its 9,5 million ounces of open hedges, already deep under water, in a rising gold-price environment. Barrick's strategy is built upon the assumption, spelled out in the company's last Annual Report, namely, that gold lease rates remain stable. This assumption has now been fatally shaken by events in the gold market during the past couple of weeks. The spectre of the supply of lease gold drying up looms large in the horizon. In consequence lease rates could explode, making one ounce of gold in hand worth several ounces in the bush (that is, locked up in ore reserves). There is no way to hedge against the risk that demand for cash gold will surpass supply of gold for lease. It is totally irrelevant what Barrick says about the flexibility of its arrangements with the bullion banks. Barrick's capital may turn out to be insufficient while bleeding gold in delivering mine output into the hedge-book for nothing. It is entirely possible that we are witnessing a dance macabre, the last contango for Barrick. Backwardation of gold remains an enormous threat to Barrick's survival. After all, Messrs. Wilkins and Sokalsky should know best. They don't want to own Barrick shares. They have voted. With their feet.

BARRICK EXECS CONTINUE TO EXERCISE OPTIONS AND SELL SHARES

I revealed already that when it comes to owning Barrick shares, the two top Barrick executives, CEO Greg Wilkins and CFO Jamie Sokalsky have voted with their feet. In retrospect it looks more like a stampede of insiders out of Barrick shares and options.

As reported by the Canadian newspaper National Post on September 21 and 25 (2007):

> ▷ Barrick executive vice president Alexander Davidson exercised 25,000 options for company shares at $23.85 each on Sept. 18 and then sold these shares for $39 each the same day. Davidson exercised 5,600 more options at the same price on Sept. 20, then sold the shares. He exercised another 19,400 options at the same price the following day, then sold the shares for $41 each.

> ▷ Patrick Carver, executive vice president and general counsel at Barrick exercised 12,100 options at $29.60 on Sept. 18, then sold these shares for prices ranging from $39.35 to $39.41 the same day. He exercised another 12,000 options at $29.60 on Sept. 20, then sold these shares for $40.30 each the same day.

> ▷ Peter Kniver, executive vice president and COO, exercised 40,000 options for Barrick shares at $23.80 each on Sept.21, then sold these shares the same day for prices ranging from $40.26 to $40.32.

> ▷ Executive vice president and CFO Jamie Sokalsky exercised 49,100 options at $30,70 each on Sept. 19, then sold these shares the same day for prices ranging from $39.45 to $39.61. This is In addition, to selling 135,000 shares between Sept. 1 and 14 as mentioned in Part 4 of this series.

Many others at Barrick have exercised options and sold company shares. The National Post comments:

> " Looking for someone to pick up the tab for a night on town? Well, you might want to track down one of the 28 executives, directors and/or officers at Barrick who since Sept. 1, 2007 have exercised and sold more than 1.2 million options for company shares. Consider the 420,050 options that were exercised and then sold in four days, from Sept. 10 to Sept. 14. They generated $3,254,651 plus $1,439,812 in total profits for the 15 Barrick officers who performed these transactions. That's one helluva dinner for starters.'

More pertinently I ask the question: what's the rush to get rid of Barrick shares? What is it that insiders do know but shareholders may not?

Barrick Throws In The Towel

It could have very well been the impending bombshell timed to explode on September 28 when Barrick CEO Greg Wilkins was to announce that the company 'has no plans to return to the futures markets to hedge its gold production'. This amazing announcement is in my opinion nothing short of an admission of guilt. Barrick's hedging policy has caused a financial disaster that was perfectly foreseeable and avoidable. Barrick executives have been warned that their so-called hedge-plan was fraudulent and involved the company with unacceptable risks. I told CFO Sokalsky in person about the errors of his ways already ten years ago. My 50-page memorandum Gold Mining and Hedging — Will hedging kill the goose laying the golden egg? that I prepared for Barrick executives is in the public domain.

Ferdinand Lips in his book Gold Wars quotes extensively from it.

Shareholders would be perfectly justified in launching class action suits against Barrick executives. Insiders are well aware of this. Hence, the spectacular stampede to dump Barrick shares that may have their origin in illegally paid bonuses. Why, these bonuses could possibly represent paper profits rather than earned profits. It is criminally fraudulent to pay yourself a bonus out of paper profits. The contingent liability encumbering paper profits could turn into real losses for which the funds paid out in bonuses should have served as cover. Apparently this is what happened to Barrick: the rising gold 'price' made paper profits from Barrick's 'hedges' evaporate while turning all remaining 'hedges' into a loss-maker. Millions of dollars that Barrick executives have recently pocketed from bonuses could conceivably be part of the cover for losses embodied by the 9 ½ million ounces of 'hedges' under water.

It is remarkable and noteworthy that CFO Sokalsky has got off from his high horse. He is no longer touting his so-called hedge plan that involved using paper profits for the purposes of window-dressing operational profits. Quite possibly company counsels have warned him that such a tactic may be deemed illegal and actionable by shareholders.

As reported by Reuters quoting an interview on CNBC, on Friday, September 28 company president Wilkins announced the end of the saga of 'hedging' in gold mining. He still appeared to be defending the practice by promising that the company is going to continue to hedge its copper production. The red herring of copper hedging will lull nobody into believing that the discontinued gold hedging strategy was unobjectionable from the legal point of view. The objection is not against the use of the futures markets in hedging; it is against the practice of selling leased metal. There is no lease market for copper so Barrick cannot sell leased copper.

***

As this contribution on the economics of gold mining has set out to show, the economics of copper mining is as different from that of gold mining as night is different from day, on account of the different behaviour of the underlying marginal utilities.

Be that as it may, Barrick has thrown in the towel. Truth has won over falsehood. President Wilkins said in the interview: 'Frankly, our investors are really looking to benefit from the upside of gold and we share that point of view.' He did not explain why it took him so long to come around to honouring the wishes of shareholders, nor did he say what other criteria than serving the interest of shareholders may guide his actions. Deafening silence surrounds the question what he is planning to do with the 9 ½ million ounces worth of 'hedges', now deeply under water as a direct result of the foolish hedging policies of management and a potential source of further horrendous losses in case the 'price' of gold advances further.

The fact is that Barrick is haemorrhaging gold and the executives are trying to cover it up. Rome is burning and Nero fiddles on the roof. A few days earlier, at the Denver Gold Group Forum, Wilkins talked to the assembled mining experts complaining about the high price of truck tires explaining how he was going to fix the problem. Not one word was said about the 9 ½ million ounces of 'hedges' under water, or how they can be lifted before they do further damage to the company and its shareholders. The CEO talks about building a truck tire factory when the gold mine is on fire. Perhaps, if he put out the fire first, then he could afford to pay the going price for truck tires.

Of course, he must have noted that 'hedging was practically anathema' at the Forum, as niftily put by Citigroup analyst John Hill. Was Wilkins just trying to be considerate in avoiding an unpleasant subject? The gold 'price' reacted to the news that Barrick has thrown in the towel by jumping almost $10 to $744, a 28-year high. That cost the company and its shareholders a cool 95 million dollars.

Still, Barrick shareholders have every reason to celebrate. I take this opportunity to congratulate them upon their victory over a fossilised management. I pledge my further support to them with my pen. I shall provide a post mortem on Barrick's unilateral hedging strategy. I have changed the subtitle of this series to: A Primer on the Economics of Gold Mining, to indicate that a new era has started in the history of gold mining. The mindless rush of gold mining companies to play 'follow the leader' is over. I could not find anybody willing to defend

Barrick's indefensible strategy of unilateral hedging. This strategy has been thrown where it belongs: to the garbage dump of history. Make no mistake about it: this was the greatest mining disaster in the history of gold mining.

Two-Legged Straddles

I shall now explain what Barrick has done wrong and how it should have proceeded instead. What I have to say is basically no different from what I told Sokalsky ten years ago. Selling gold futures at price spikes in excess of annual output is no hedging, it is naked forward selling. As events have proved, I was right: naked short selling is a foolish strategy as it can make even the #1 gold miner suffer, not just a loss of face, but also the loss of billions of dollars.

Consider two hypothetical gold mines, AXY and XAB. Compare their operations which are very similar yet fundamentally different. Both mines work with two-legged straddles having a short and a long leg. With their short legs they both enter the gold futures market. The difference is in where they put the long leg. I wish to emphasise that this example is schematic, that is, oversimplified for easier comprehension. The actual situation is considerably more complicated, but simplifying it does not affect the underlying principle. AXY enters the long leg of its straddle into the bond market; XAB keeps the long leg anchored in the gold mine itself.

From this it should already be clear that XAB's are true hedges in the sense that they are rooted in mining. By contrast, AXY's hedges are false.

The gold mine has been turned into a hedge fund. At any rate, its 'hedges' have nothing to do with gold production. AXY needs gold only as a source of cheap financing for its gambling ventures.

Fraudulent Hedging

Suppose there is a $10 upwards spike in the gold 'price'. AXY reacts by selling 100 gold futures contracts. In doing so it locks in a selling price for gold, gold that it arranges to borrow from a bullion bank at 1 percent per annum interest, in order to sell it and invest the proceeds at 6 percent in the bond market for a net income of 5 percent per annum.

AXY does not think that it is in any danger on account of a possible advance in the gold 'price'. 'What goes up must come down'. In any case it reasons that the gold sold forward is in hand: it can be scooped up from its mines at any time. But as we have seen, this is a fundamental mistake. AXY does not have the gold in hand: it only has a bird in the bush. The hedge is fraudulent because the 5 percent net interest income is commingled with operative profits, disregarding the contingent liability that AXY still has on its open 'hedges'. As we have observed, it is criminally fraudulent to represent paper profits as earned profits.[13]

True Hedging

The other gold mine XAB reacts the same way to the initial $10 upwards spike in the gold 'price': it also sells 100 contracts of gold futures, the short leg of the straddle. The difference, as already suggested, is in the long leg which in this case is entered into the actual production of gold from the mine.

In more details, XAB is alive to the opportunity offered by the fact that the upward spike in the gold 'price' has promoted some of its submarginal grades of ore into the payable category. To fix our ideas suppose that XAB has a submarginal vein of gold bearing ore it affectionately calls Moonbeam. Even though submarginal, Moonbeam it is not barren. It is pregnant with profits which XAB wants to capture.

A godsend, XAB finds that Moonbeam is now payable, thanks to the $10 upwards spike in the gold 'price'. The trouble is that the godsend may be available only for a couple of minutes and it is not possible to get the gold out of the ore and take it to the market in such a short space of time. No problem. That is where hedging, in the true meaning of the word, comes in. Using the facility offered by the gold futures market XAB can lock in the spiking price now; mine and deliver the gold later. Geologists at XAB know exactly how much of Moonbeam ore should be earmarked and mined in order to come up with the right amount of gold that must match the amount sold forward. The mine goes ahead and produces the gold. Never mind if the 'price' of gold has fallen back in the meantime. The higher selling price is locked in. When the gold produced from Moonbeam ore is sold, the mine lifts its hedges, i.e., covers the short position in the futures market.

In effect, XAB has sold gold at a profit from ore that, absent hedging, represents zero value. It looks like prestidigitation, but it isn't. It is the same idea as harnessing energy from the tide-and-ebb movement of the oceans. XAB harnesses the fluctuating gold 'price' which represents energy. The energy of tides, given the skill of engineers, can be put to use. Likewise, the skilled gold miner can squeeze gold out of worthless rock. That's the challenge of the profession, challenge that not every gold miner can meet.

Notice that XAB does not care if the 'price' of gold has increased between its selling of gold futures and its selling cash gold later. It is true that any increase generates a loss on the short leg, but it is compensated dollar for dollar by the higher price it will receive for the gold extracted from Moonbeam. XAB only cares about the opportunity of selling gold profitably, gold, the production of which in the absence of hedging would involve the mine with a loss. If, on the other hand, the gold 'price' fell back, then the short position of XAB in the gold futures market would show a profit. That profit could be taken immediately.

Suppose that the chance of the gold 'price' moving up or down after every $10 spike is 50-50. Then the mine will enjoy an extra income from its hedging operations because 50 percent of its hedges will be closed out profitably without even touching any gold bearing ore. The other 50 percent is just as beneficial making it possible to extract gold profitably from submarginal grades of ore. Herein you have a win-win strategy. Quite unlike Barrick's which is a lose-lose strategy — except in a bear market for gold.

Fool's Gold Future

This being a post mortem I want to explain most carefully what has made the boat of Barrick hit the reef. The #1 gold miner did not understand the subtle difference between selling gold futures and selling borrowed gold.

While both come under the heading 'selling gold forward', there is an important difference. The gold mine selling gold futures has not sold the gold, so any possible mis-judgement in timing is self-correcting. On the other hand, the gold mine selling borrowed gold has thereby finalised the terms of the sale. Only delivery is put off. The self-correcting feature is missing. Any error in timing could be disastrous.

Barrick is totally ignorant of (true) hedging. Observe the difference between two operations:

(1) Selling gold futures for hedging purposes is one thing. It simply means booking a selling price now, with the actual sale of newly mined gold to follow later. A subsequent increase in the 'price' of gold is not hurting because the gold mine has retained the right to sell gold at the higher price later.

(2) Selling borrowed gold is another thing altogether. The actual sale of newly mined gold at a fixed price has been consummated, only delivery remains. Every cent of an increase

in the 'price' of gold is hurting because the increase means that the gold has been sold at the wrong price.

AXY acts as a hedge fund. Its straddles are fraudulent. Even if the financial results are positive in the end, it cannot report, still less pay out, a profit. Profits are paper profits. They will not be finalised until the 'hedges' are lifted. There is a contingent liability which can turn into real losses if the gold 'price' has a subsequent run on the upside. Paying out paper profits in bonus is a criminal fraud. The fact that AXY is a gold mine has nothing to do with its adventures in the world of gambling. Any hedge fund can do it (and will probably do a better job of it). The problem plaguing Barrick now is that it has commingled paper profits from gold and bond speculation with operating profits from gold mining and has, apparently, dipped into its treasury and paid hefty bonuses to executives and directors. The money is gone, but the contingent liability remains. When the gold 'price' increases, it becomes a loss that gets larger with every cent of an increase in the gold 'price'. The potential loss is open-ended.

Double Jeopardy

No wonder that the 28 Barrick executives are in such a mad hurry to cut and run before their bonuses are attached by court injunction in a possible class action suit. Damn whoever invented bonuses in the form of options. Cash bonuses would not have left such a stinking paper trail.

By contrast, consider XAB. It acts as any proper hedger does who is involved in the production of real goods. Its straddles are true hedges: they aim at benefiting the company from favourable price hikes by producing gold from ore body whose market value is zero in the absence of a hedging strategy. This operation is completely independent of the fickleness of interest rates and of the variation of the gold 'price'.

Note that the profitability of the 'hedges' of AXY is exposed to 'double jeopardy'. It depends on the assumption that neither interest rates nor the gold 'price' will rise. Should either do, the 'hedges' will show an immediate loss. Higher interest rates make the market value of bonds fall, hurting the long leg of the straddle. A higher gold 'price' will increase the cost of lifting the straddle.

Maximising The Life Of The Gold Mine

But the main difference between the two strategies has to do with the fact that true hedging (the strategy of XAB) extends the working life of the gold mine, while fraudulent hedging (the strategy of AXY) short-ens it. True hedging spares the richest ore bodies and shifts mining towards the submarginal grades or ore. This also means the most effi-cient deployment of the capital of the mine.

Barrick-type hedges result in a ruthless exploitation of the mining resource. Naturally, AXY wants to squeeze the maximum amount of cash out of its 'hedges', regardless of the damage it may cause to the longevity of the mine, because it wants to buy as many bonds as possi-ble. In consequence the richest grades of ore are extracted first and the mine is exhausted prematurely. When it is forced to close down, it will still have a lot of valuable gold-bearing ore left behind.

Economics Of Gold Mining

The economics of gold mining is as different from that of base metal mining as day from night. The aim of a copper mine, for example, is to maximise profits without regard for the working life of the mine. The reason is that the marginal utility of copper is declining. This means that if you do not market your copper at the earliest opportunity, then competition grabs your market share and runs with it. *Tarda venientibus ossa* – says the Latin proverb (late-comers to the meal get the bones). In the case of copper miners, late-comers have to sell at a lower price.

By contrast, the marginal utility of gold is declining so slowly that it is practically constant. There is no pressure on the miner to rush his product to the market. His concern is to get as much gold throughout the mine's extended working life as possible, regardless how long it may take. If it takes longer, no harm done. The mine stands to benefit from deliberate currency debasement practiced by governments. De-basement has the unintended effect of promoting the submarginal ore bodies of the gold mines to the payable category.

Incidentally, this is the secret of the popularity of owning gold min-ing shares in spite of the meagre returns to invested capital. Gold min-ing shares have a built-in option-feature. The option expires when the gold mine is exhausted. Thus, given two identical gold mines with ex-actly the same geological features, the one worked more conservatively will command the higher share price and the higher market capitalisa-tion, because the underlying option has the longer maturity date. The market will assign the lowest market capitalisation to the gold mines that go after the highest grade of ore, even if the dividends paid by that mine are higher.

Having said that, we find that the hedging strategy of XAB still has shortcomings and calls for further improvements. Both AXY and XAB are using unilateral hedging strategies. As a side-effect speculators are invited to converge on the short side of the market and compete with the gold mines to nip every gold rally in the bud. What is needed, clearly, is bilateral hedging and its four-legged straddles to eliminate that threat.

Endnotes to Chapter 44

[1] See chapter 48, Deconstructing Ideologies.

[2] Certainly, Krugman does not. But then, he's paid for his performances.

[3] In Aristotle's time it was next to impossible. Aristotle drew a parallel with cattle, that does multiply, for reasons well known.

[4] Virgil, *Aeneid*, ii.49

[5] The legal experts will recognise how an Actio Pauliana will/may bring relief to the defrauded parties (Actio Pauliana is the name for a recovery claim in Roman Law, i.e. Europe, South Africa and parts of Indonesia.

[6] See volume II for a better grasp of the trading terms or trading jargon and its meaning.

[7] Which does not prevent a situation were silly ideology have completely taken over, in which case, no 'conspiracy' is needed. The flock of followers behaves with self-censure and will religiously act in unison. See Chapter 48 'Deconstructing Ideologies'.

[8] See Volume II for an explanation of the trading terms.

[9] That would depend on many factors such as crop, crop rotation, fertility of the soil, climate and location, availability of water, etc...

[10] Technically, there exists no such thing as a 'price' of gold. It is an oxymoron. Gold is the monetary unit under a gold standard and it is expressed in terms of itself or in terms of silver. When the gold standard becomes adulterated with greenbacks or fiat, the phrase 'gold 'price'' is just meaningless, for it takes the world on its head like the tail that wags the dog... See also chapter 49 on deconstructing ideologies for an explanation of turning things on their head.

[11] The gambling casinos in casu are the bond and stock markets.

[12] Reuters, August 3, 2007.

[13] It certainly, makes a *fiscal* difference...

⚞ Chapter 45 ⚟

Futures Markets, Basis, Contango, Backwardation

The Last Contango

When the silver corpse stirs, money doctors run. People from around the world keep asking me what advance warning for the collapse of our international monetary system, based as it is on irredeemable promises to pay, they should be looking for. My answer invariably is: 'watch for the last contango in silver'.

It takes a little bit of explaining what this cryptic message means. Contango is that condition whereby more distant futures prices are at a premium over the nearby. The opposite is called backwardation which obtains when the nearby futures sell at a premium and the more distant futures are at a discount. When contango gives way to backwardation in *all* contract spreads, never again to return, it is a foolproof indication that no deliverable monetary silver exists. People with inside information have snapped it up in anticipation of an imminent monetary crisis.

'Last contango' does not mean that the available supply of monetary silver has been 'consumed' by industrial applications, as trumpeted by the cheerleaders of the get-rich-quick crowd. Such a notion is at odds with the fact that silver has always been and still is, a monetary metal. Huge stores of monetary silver still exist, *but are kept out of sight* and availability by their current owners who, for obvious reasons, want to remain anonymous. 'Last contango' is the endgame of the grand tug-of-war between the money doctors and 'We, the People'. The doctors exiled silver from banking to the futures market hoping that it will drown there in a sea of paper silver. But the silver corpse stirs. People withdraw ever greater chunks of cash silver from exchange-approved warehouses. The money doctors run scared. If futures trading in silver is unsustainable and must end in default, then the flimsiness of the house of cards built of irredeemable promises will be exposed for all to see. Following the last contango in Washington the money doctors, led by Helicopter Ben, will follow the example set by the 18th century Scottish adventurer John Law of Lauriston. He left Paris in a hurry. In a disguise. Disguised as a woman.

Don't Kill The Goose Laying Silver Eggs

My main argument justifying the claim that the bulk of monetary silver has not been consumed is that silver, just as gold, is far more useful in monetary than in industrial applications. Provided, I hasten to add, that you know what a monetary metal is and you also know how to make it yield a return. Admittedly very few people do and fewer still are willing to share their knowledge with others. Nevertheless, monetary applications of silver are real. Industrial applications kill the goose that lays silver eggs. We must also remember that silver consumption is a relative concept. In Newfoundland tiny silver pieces half the weight of a silver dime with 5 cent denomination had been in circulation before 1949. After the country was absorbed into Canada, these pieces were threaded onto a chain to form bracelets and necklaces. You may, of course, say that silversmiths have 'consumed' silver but, clearly, these pieces could re-enter circulation if circumstances warrant it, as quickly as overnight. While the labour component of the price of silver cutlery and plate may be greater, again, this is relative. At a higher silver price it may become negligible. There is hardly any form of silver consumption the product of which could not be recycled, provided only that the silver price is high enough.

The Hairy Tale Of Naked Short Interest

Every time the silver price rallies, selling appears and the price falls back. 'Aha', the cheerleaders cry, the 'silver managers are at it again. They are selling silver naked!' Since the silver managers issue no denial, it is taken as a confirmation of the hairy tale of naked short selling.

According to this fable the silver managers gang up against silver investors in an effort to drive down the silver price, so that they may cover their naked short positions at a profit. But if this were true, wouldn't they sell into weakness rather than into strength? The fact that an increase in the short commitment invariably occurs on rallies and it is then reduced on subsequent dips clearly indicates the absence of malicious intent. Traders simply take advantage of the variation in the silver price in order to derive profits from it, much the same way as hydro plants take advantage of the tides in order to harness its energy. Nobody suggests that the tide-ebb cycle is caused by the hydro plants. It is interesting that the cheerleaders don't complain when the silver managers buy on dips. They put a different spin on it. Purchases are described as the last desperate attempt of the silver managers at short covering.

Soon enough this fable of a huge phantom naked short position will be put to the test. According to the cheerleaders the short interest should cave in under the burden of unbearable losses. The silver managers will throw in the towel and panic-covering will cause the silver price to go to four digits, non-stop. 'Patience, fellow silver investors, patience! Hang on just a wee-bit longer! After this last sell-off the price will go straight up!' Well, we have heard that battle-cry often enough, long enough. It is getting monotonous, perhaps a little boring as well.

So where do we go from here? The cycle of profit-taking bargain-hunting-short-covering will, of course, continue as before. Volatility will grow, quite possibly faster than the moving averages, maybe far exceeding anything we have seen so far. The silver price could be up $100 one day and down $100 next day, so that a relative top may be indistinguishable from an absolute top. Lots of investors will be bumped from the band-wagon prematurely and they may find it impossible to climb back. But silver to go to four digits in one fell swoop? No way. Unless Helicopter Ben's deeds are as good as his bluffing and the air-drop of Federal Reserve notes does start in earnest.

Hedging Or Streaking?

I do not deny that naked short sellers exist. They do. I prefer to call them 'streakers'. Remember 'streaking', the fad of the 1970s? Young men derived excitement through exhibitionism as they ran short distances stark naked in busy streets. If the commercial traders ever run naked, it is likewise for fleeting moments only. They cover at the first opportunity. Then they may streak again and cover again. It must be exhilarating. I am not so sure about its profitability, though.

I go further. What passes as 'hedging' by gold and silver mining concerns is also streaking. If the miners were hedgers, then they would plow output into a monetary metal fund and write covered call options against it. But this is not what they do. They sell forward their future output, essentially selling naked, sometimes going out as many as 5 years. Then they cover part of their short position through purchases of call options. You can hedge cash gold, but you cannot hedge gold locked up in ore deposits deep underground that will take 5 years to bring up and unlock!

Hungry Pig Dreams Of Acorn

To call the gold miners' forward selling 'hedging' is a gross abuse of language. [1] It should not be permitted by the watchdog agencies. It is an instance of wilfully misinforming the public. According to a Hungarian proverb 'hungry pig dreams of acorn'. The wheat farmer selling wheat futures before harvest is not hedging. He is selling forward in order to lock in a favourable price. He is barred from selling anything in excess of his current crop. It would be tantamount to selling dreams. Likewise, the gold miner should also be limited to selling forward one year's production.

In any case, it is not the producer who hedges but the warehouseman. If the producer calls his forward sales 'hedges', then he is obfuscating. He wants the buyers of futures contracts to believe that they are buying something more substantial than the dreams of a hungry pig.

Streaking as practiced by gold and silver mining concerns, in contrast with hedging proper, is a deeply flawed strategy animated by Keynesian and Friedmanite precepts. The basic assumption is that spikes in the gold and silver price are an aberration and, hence, must be temporary. Prices, as everything in economics, are bound to revert to the mean. The regime of irredeemable currency is here to stay. The money doctors have perfected methods whereby we can avoid the pitfalls into which the early pioneers of fiat currency fell. Take, for instance, the helicopter. The money doctors of the French Revolution had to labour without the benefit of air drops of assignats.

Helicopter And Guillotine In Aid Of Monetary Policy

This is not the place to refute Keynesian and Friedmanite fallacies. Suffice it to say that the helicopter is a dubious asset in the hands of the Federal Reserve Chairman anxious, as he is, to get his freshly printed 'IOU-nothing' notes into the hands of the public instantaneously. On the liability side the Chairman does not have the benefit of another great invention readily available to the managers of the assignat, namely the guillotine. As is known, during the French Revolution the guillotine was used, among others, for the purpose to cap the 'price' of gold with good effect. So much for hi-tech. As for lo-tech, absolutely nothing has been learned by monetary science during the past 200 years to justify the claim that money doctors can indefinitely entice people to give up real services and real goods in exchange for irredeemable promises to pay. The dictum of Lincoln still stands: you can fool some people all the time; you can even fool all the people some of the time; but you cannot fool all of the people all of the time.

Money is not what the government says it is but what the market treats as such. Silver and gold have been demonetised by the government through trickery and chicanery: silver in the 1870s and gold a century later, in the 1970s. Markets have never ratified these government measures and, presumably, never will in view of the disastrous record of fiat currencies. Witness the helicopter and the guillotine, the carrot and stick of monetary policy.

The principle of reversal to the mean doesn't work for monetary metals. Silver and gold mining concerns will find to their chagrin that their streaking strategy is backfiring. They are facing horrible losses on their naked short positions. They can thank their plight to their Keynesian and Friedmanite mind-set and to the brainwashing that passes as research and education in economics departments at all the universities and think tanks of the world today.

Basis, The Best Kept Secret Of Economics

How many gold mining executives are familiar with the concept of basis? Maybe one in ten. And how many can use it effectively in marketing gold? Maybe one in a hundred. Don't look for a chapter on basis in Samuelson's Economics. It is not there. Don't try to find its definition in Human Action of Mises. It is not there either. You have to go to obscure manuals on grain trading produced by professionals for the benefit of professionals to learn what it is. [2] As far as I can tell no economist has ever written about it for the benefit of laymen.

The basis earns its name by serving as the most basic trading tool and precision instrument of the grain elevator operator. In buying and selling grain he is not guided by the price and its variation. He is guided by the basis and its variation. He stands ready to buy or sell 24 hours a day, 7 days a week. If you wake him up in the dead of the night with an offer, he won't ask your price. He will ask your basis. If he likes it, then it's a deal, regardless of the price. Professional buyers and sellers of grain do not quote their bid/asked price. They have no use for it. They quote their bid/asked basis.

Recall that basis is the spread between the nearest futures price and the cash price. The grain elevator operator buys cash grain during the harvesting season to fill his elevators to the brim. He tries to buy cash grain at the widest possible basis (known as carrying charge). He is planning to sell it when the basis is getting narrower. His profit is just the shrinkage of the basis. What is the explanation of this peculiarity? When the grain elevator operator buys cash grain, he sells an equivalent amount in the futures market. He must hedge his inventory because the capacity of his elevator storage space is so huge that even a minor fall in the grain price will wipe out his entire capital, if his cash grain is left unhedged.

During the growing season the basis keeps falling as inventories are being drawn down. The grain elevator operator tries to sell cash grain at as low a basis as possible, because he expects to replace it at a wider basis when the new crop becomes available. It goes without saying that in tandem with selling cash grain he lifts his hedges, i.e., buys back his contracts to deliver cash grain in the future. I repeat, from the point of view of profitability, the prices at which he bought and sold cash grain don't matter. The only thing that matters is the variation of the basis. Sometimes he buys cash grain at a higher and sells it profitably at a lower price. How can he get away with this prestidigitation? Well, he has correctly anticipated that the basis will shrink faster than the price will fall. He is aware that he cannot predict the variation of the price, which is at the mercy of nature. But he may divine the variation of the basis that depends on human need, which is more predictable.

Rationing Warehouse Space

Moreover, the basis also helps the grain elevator operator to decide what type of cash grain to buy and store. Other things being the same he will buy the grain with the higher basis and sell the one with the lower. In this way he can maximise his profit derived from the shrinking basis. If the basis is higher for wheat than for corn, then he will keep buying cash wheat in preference to corn until the basis for corn catches up. Or, suppose, the news is that corn blight has hit the growing regions. The astute grain elevator operator will respond by accelerating his sales of cash wheat, in order to make room for more corn in his elevators.

The best way to think about the business of the grain elevator operator is to assume that he is marketing warehousing services, including the rationing of warehouse space between competing uses. His guiding star is the basis. High and rising basis tells him for which purposes the demand for scarce public warehouse capacity is the most urgent. Low and falling basis tells him for which purposes the demand is slack, as people prefer non-public solutions for their storage problem, e.g., by keeping supplies closer to home, as often happens in troubled times. Including digging holes in one's own backyard.

The idiosyncrasies of the basis with regard to monetary commodities, since they can be buried in holes, are quite different from those with regard to non-monetary commodities, which cannot. This will be the subject of the last of this 3-part series on the basis.

Acknowledgement

I am grateful to Dr. Theo Megalli for calling my attention to the work of the German monetary scientist Heinrich Rittershausen (1898-1984)

Backward Thinking

The father of backward thinking on backwardation is undoubtedly John Maynard Keynes. In his 2-volume Treatise on Money published in 1930 he developed a theory of the futures markets and introduced the concept of normal backwardation. As the name suggests, backwardation is considered as the 'normal condition' of the futures market so that, by implication, contango is 'abnormal'. According to Keynes backwardation, or discount on the futures price as compared to the spot price, is a necessary incentive that is supposed to persuade speculators to buy forward. In his view the discount is just the 'insurance premium', as it were, that speculators collect for shouldering the risk that the price of the commodity may fall during the time-span to delivery.

It would be hard to misconstrue the meaning of backwardation in a way worse than Keynes' 'normal backwardation' does. His theory turns reality upside down. Again.

The truth is that the normal condition of the futures markets is that of contango whereby the futures price is at a premium compared to the spot price. The premium accrues to the warehouseman who carries the physical commodity while hedging it by selling an equal amount of futures.

The basis, or difference between the futures price and the spot price, is the signal telling the warehouseman about the state of demand for warehouse space. One may even say that the (positive) basis is the market price of available space in the warehouses. It tends to be low when warehouses have a lot of vacant space to fill and high when they are close to full. Not only does it help to allocate scarce warehouse space between competing uses; the basis also guides the warehouseman telling him how fast he should fill his vacant warehouse space, or how fast he should make space available for alternative and more urgent uses; in other words, to decide which commodity to buy and which to sell. Other things being the same the warehouseman should buy the commodity with the higher and sell the one with the lower basis. Without the signal from the basis and the variable contango he would be in the dark shooting from the hip.

At any rate, backwardation is always indicating an abnormal condition: that of a shortage, whether it is due to insufficient production or prodigal consumption, or whether it indicates lack of foresight to carry sufficient supplies to cover future needs.

Keynes' celebrated faux pas in introducing the misnomer 'normal backwardation' is second only to that of Karl Marx. As is known, Marx has made the worst blunder in the history of economic thought when he created his theory of value. According to him, labour is the exclusive source of value, so the value of merchandise is directly proportional to labour content.

Thus, then, the government can create 'value' by having bottle-caps buried in deep holes and let people prospect for them and dig them up at great cost in labour – as has in fact been suggested by Keynes. This shows the common thread in the thinking of these two 'defunct' economists.

The Keynesian mindset is obsessed with the idea of overproduction and with the need to fight it by all available means. At the same time it dismisses the idea that in the real world scarcity is the basic human problem one should worry about.

***

Keynesian economists never quote their mentor's theory of the futures market as it is a *major embarrassment*. [3] Moreover, it is hard to disagree with James Turk that much of what floats around on the internet about backwardation is total rubbish. It would seem neither the Prophet nor the general public have any idea.

A deep level of ignorance about 'basis' and 'backwardation' is the chief cause of the fiasco – and Turk is silent on this – of the gold mining industry falling into the trap laid by the government. It was the trap of 'hedging', more precisely, the selling of mine output forward up to fifteen years in advance. It was an insane collective hara-kiri of a major industry. It failed miserably because it left the reaction of speculators out of the equation. [4] Yet it was perfectly predictable that the reaction would be negative – from the point of view of the industry itself. Speculators would abandon their traditional perch on the long side of the market and they would hop over to the short side. Gold mines and speculators would fall over themselves in competing for the privilege of being the first in selling gold short.

The net result was that the gold 'price' was clubbed down every time it was trying to climb out of the hole. Gold prospecting was stifled. In addition, the grip on the world of the regime of irredeemable currency was reinforced – just as wished by the governments. Other results included the premature depletion of the ore reserves of the mines, the looting of shareholders by management, the insanity and waste involved in producing gold at peak rates of output only to squander it at $250 an ounce, as recently as 1999.

Had gold mining executives educated themselves about the gold basis and the threat of backwardation in gold, the disaster would have been avoided. Based on the correct principles of bilateral hedging, the mines would have developed a marketing strategy motivated by the trading of the gold basis – instead of trading the gold 'price'. The vanishing of the gold basis would have prevented these executives from making the worst blunder: selling (borrowed) gold and buying the futures. They would have saved a bundle for their shareholders to whom the losses caused by the vanishing basis were charged. They could have maximised the useful life-span of their mines, instead of maximising short-term paper profits of dubious value. Gold mining executives, just like the American bankers, are very good at paying themselves huge salaries and bonuses. They are not nearly as good at admitting their mistakes and learning from them.

✷✷✷

According to Turk there have been three episodes of backwardation in gold as follows:

(1) The first occurrence was November 29, 1995. That backwardation lasted for a day and was probably the result of a hedge buy-back by Barrick Gold.

(2) The next occurrence lasted for two days, September 29-30, 1999. It was caused by a mad rush for physical gold to cover short positions in the wake of the Washington Agreement on central bank gold sales.

(3) The third occurrence happened last month and continued for three business days, November 20, 21 and 24. Turk says that no special event triggered this latest backwardation.

Turk does not consider the possibility that the November episode could have been a premonition of a more durable backwardation on the way. He does not recognise the backwardation at the Comex that started on December 2 and lasted for two weeks, in spite of the fact that it has been confirmed by the Tokyo Commodity Exchange where backwardation was in force, not only between spot and nearby but between more distant futures as well.

The key to understanding the present upheaval in the world economy and the relevance of backwardation to it is that, regardless of official propaganda, gold circulation (such as it is) never ceased to be an important part of the world's trading system.

Backwardation means that gold circulation is stopped in its tracks, which is deflationary in the extreme, greatly contributing to the contraction of world trade.

Backwardation in gold causes and is caused by, the cascading contraction of *world trade.* [5] It is preposterous to suggest that no special event triggered the backwardation in gold. The special event was the onset of Great Depression II, just as sabotaging the gold standard by Britain on September 1, 1931, heralded the onset of Great Depression I.

The problem with Turk's analysis is that he considers backwardation in gold in isolation, taken out of the context of the vanishing of the gold basis that has been going on for at least three decades. This is like trying to understand the eruption of a volcano while deliberately ignoring prior rumblings. Given the secular decline of the gold basis, it should be easy to interpret the backwardation episode last month as a warning of the crisis caused by the realisation that the world was walking into a gold trap. The gold basis was bound to enter negative territory, because its relentless decline indicated that ever more gold was going into hiding, while it became ever more difficult to coax it out of hiding.

This is not a crisis of Comex. This is a crisis of the international monetary and payments system trying, as it is, to reduce global debt with irredeemable promises issued by central banks. This is a crisis caused by mainstream economics in putting monetary science beyond the pale and cheering on the government for driving gold, the ultimate extinguisher of debt, out of the monetary system.

Borrowing Carl Menger's admirable phrase 'police science,' [6] alias Keynesian economics, must bear full responsibility for conceiving, giving birth to and raising to maturity Great Depression II. In an earlier article Backward Thinking on Backwardation I explained that backwardation in gold is the flip-side of the phenomenon of a drastic contraction of world trade and employment. This brings out the danger in denying the fact of gold backwardation or to belittle its significance, as most observers seem to be doing. I am reminded of the saying of the Swiss educator F.W. Foerster: 'if you don't use your eyes for seeing, later you will use them for weeping.' In this article I want to enumerate the reasons why I believe that permanent backwardation in gold would bring about the descent of our civilisation into lawlessness similar to that following the collapse of the Western Roman Empire.

The consensus seems to be that, even if backwardation in gold occurred at one point, it would not be a significant event given the zero-interest environment. Forward thinking on backwardation shows that this is wrong.

Tom Szabo observes: 'If somehow short-term interest rates were to go into significant backwardation, it should be no surprise that gold and silver may go into significant backwardation. THIS WOULD NOT BE A SIGN OF IMMINENT MONETARY COLLAPSE [his emphasis]. In fact, a pretty strong argument could be made for the opposite – that the negative interest rate is a sign of excessive monetary demand (in relation to demand for capital goods and investments). I've looked but have been unsuccessful in finding an historical example of a monetary collapse that occurred while money was actually in high demand. Of course, high demand for money could be extremely deflationary and the only known cure for this is to create a high supply of money, otherwise known as hyperinflation.'

While I would disagree with the use of the word 'imminent' in describing the coming monetary collapse, I must maintain my stand that a durable backwardation, such as we have experienced for two weeks earlier this month, is a premonition that there will be repeated episodes of the same kind, ever more frequent, ever deeper, ever longer, each episode significantly weakening the monetary system – regardless of the zero or negative short term interest rate. (Let us leave the question aside that zero or negative interest rates in and of themselves show an alarming pathology of the monetary system!)

I have argued that we must carefully distinguish between a fiat money regime with an undisturbed flow of gold to the futures market; and a fiat money regime where the flow of gold to the futures market has been blocked by an unprecedented surge in the demand for cash gold.

> ▷ In the first case confidence in fiat money is high; in the second, it is low and waning fast.

> ▷ In the first case paper gold is an effective substitute for physical gold in most applications; in the second, paper gold has been unmasked as a fraud and discredited beyond repair.

> ▷ In the first case the economy works pretty well the same way as under a gold standard; in the second, all hell is turned loose as the exchange of goods and services is on the decline and autarky on the rise.

Tom thinks 'it is incorrect to claim that gold and silver could be in true backwardation without at least some inversion of the futures price curve where the nearer contracts are trading at a higher price than the further out contracts. Well, exactly that's what has happened at Tocom during the first two weeks of this month and is happening still. Tocom publishes its trading summary at the close of trading every day on the

Internet:

I don't understand how Tom could miss it. Backwardation is jumping off the internet page covering the standard kilo bar contract, even as I write this. Tom is complaining that the spot price for gold is difficult to ascertain: 'the spot price for gold is elusive... because they are third-party quotes that suffer from a variety of problems that can make them unreliable and imprecise.' I disagree. You just have to be plugged into the right feeds at Bloomberg. My spot price quotes include all the five price fixers at the LBMA, plus everybody else worthy of quoting... The spot gold 'price' one ought to use, is the best or highest bid (and the best or lowest offer) from 300 banks world-wide. The data we use is directly from the exchange and the prints we see for the carry available are super precise. We can get e.g. 90¢ per oz profit on the December contract versus our spot quotes that come from every bank on earth... Everybody of note is inferring that gold is in backwardation because of the zero interest. Let us explore that a little further. One can achieve 0.25% annualised by carrying gold for 190 days till June 26, 2009. 190 days in maturity is about equivalent to a 6-month T-bill with a current yield of 0.18%. The cost of carry for 190 days is $0.25 - 0.18 = 0.07\%$. If we compare this with the cost of carry for 11 days till December 27, 2008 and, again, for 69 days till February 27, 2009, then we get that the cost of carrying gold is as follows (all percentages are annualised)

for 11 days	1.005%
for 69 days	0.9%
for 190 days	0.07%

That is pathological without any need of further explanation! It costs more to carry gold for shorter periods of time than for a longer period – according to the futures market. That puts a hole in the zero interest-rate argument and explodes the explanation that the extra-low contango or outright backwardation in gold is nothing more than 'normal backwardation' of a non-monetary commodity!'

Tom says that he does not see things evolving in the same catastrophic manner as I do. For example, he believes that 'there will always be willing buyers and sellers of gold in some quantity if the price (in irredeemable fiat currency) is right.' Buyers – si, sellers – no! That's just the whole point. The lack of credibility of irredeemable currency will be such that no one in his right mind will accept it in exchange for gold, the ultimate liquidator of debt. Previously, people were willing to trade their gold because they could always replenish their supply from Comex warehouses. That means, in other words, that the irredeemable dollar could still be used as a liquidator of debt (i.e., gold still has a competitor). But let them close the Comex gold warehouses. This is a quantum jump; it means that the irredeemable dollar can no longer be used to liquidate debt, e.g., debt incurred by those holding short positions in gold futures. It is essential not to belittle the import of this observation.

Tom thinks that I am an alarmist in believing that the permanent closing of the gold window at the Comex will mean a cessation in gold mining, loss of segregated metal deposits and institutionalised theft of ETF holdings.

To answer this I have to go back to the collapse of the Western Roman Empire after the abdication of the emperor *Romulus Augustulus* [7] on September 4, 476 A.D. It was followed by the Dark Ages when the rule of law, personal security, trade of goods against payment in gold and silver could no longer be taken for granted. Gold and silver went into hiding, never to re-emerge during the lifetime of the original holders. It is plausible to see a causal relationship between the fading of the rule of law and the complete disappearance of gold and silver from trade. Virtually all observers say that the first event caused the second.

I may be in a minority of one to say that causation goes in the opposite direction.

The disappearance of gold and silver coins as a means of exchange was a long-drawn-out, cumulative event. In the end, no one was willing to exchange gold and silver coins for the debased coinage of the empire. At that point the empire was bankrupt; it could no longer pay the troops that defended its boundaries against the barbarians threatening with invasion.

This is not to say that the empire did not have other weaknesses. It did, plenty of them. But the overriding weakness was the monetary weakness. Centuries after centuries the Mint of the empire could attract less and less gold and silver. Because of this, the empire was forced to debase its coinage and the deterioration continued until the bitter end, when the gold flow to the Mint completely dried up.

Compare this with the Eastern Roman Empire that lasted until the fall of Constantinople to the Ottoman Turks in 1453 A.D., or almost one thousand years longer than the Western half and during most of this time it could keep its Mint open to gold, producing the gold bezant, which also became the coin of the Muslim world. Is this difference between the two empires trying to tell us something about the importance, from the point of view of political and economic survival, of keeping the Mint open to gold? The history of the monetary system of the United States shows an ominous parallel to that of the Western Roman Empire. As long as gold and silver was still used in trade at least to some extent, the Western Roman Empire was limping along. The modern equivalent of the disappearance of gold and silver is epitomised by the progressive vanishing of the gold basis. There is simply no continuous transition from the paper dollar cum contango to the paper dollar cum gold backwardation, Tom's prayer notwithstanding. The transition will necessarily involve *a sudden* and *fatal weakening* of the legal system. Remember, the legal system works only as long as most citizens are law-abiding. It breaks down as soon as the majority of the citizens find that the law protects thieves in high places, but offers next to no protection for the honest hard-working middle class. I am not going to elaborate here on the proposition that irredeemable currency is a system that protects thieves in high places, but robs the little guy by plundering his savings. Tom notes that it may be technically possible to delay the collapse of the fiat money system by 'allowing' gold to appreciate in a hyper inflationary scenario. That is precisely the phase that will end with the entrenchment of backwardation in gold. Thereafter one can no longer talk about an 'appreciating gold 'price', or any gold 'price' for that matter, as the pricing mechanism will have self-destructed, at least as far as the 'price' of gold is concerned. As Tom himself observes in the same article, local prices in India, China and in the jungles of Papua are not relevant. Only gold 'price's in New York and London are and the arbitrage between the two. I have nowhere said that the *end* of the fiat money system will follow the closing of the gold window at the Comex *in a matter of days*. Sure, finance ministers and central bankers will try to 'muddle through'. It is not possible to predict how long the death throes of fiat money will continue. Tom may be right in suggesting that it will take many years and claims of an imminent monetary and economic collapse will again turn out to be wrong. But where Tom is certainly, mistaken is his suggestion that all this agony will take place while the Last Contango in Washington is still going on.

> You can't have contango and backwardation at the same time. Backwardation is like a black hole, once it grabs a currency, it will swallow it and gold quoted in that currency will never return to contango.

I think Tom's greatest mistake is to interpret the move into backwardation, or gold to enter the 'fever phase', as 'gold's regaining fully-recognised monetary status'. Unfortunately, just the opposite is the case. Whether officially recognised or not, gold's monetary status was never in doubt. Gold has always been the monetary commodity par excellence, due to the fact that it has constant marginal utility (or, if you will, the fact that the marginal utility of no other commodity declines at a rate slower than that of gold). What we are witnessing is a transition that deprives gold of its monetary qualities.

> Gold in hiding cannot and will not act as money.

More to the point, absent gold, nothing else can or will. The disappearance of money, that can be trusted, fatally undermines the legal system, the sanctity of contracts, *habeas corpus*, any and all provisions of law and order that we take for granted. Under these conditions nobody can operate a gold mine, nobody can run a gold refinery, nobody can guarantee segregated gold deposits and nobody can prevent the institutionalised theft of ETF holdings. Welcome to the Madoff economy! (See: Paul Krugman's column in The New York Times 'Jail one Madoff, two others will jump into his shoes.') As a consequence of the permanent backwardation in gold, we shall have a world gone **Madoff**.

Endnotes to Chapter 45

[1] We will come to abuse of language in chapter 48, Deconstructing Ideologies.

[2] E.g. Sherry Lorton & Don White, *The Art of Grain Merchandising*, 1994, White Commercial Corp.

[3] Avoiding embarrassment would have been a lot easier by selecting the right people to receive a doctorate or academic title to begin with. Such a treatise ought not to have passed at all for its compilation of logical fallacies, innuendo and poor research, not to mention hare-brained 'theories'.

[4] Keynes is being credited no less for the 'theory of speculation' and look...when applied by the very governments he advised on it,... it fails! Of course, that is because it was thoroughly wrong from the beginning.

[5] Watch out for possible increasing trade barriers, tariffs and other stumbling blocks, decreasing trade and increasing backwardation.

[6] Cfr. Chapter 48, Deconstructing Ideologies, under 'Modern Spells', The Thought Police.

[7] *Augustulus* appears to be his diminutive, mocking name.

~~%~~ Chapter 46 ~~%~~

Economic Cycles

E conomists [1] recognise four major cycles, or regular fluctuations, in the economy as follows:

(1) Kitchin's short-wave cycle of average duration 3-5 years, discovered in 1930;
(2) Juglar's cycle of average duration 7-11 years, discovered in 1862;
(3) Kuznets' medium-wave cycle of average duration 15-25 years, discovered in 1923;
(4) Kondratiev's long-wave cycle of average duration 45-60 years, discovered in 1922.

Joseph Schumpeter, who was born in Austria and came to the United States where he also served as President of the American Economic Society in the 1950s, was an outstanding student of economic cycles. He believed that the various cycles are inter-dependent, in contrast with the view of others such as Forrester, who believed that the cycles act independently of one another. Schumpeter baptised three of the four cycles by naming them after their discoverers. The exception was Kuznets' cycle, which he did not recognise.

At any rate, Kuznets got a 'consolation prize' for being passed over by Schumpeter, namely the Nobel Prize for economics. Moreover, he is the only Nobel-laureate among the four name-giving economists. Kuznets noticed that residential and industrial buildings have an average useful life of 21-23 years. His medium-wave cycle is about fluctuations caused by the amortisation-cycle and the problem of replacing ageing buildings. It is interesting to note that all the students of cycles among the four whose name begins with a K were Russian.

Kondratiev's Long-Wave Cycle

The long-wave cycle in the capitalist economy was discovered by the Soviet economist N. D. Kondratiev (1892-1930) in 1922. He had been anticipated by J. van Geldren in 1913 and, even earlier, by Jevons in 1878 and H. Clarke in 1847, among others. Independently of Kondratiev, De Wolfe proposed a theory involving the idea of a long-wave cycle in 1924.

As we have noted above, some important students of cycles believed that they were inter-dependent. In particular, they noted that the average length of each of the four cycles is slightly longer than double the length of the immediately preceding shorter cycle. In the 1930s historians F. Braudel, F. Simiand and E. Larousse looked at changes in the 'secular trend' that were taking place roughly every 100 years. This suggests that Kondratiev's cycle might also be followed by a centennial cycle of approximately twice the duration.

Kondratiev's methodology involved the analysis of 21 statistical series, that is, 21 economic indicators such as the price index, the rate of interest, wage rates, rents; volume of production, consumption, exports, imports, employment, etc., as well as their standard deviations. In studying volumes Kondratiev used per capita data. He calculated deviation from the trend through the method of least squares. In order to filter out noise caused by the shorter cycles he employed nine-year moving averages. He took his data-base from the French, British, German and the U.S. economy.

Only in 6 of the 21 series could Kondratiev not confirm the presence of a long wave-cycle. Significantly, in the case of the price level and the rate of interest the evidence was strong. Kondratiev's ultimate conclusion was that he obtained sufficient empirical basis to support the hypothesis of the existence of a long-wave economic cycle in the capitalist economies he studied, with an average duration of 54 years. He allowed a 25 percent deviation from this average. In particular, Kondratiev identified three historic waves:

(1) First wave: rising phase from 1780-90 to 1810-17; falling phase from 1810-17 to 1844-51
(2) Second wave: rising phase from 1844-51 to 1870-75; falling phase from 1870-75 to 1890-96.
(3) Third wave: rising phase from 1890-96 to 1914-20; falling phase started 1914-20.

Kondratiev was exiled to Siberia by Bolshevik officials who flatly rejected his conclusions. To the faithful communist, there could only be one falling phase of the capitalist economy, followed by the socialist revolution and the dictatorship of the proletariat. And, following that, there was to be only one rising phase, leading to eternal bliss under communism.

Kondratiev died in the Gulag in 1930 at the age of 38. His work was later updated by other economists using his original methodology. They found that the falling phase of the third wave ended 1947-48 and that there is a

(4) Fourth wave: rising phase from 1947-48 to 1973-80; falling phase started 1973-80.

Jackson's Linkage

In 1947 the British-born Canadian economist Gilbert E. Jackson studied the behaviour of just two economic indicators, that of the price level and the rate of interest. He found that the two are linked. Sometimes the price level leads and the rate of interest lags; at other times, the other way around. In his own words just like two hounds on a leash holding them together, while one can get a little bit ahead, they cannot come apart, the leash obliging them to follow the same path, uphill or down. Jackson's calculations yielded the same long-wave cycle established by Kondratiev. He called this phenomenon 'the linkage'.

Jackson was probably unaware of Kondratiev's work. Therefore, it is quite remarkable that two economists working independently came to virtually identical conclusions. Yet Jackson's contribution is all the more significant as he focused on just two economic indicators instead of twenty-one, to get the same conclusion. Jackson's methodology used British data, namely wholesale prices in Britain and the yield on British consols for a period of over 150 years from 1782 to 1947. In order to iron out short-term fluctuations in the data-base due to the business cycle and other factors, Jackson replaced the raw figures by eleven-year moving averages. He then charted both indicators in the same coordinate system showing two curves with the rising trend of both curves indicating an inflationary spiral and their falling trend the deflationary spiral, alternating with one another. We reproduce Jackson's original chart at the end of the paper. As the chart clearly shows, sometimes prices lead and sometimes they lag the rate of interest. Neither Jackson, nor anyone else who studied the phenomenon of linkage, could offer a full theoretical explanation. The most they could say was that it appeared to be an 'accidental coincidence'.

Jackson's results were published in 1947 in a paper 'The Rate of Interest' that was barely noticed by the profession at the time. By now it is largely forgotten in spite of the renewed great interest in Kondratiev's long-wave cycle to which Jackson's linkage is closely related. Nobody ever bothered to update Jackson's chart using his original methodology.

Since prices and interest rates are by far the two most closely watched and studied economic indicators, the possibility of a connection between the two has attracted a great deal speculation among economists. A host of excellent thinkers such as Knut Wicksell, Wilhelm Röpke, Gottfried Haberler, to mention only three who have studied it, found the phenomenon of linkage 'puzzling'. Irving Fisher went as far as saying that 'it seems impossible to interpret [the linkage] as representing an independent relationship with any rational basis'. In their 1932 book *Gold and Prices* G. F. Warren and F. Pearson claimed that they have found the causal relationship explaining linkage. They asserted that rising (falling) prices are the *cause* and high (low) interest rates are the *effect*. They argued that creditors note the rise in the price level and demand compensation from debtors for the loss of purchasing power in the form of higher interest. Conversely, when the price level falls and the purchasing power of the currency rises, competition of creditors forces reduction in lending rates.

Jackson rejected this line of reasoning. He pointed out that linkage works both ways. While sometimes the price level leads and the rate of interest lags giving impetus to lenders to change the lending rate, at other times the rate of interest leads and the price level lags. Do Warren and Pearson suggest that lenders are clairvoyants who can divine what direction prices will take in future years?

The Propensity To Hoard

Mainstream economics bypasses the problem of hoarding altogether. It suggests that in the modern economy with a well-developed capital market hoarding is either non-existent, or if it is practiced at all, then the practice is confined to boorish and uninformed people whose action can be safely ignored as unimportant. However, economists can dismiss the phenomenon of hoarding and its consequences only at their own peril.

There may be more to hoarding than boorishness. It is well-known that informed producers regularly use sophisticated inventory-management techniques involving the speeding up or the slowing down of input and output at either end of their production line. The means of hoarding are just as ingenious as its objects are varied. The practice is certainly not confined to housewives buying more sugar to fill up their pantry, nor to small-time smugglers holding contraband merchandise in mountain-caves. They also include big multi-national firms using the most up-to-date techniques such as inventory-padding or the deliberate use of leads and lags in warehousing. In recent times cutbacks in production quotas of highly marketable goods such as crude oil have been utilised for the same purpose with dramatic effect. The Japanese are known to import far more lumber and coal from Canada than they need for current consumption. Having treated the excess with an impregnating solution, they sink the lumber and coal to the bottom of their mountain lakes. Nor is hoarding of fuel confined to energy- poor countries. The U.S. government is filling up disused salt mines with crude oil. They call it 'strategic stockpile', but in the vernacular it is called hoarding, even if the word has a pejorative or boorish connotation.

The supertanker construction boom in the 1970s was not an exercise in efficient transportation. Its purpose was to build floating warehouses. The supertankers filled to the brim with crude set sail without the captain having the slightest idea of its final destination. If the highest bid for the crude in the tanker was not high enough, no problem. The supertanker just had to keep cruising a little longer. Futures and options trading opened up new avenues for the general public to participate in the hoarding game. These examples illustrate the phenomenal increase in the propensity to hoard in the period preceding 1980, which was manifested not only in rising prices but rising interest rates as well. Since 1980 the world has been experiencing a fall in the propensity to hoard and even 'dishoarding' previously hoarded goods. The process of reducing stockpiles at falling prices, which have been built up in expectation of higher prices, is a painful one.

It would be an impossible task to estimate, However, tentatively, the size of existing stockpiles of goods held not for impending consumption but, rather, for some other reason, notably in protest against low interest rates, reckless government spending and the banks' plundering the savings of individuals. This is where the statistician must plead ignorance. The only way to grasp the hoarding instincts and habits of people is through theoretical understanding.

The divorce of hoarding from saving took place in response to the conspiracy of the banks, aided and abetted by the government, in order to defraud and dispossess the saving public. Over long periods of time the propensity to hoard has been gaining ground as an independent economic force at the expense of the propensity to save (i.e., save money) in response to deteriorating bank practices, in particular, the banks' sheltering of illiquid government debt in their balance sheet and the government's protecting the banks against depositors withdrawing the gold coin.

By now the U.S. has reached the point that the savings rate is negative. It is wrong to blame the American people for this unfortunate state of affairs. The blame should be assigned to American politicians and officials who have corrupted the monetary system to such an extent that people refuse to put their savings into instruments the banks have to offer. No one knows what the savings rate would be if the value of marketable goods hoarded by Americans could be calculated.

Gold As The Monetary Metal

What makes gold the monetary metal par excellence is that it is the most hoardable commodity. This means that the opportunity cost of hoarding gold is lower than that of hoarding any other commodity. Gold is held in the balance sheet even if the promise of return to capital is nil. No other commodity is held in the balance sheet unless there is some promise of return to capital. This property puts gold outside of the power of governments. The pronouncements of the government about the 'demonetisation of gold' is empty gesture. More anti-gold propaganda will only increase the propensity to hoard gold.

Consider the proposition that the greater is the propensity to save, the lower will be the rate of interest be. This proposition in itself is not controversial. The mechanism whereby the flow of savings regulates the rate of interest under a gold standard is quite transparent. Savers who feel that the rate of interest is too low will exchange their bank notes and deposits for gold coins. In this manner savers retain direct control over the level of bank reserves as they confront the bank with the choice of either raising the lending rate or contracting bank credit. Thus, the mechanism that regulates the rate of interest is the savers' privilege to hoard gold. Any effort to tamper with this mechanism is certain to introduce distortions in the economy.

Governments in their wisdom have removed the gold coin as a regulator of bank reserves. They did this in order to disenfranchise savers who no longer have a say in setting the rate of interest. The government and the banks usurp this privilege. The government wants to project an image of itself as a 'do-gooder' in keeping the rate of interest low, purportedly in order to benefit the general public. The banks, in their turn, want to pursue a credit policy motivated by political rather than economic considerations. No cost-and-benefit analysis has ever been carried out and the costs have been conveniently ignored. To be sure, there are costs connected with pushing gold out of the monetary system.

As the government has assumed power over monetary policy in contemptuous disregard of the expressed wishes of the savers (to say nothing of the provisions of the Constitution), it aggrandises power. Since by its very nature the power to issue money is unlimited, the new monetary regime flies in the face of the principle of representative government of limited and enumerated powers.

But for our purposes more important than the destruction of the gold standard is the abridgement of the savers' rights and privileges that has predated their total disenfranchisement by several hundred years. The banks have always kept a bag of tricks on hand (other than raising the rate of interest) to dissuade their depositors from taking the gold coin. When they reached the end of the rope, they could always count on the government 'to go off gold' in order to save the banks' face – and skin – in declaring the banks' bad liabilities legal tender. Thus, the banks were rewarded, rather than punished, for their wrong-headed credit policies. No wonder that more credit abuses were heaped upon credit abuse for the centuries.

Double Standard Of Justice

The legal right of savers to demand gold coins in exchange for their bank notes and deposits whenever they get worried about the condition of banks or about the profligate spending habits of the government is eminently just and equitable. It is the little man's protection against the powerful and mighty without which, as history has made abundantly clear, the former would get plundered by the latter for all his worth.

This protection has been compromised by a double standard that was surreptitiously introduced in contract law. Creditors were free to press for the liquidation of firms that have failed to perform on their contractual promises. Originally there were no exceptions. Later, however, the banks got exempted from this provision of contract law. They were made immune against the wrath of their creditors, including depositors. A bank that refuses to pay gold on its sight liabilities could no longer be sued for breach of contract.

There is no defensible justification in jurisprudence for extending special privileges to banks, or for protecting them against the consequences of their own folly. A law setting up double standard of justice is bad by definition. The argument that bank failures cause too much economic and social pain is spurious. All should stand equal before the law. Compromising this principle lets the bad effects of bank policy accumulate and will ultimately cause far more harm and economic or social distress than the immediate punishment of the bank that has gone astray.

Later the banks got still more protection from the government in the form of compromised standards of inspection. When they overstate the value of their assets and understate that of their liabilities, bank examiners look the other way. 'See no evil, speak no evil'. Banks can get away with fraudulent accounting practices that would trigger harsh punitive action if practiced by other firms. Bank examiners exonerate guilty banks upon the tacit approval, if not at the outright request of the government.

Economists are not famous for their curiosity about this peculiar tolerance for fraud that governments the world over have displayed for centuries. Yet the explanation is rather simple: 'If you scratch my back, then I shall scratch yours.' The banks have ample opportunity to return the favour of the government when they are expected to buy up treasury paper, which the market is no longer willing to take at the yields offered and to deliver similar sweetheart deals.

It would be naive in the extreme to assume that the savers meekly acquiesced in such acts of double-dealings and coercion. They could not prevent the government and the banks from sabotaging and ultimately destroying the gold standard. But they could do something about it. Instead of (or In addition, to) hoarding gold, savers thereafter started hoarding other marketable commodities. The list of marketable goods is endless. There are the conventional ones such as salt, sugar, spices, spirits, tobacco, tea and coffee. To this, one has to add the non-conventional ones, energy carriers such as crude oil and narcotics such as heroin and cocaine. (Note that as long as governments tolerated the gold standard there was little problem with drug trafficking. The suggestion cannot be easily dismissed that the escalation in illegal drug trade in the twentieth century was in direct response to the destruction of the gold standard.)

Causes Of The Kondratiev Cycle

We can now present our own explanation for the linkage and, simultaneously, our own description of the genesis of Kondratiev's long-wave cycle. Frustrated savers sell their bonds and put the proceeds in marketable commodities. Thus, rising commodity prices and falling bond prices are linked and they reinforce one another. The linkage is best described as a huge speculative money-flow. The money-tide begins to flow at the commodity market while ebbing at the bond market. This epitomises the inflationary phase of Kondratiev's long-wave cycle.

But falling bond prices are tantamount to rising rates of interest. Thus, a rising price level and a rising interest-rate structure, if they do not march in lockstep, at least they are closely linked. The money-flow from the bond to the commodity market, while it can go on for decades, will not last indefinitely. Holders of commodities will find that it is not possible to finance ever increasing inventories at ever increasing rates of interest. At one point they will panic and sell. Not all can get through the exit doors at the same time, however. Some will get trapped. Inventory reduction is a long-drawn-out and painful affair. This means that the speculative money-flow has reversed itself. Now the money-tide begins to flow at the bond market while ebbing at the commodity market. Prices of commodities fall while bond prices rise. Again, rising bond prices are tantamount to falling interest rates. The falling price level and the falling interest-rate structure are linked and they reinforce one another. This reversed money- tide epitomises the deflationary phase of the Kondratiev cycle.

Note the role of speculation in all this. Speculators are prominent in both the inflationary phase in which they go long in the commodity and short in the bond market, as well as in the deflationary phase in which their long and short legs are switched around. Just about the only way to make money in a depression is to speculate in the bond market on the long side. The bull market in bonds in a deflation is completely ignored by mainstream economists. Yet this is the key to the understanding of the reversal of the money-tide. Speculators do arbitrage between the bond and commodity markets. When they think that the saturation point has been reached, they reverse their position. They replace their existing straddles with the opposite ones. That is, they enter their long leg in the commodity and short leg in the bond market. This then heralds the end of the deflationary and the beginning of the inflationary phase.

The linkage and Kondratiev's long-wave cycle are explained in terms of fluctuations in the propensity to hoard. Since hoarding gold, the natural conduit, is obstructed by the banks and the government, the propensity to hoard manifests itself as the hoarding of other marketable goods. Already in 1844 Fullarton recognised that gold hoarding is just a protest-vote of the savers against low interest rates, the banks' loose credit policy and profligate government spending. Nevertheless, almost a hundred years later John Maynard Keynes looked at gold hoarding as a psycho-pathological aberration. He invoked the authority of David Ricardo. But Ricardo had also missed the economic significance of gold hoarding and he proposed the gold bullion standard to combat it.

To explain gold hoarding with psycho-pathology is nothing but scientific obscurantism. Keynes had a hidden agenda. He wanted to forge a weapon against the gold standard out of the fact of gold hoarding. The British economist was a bully. He was determined to sell the idea that the gold standard was unworkable, first to F.D. Roosevelt and then to the rest of the world. In this he did succeed.

Mainstream economics is still at the retarded level of Keynes when it comes to assessing the gold standard. It refuses to recognise the protest-aspect of gold hoarding, it is forgetful about the axiom that saving must precede spending and it ignores the fact that without saving there is no economic development. Gold is the leash on which the frugal must keep the prodigal. It is this leash that the banks and the government have always wanted and eventually managed, to escape from when they first sabotaged and then junked the gold standard. Although the sabotage started several hundred years ago, the world economy being run entirely without the leash of the gold standard has only a brief history of barely 30 years. It is not a glorious history.

In the great tug-of-war between the frugal and the prodigal the former appears to be the perennial loser. This is explained by the fact that the playing field is not level but tilts against the frugal, that is, the saving public. This includes not just creditors but, above all, the little man who is forced to keep his meagre savings in the form of cash, i.e., paper money open to plunder by the prodigal which is the consortium of the banks and the government. In spite of this bias we cannot take it for granted that the tug-of-war will end with the ultimate defeat of the frugal, just because the prodigal has succeeded in knocking the weapon of the gold coin out of his hand. The frugal has something else up in his sleeves. It is the propensity to hoard, an extremely efficient weapon which, however, is not free from some very dangerous side-effects.

A jump in the propensity to hoard can siphon off enormous amounts of money from the bond market. This will make the rate of interest jump, too. The last time it did that was in the years 1971-81. Those ten years that shook the world heralded the deflationary spiral in Kondratiev's long-wave cycle, the spiral that is still continuing.

Contra-Cyclical Policy

As already noted, the rise in the propensity to hoard has its limits. The hoarding of goods reaches its saturation point when it dawns on people that a high price structure and a high interest-rate structure cannot be maintained in the presence of high inventories. Declining marginal utility kicks in, ending the inflationary and ushering in the deflationary spiral. The long and painful process of inventory liquidation begins. The money-flow from the bond to the commodity market makes an 'about face'. The deflationary spiral may turn into a depression in which innocent firms start falling like dominoes.

Keynes' contra-cyclical policy should properly be called 'counter-productive policy'. It has been dogmatically applied by central banks since the 1930s only to make things worse. Following the Keynesian script, during the deflationary spiral the central bank is trying to contain weakening prices through open market purchases of bonds. Bond prices rise, in other words, the rate of interest falls. Bond speculators take the clue and they buy the bonds, too. Linkage causes the price level to fall (or at least stay weak). The central bank is unable to stem the deflationary tide of money flowing from the commodity to the bond market. In fact contra-cyclical monetary policy just pours oil on the fire.

Exactly the same is true of the inflationary spiral. The main worry now is the high rate of interest. To bring it down the central bank resorts to open market purchases of bonds. In doing so it puts new money into circulation which it hopes will flow to the bond market. Instead, it quickly finds its way to the commodity market and bids up prices there. Linkage does the rest. Higher prices bring about higher interest rates. Contra-cyclical policy fails in this case as well.

In the deflationary spiral the central bank combats weakening prices. This causes the rate of interest to fall, which leads to still lower prices. In the inflationary phase the central bank combats high interest rates. This causes prices to rise, which leads to still higher interest rates, all because of the linkage. The contra-cyclical policy of Keynes backfires in either case. For example, during the 1947-80 inflationary spiral the rate of interest rose five-fold and the price level ten-fold in the United States, in spite of vigorous contra-cyclical intervention by the Federal Reserve banks. Dr. Keynes prescribed medication that made the condition of the patient worse. He was ignorant of the linkage.

To recapitulate, the long-wave economic cycle is caused by a huge speculative money-flow back-and-forth between the bond and commodity markets. The flow is further aggravated by mindless contra-cyclical intervention. The oscillating money-flow is induced by fluctuations in the propensity to hoard. It is futile trying to correct these money flows. At best one can re-direct them into channels where they can do no harm. Keynes was so obsessed with gold hoarding that he missed the hoarding of other marketable goods, a problem potentially far more menacing. Keynes was the *high priest* of anti-gold agitation. He preached that if 'the gold coin was kept away from man's greedy palms' then there would be no gold hoarding, no economic contraction, no deflation, no unemployment. His was a colossal mistake, the kind that only a doctrinaire could make.

After the destruction of the gold standard by the government hoarding did not cease. It only changed form. The benign tumor turned malignant. Not only did the withdrawal of gold coins from the monetary bloodstream through government coercion fail to stop deflation: it set off a huge suction pump in the bond market siphoning money off from every nook and cranny of the economy. In particular, it created a devastating liquidation and depression from which only a world war could pull the economy. We can't help but notice that gold is the philosopher's stone. In its possession the propensity to hoard is directed into its proper channels. Without it the world economy becomes a plaything in the hands of bond and foreign exchange speculators.

Competitive Devaluations

Since 1981 the world appears to be in the grips of a deflationary spiral, right on schedule as predicted by the Kondratiev cycle. This spiral hasn't run its course yet. Some liquidation has taken place, but the worst seems still to come. The politicians and economists congratulate each other for 'having squeezed inflationary expectations out of the system'. Whatever they have squeezed, the inflationary and deflationary spirals are not caused by expectations, but by actual money-flows between the commodity and bond markets. The international monetary system is still the same rudderless ship it has been since 1971 and it is still exposed to the same monetary storms. The only difference is that the direction of the gale has changed.

The dangerous deflationary spiral threatening the world's prosperity started in Japan where the stock market collapsed followed by the real estate market. The sun has set on the Land of the Rising Sun. The next sunrise is probably a long way off. The devastation caused by deflation in the Japanese economy is of the same order of magnitude as that in the American during the previous cycle in the 1930s. Both **deflations can be characterised as an irresistible money-flow from the commodity to the bond market**, drying up resources in all departments outside of the bond market. In Japan, the rate of interest fell practically to zero. Ten years ago the Japanese government reacted in the same way as the American in 1933. It devalued the yen by fifty percent. This measure has been just as futile as the devaluation of the dollar was seventy years ago. It triggered competitive devaluations of the world's currencies in the 1930s. The yen-devaluation has the same effect. It was the cause of the collapse of the ruble and other Asiatic currencies. Right now it is the turn of the U.S. dollar to devalue. It remains to be seen whether the euro will also succumb to the temptation.

The Japanese deflation-tumor could very well metastasise across the Pacific. There is a carry-trade between the Japanese and American bond markets. Overpriced Japanese bonds are sold and the proceeds are put in the relatively underpriced American bonds. Note that this carry-trade is not hindered but rather helped by the devaluation of the dollar. At any rate, the outcome is a further fall in the rate of interest in the U.S. The deflationary spiral is alive and kicking. The stock market boom in the 1990s was not justified by increases in productivity and profitability any more than it was in the 'roaring twenties'. If the stock market crashes, the already irresistible money-flow to the bond market would be reinforced, just as after the 1929 crash. Falling interest rates would cause over-indebted firms to scramble in an effort to get out of debt. Credit-collapse may ensue. Already, the long-term rate of interest has been pushed down from 16 to 6 percent. The danger is that it may keep falling to 3 percent or lower, due to the speculative orgy in the bond market. Like a gigantic vacuum cleaner, the bond market siphons off resources from the real economy, just as it did in the 1930s. As noted already, it is not generally realised that **a depression, creates boom-conditions for the bond speculator** who makes a killing while everyone else is bleeding to death.

Mutations And Catastrophes

Kondratiev's long-wave cycle forces us to give up the earlier, optimistic models of uniform growth of the capitalistic economy, at least until the world is ready to return to the principles of classical liberalism and limited government, including its harbinger the gold standard. The following is a paraphrase of the thoughts of the Hungarian philosopher Béla Hamvas [2]

> " ... Our government, without the limitations imposed upon it by the principles of classical liberalism, makes for a fair-weather system. Under such a paternalistic, omnipotent and omniscient government modern civilisation may appear to work productively and humanely enough, that is, as long as the fair weather lasts.
>
> ...But let drought strike, or let flood engulf the land. Then our democratic unlimited government will at once show its feet of clay. No sooner does social disturbance, civil strife, or distrust raise its face than will centralised government lose its grip and get entangled in one crisis after another, all of its own making. The government that was omnipotent in fair weather would be helpless in foul. The government that was omniscient during the smooth evolutionary phase would plead ignorance at the first sign of a mutation. The fair-weather system of unlimited government is forever unable to cope with catastrophes.
>
> ...Older schools of evolution did not assume continuous progress. They were not given to thinking in terms of growth curves rising uniformly forever. They made allowance for mutations, they admitted the possibility of setbacks, abrupt reversals and tumbles. Older philosophers assumed that nature abhorred uninterrupted continuity, as much as she abhorred vac-

uum. They knew that in nature there was no continuous transition from the lower state to the higher. We should do well to remember the teachings and emulate the humility of those older philosophers. They were wise men, immeasurably wise. Certainly, far wiser than ourselves. Their thinking had one great advantage: they were not afraid to warn of the day when the weather would turn from fair to foul. They dared to think mutations. They dared to think catastrophes. While they were aware that dull times called for dull theories, they believed that critical times called for theories altogether alien to and different from those dull theories. In critical times you must think deeper, you must be wiser and more imaginative.

...We are in the habit of slighting and disparaging the accomplishments of older philosophers. We seem incapable of benefiting from their wisdom. They bequeathed a theory of limited government to us, a theory we have passionately rejected in favour of dull theories suitable for dull times... Yet the days of fair weather are numbered... We have lost our compass and the sea is growing stormy... Our boat of government omnipotence is now in waters teeming with dangerous reefs under the surface... We are in deep trouble... Que sera, sera...."

What Is To Be Done?

We need not conclude our review on such a pessimistic note. We are able to temper the deleterious effects of Kondratiev's long-wave cycle, even though we are unable to eliminate it. If we cannot legislate the propensity to hoard out of existence, we may at least confine it to its proper channels and secure it with a safety-valve. The role of gold in the world is to provide just such a safety-valve. God created gold in order to render the propensity to hoard harmless. Gold hoarding has no effect on essential consumption, its only effect is on jewellery consumption. Under a gold standard there is no bond, still less foreign exchange speculation. The only road to stabilisation is to put speculation into its proper place, confining speculators to fields where they can do no harm, but they may do some good: to the market of agricultural commodities with supply controlled by nature, not by man. The greatest blunder that Keynes committed was that he failed to foresee the forces that his policies would unleash. In particular, he was oblivious to speculation unleashed in markets where supply is not controlled by nature but by man (read: governments and central banks), such as the bond and foreign exchange markets.

The significance of a gold standard is not to be seen in its ability to stabilise prices, which is neither possible nor desirable. It is, rather, seen in its ability to stabilise the rate of interest at the lowest level that is still compatible with the requirements of the saver. The stabilisation of the rate of interest and foreign exchange will then impart as much stability to the price level as is consonant with a dynamic economy. By letting the saver withdraw the gold coin (read: bank reserves) when the rate of interest falls to a level he considers unacceptable, the irresistible speculative money-flow to-and-fro between the commodity and bond markets –the engine of inflationary and deflationary spirals – would be shut down at source.

Benign bond/gold arbitrage would replace the malignant bond/commodity speculation. Since the former is self-limiting while the latter is self-aggravating, economic stability would be enhanced.

The alternative to a gold standard is too horrible to contemplate. Unemployment more devastating than that of the 1930s, an earthquake shaking the international monetary system to its foundations, the construction of protective tariff walls and, in the end, a world war in which governments hope to find an escape route from economic chaos.

Endnotes to Chapter 46

[1] Except for Krugman and the cult of the Prophet. Although, some informally admit to the existence of economic waves.

[2] Secret Minutes, 1962, see: The Works of B. Hamvas, vol.17, Budapest: Medio, p 104-106, in Hungarian.

Exploding The Myth Of Silver Shortage

What Does the Negative Silver Lease Rate Really Mean?

On Thursday, September 20, 2007, the lease rate of silver suddenly dipped into negative territory. It fell to minus 0.1 percent per annum. I wish Ted Butler stopped talking about silver manipulation and telling fairy tales about raptors and dinosaurs and instead explain the behaviour of silver lease rates and the silver basis to his readers. In particular, explain negative lease rates and basis. It may be more helpful in promoting an understanding of the silver market.

I have a long-standing disagreement with silver analyst Ted Butler. I hold the view that silver is a monetary metal, second only to gold in importance. Supply-demand analysis of price is not applicable to silver, still less to gold. The reason is that supply and demand are undefinable in case of a monetary metal. There is no way to quantify speculative supply and demand, Speculators make split-second decisions to become a seller from a buyer or the other way round.

Making price predictions for the silver price on the basis that it is allegedly scarcer than gold does not make sense. Silver has been, is and will continue to be cheaper than gold for a monetary reason that is just the opposite of the scarcity argument. The monetary stockpiles of gold are much larger than that of silver. Therefore, there is less of a threat for the value to drop on account of new additions to the stockpile in the case of gold than in the case of silver. It is not the absolute change in mine output, for example, that has an impact on the value of a monetary metal, but the relative change as a percentage of existing stockpiles. For this reason gold is more valuable than silver: the huge stockpiles of gold make the impact of a change smaller. Ergo the value of gold is more stable. In technical language, the marginal utility of gold declines slower than that of silver.

As a consequence, the specific value of gold is higher. This means that the value of unit weight of gold is higher than that of the same weight of silver. Once this fact has been firmly [understood] by the markets, it is not likely to change for the following simple reason. The monetary metal with the higher specific value is more portable, both in space and time. In more details, the cost of transporting the unit of value as represented by gold is lower. For example, if the bimetallic ratio is 15, then the cost of transporting the unit of value as represented by silver is about 15 times higher. Roughly the same rule applies to the cost of storage as well. This makes gold the superior monetary metal, as it is more suitable for the purposes of transferring value in space as well as in time than silver.

But silver is still a monetary metal and for certain application, such as parcelling out value in ever smaller bits, for example, silver could be superior to gold. And, of course, when it comes to industrial applications, silver has a very impressive array of those. In many cases there is no substitution for silver. However, do not make the mistake to think that gold has no industrial applications. It does but, because of its high specific value, these applications are mostly submarginal and as such they are ignored. In 1922 Lenin gave a textbook example of such a submarginal application of gold that became famous. He told a meeting of Communist party activists that, after the final victory of Communism world-wide, gold will be used for the purpose for which it is so superbly fitted, namely, to plate the walls of public urinals. He did not say that his plan could not be realised in the worker's paradise because workers would pick the gold plate of urinals just as fast as the government was installing them.

Another common mistake people make when comparing gold and silver is to say that gold is 'not consumed' and therefore, practically all the gold produced is still available while silver is 'consumed' and, hence, is getting scarcer relative to gold all the time.

The truth is that both gold and silver are consumed, for example, in the arts (including jewellery). The difference is in the cost of recovery and refining, relative to the underlying value.

Precisely because the specific value of gold is higher, the cost of recovery for gold is lower, so much so that gold in the form of jewellery is often lumped together with monetary gold for statistical purposes. By contrast, silver plate could not be lumped together with monetary silver. By the same token, the cost of refining gold is lower than the corresponding cost for silver expressed as a percentage of the underlying value.

Returning to the silver lease rate, this is not the first time it dipped into negative territory. happened. The 30-day lease rate was pretty consistently negative between May 25 and August 4, when it shot up and reached a high of plus 0.4 percent on August 31. The fact that negative silver lease rates are not impossible, but a well-observed fact of the silver market has exploded the myth of a world-wide shortage of silver.

Come to think of it: lessors of silver were willing to pay lessees a premium to borrow the metal. Before you rush over to ask lessors for free silver, you had better come to a correct understanding what negative lease rate means. The collapse of the silver lease rate on September 20 to negative territory meant panic short covering in silver. The shorts anticipated an imminent and substantial rise in the price of silver and were running for cover.

How did they know that the silver price was poised to rise? They were not led by crystal balls. They acted on the historic correlation between gold and silver prices which customarily move 'in sympathy' with one another. On September 10 the gold 'price' was getting ready to break the resistance level at $700, while the silver price lagged far behind in relative terms. The peak 'price' of gold for the past 27 years, $730 an ounce, was well within earshot. The corresponding peak silver price for silver, $15, established in July, 2006, was not within earshot. Gold had a fair chance to make a new high soon, while silver, selling at $12.75, didn't. Nevertheless, if gold moved, it was reasonable to assume that silver would play catch-up. In the event the price of silver moved some (on Friday, September 21, it closed at $13.50) and, according to analyst Clive Maund, 'was set to go through the roof.' [1]

The point is that if this happens, the price move will not have been caused by any kind of shortage of silver. The notion that we have a silver shortage is preposterous. Most of the silver produced by the mines and sold by the U.S. Treasury during the past 60 or so years still exists in monetary form. Monetary silver is owned by private individuals, who entrust it to commercials skilled in making monetary silver yield a return. This is the reason why silver and gold are monetary metals: they can yield a (more or less consistent) return to their holder if traded adroitly and professionally. This fact may not be too well known, but it is true nevertheless: 'damonetisation' has done nothing to destroy the unique ability of monetary metals to earn a return. Without a doubt, the best way of making this happen is through playing the short side of the market. To sit on a long position of silver will not hatch the silver egg and is not a very intelligent way to make silver yield a return. A better way is covered short selling which to the uninitiated appears to be naked short selling. It is not.

The commercials are neither stupid nor suicidal. They are professionals who make it their business to call the tops and bottoms in the price moves of monetary metals. It is well-known that they have an excellent track record in calling the market. This is not because they are vicious people who manipulate the market to their own advantage enticing the poor bulls to enter the slaughter-house. They use methods that are well-known, pretty standard among professionals and can be learned from textbooks. Using these methods they can turn the variable silver price to their advantage (or to the advantage of their clients on whose behalf they trade). You can join their ranks if you are willing to study those methods and go through the training which may be too rigorous to your taste.

If you are envious or have moral objections against other people being able to make money consistently by trading the monetary metals, then you should lodge your complaint with the government which is responsible for 'demonetising' first silver (1873) and, a hundred years later, gold (1973). Before 'demonetisation' there were no commercials, speculators and scalpers who made money by betting on the variation in the price of monetary metals. If they had tried to make a living that way, they would have starved to death. The prices of monetary metals were stable.

Whenever the price of silver significantly lags the rising 'price' of gold, then there will be panic short covering and the leased silver will be returned to the lessors in a hurry. If the lessors were not prepared for this avalanche of silver (because they expected that the leases would be rolled over), then they may not be able to absorb the silver flowing back to them. In this case the silver lease rate drops dramatically and may even dip into negative territory.

It is important to be able to interpret this correctly. As I said, silver is delivered faster by the lessees than the lessors are able or willing to absorb it. Admittedly it is a market aberration, but whatever it means, it does not mean a shortage of silver. Far from it. It indicates a relative redundancy of silver that momentarily cannot find lessors in view of an impending rise in the silver price.

Rumour-mongering about present or future silver shortages do not bring credit to the analyst. He should go back to his textbooks and study the market in greater depth. Above all, he should learn the elementary differences between monetary metals and non-monetary commodities.

At NASoE we study paraphernalia such as the gold and silver basis, the gold and silver lease rates and their variation. In addition, we look at changes in the NAV (net asset value) of gold and silver ETF's (exchange traded funds). We think the best way to make a profit consistently on silver and gold holdings in troubled times is bimetallic arbitrage. At its crudest, this means selling silver to buy gold when the bimetallic ratio (gold 'price' divided by silver 'price') falls, selling gold to buy silver when it rises. However, as a consequence of concentrated propaganda gold sales by central banks and governments, not only the gold 'price' but also the bimetallic ratio is falsified. Therefore, there is need for refinement and for other clues In addition, to the bimetallic ratio. We believe that such more refined clues can be derived from the variation in the basis, the lease rate, the NAV of ETF'S and the like.

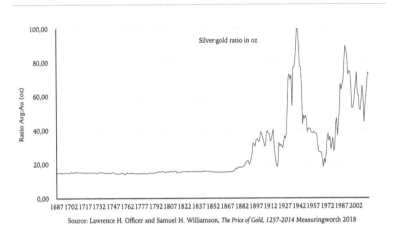

Source: Lawrence H. Officer and Samuel H. Williamson, *The Price of Gold, 1257-2014* Measuringworth 2018

Fig. 1 The silver:gold ratio since 1687 till 2018

Endnotes to Chapter 47

[1]   www.321gold.com, September 20, 2007

≫⊚ Chapter 48 ⊚≪

Deconstructing Ideologies

P. VAN COPPENOLLE

Prof. Carl Menger dedicated an entire book to what he considered the appropriate methodology for the thinker in the human and social sciences, of which the field of theoretical economics forms a subsection.

If the methodology has been handed to us as a finished product, why expand on it? Times have not changed since Menger exposed the fallacies of positivist theories. The scorn heaped on subjectivism from positivist corners has increased, even after positivism was found wanting. And not only in the subsection of theoretical economics.

This contribution is intended for the scholar in the hope it will shed more light or provide a deeper understanding on the justification for what is called a 'subjectivist' methodology in theoretical economics. The concept of a 'subjective' instead of an 'objective' science baffles most neophytes in economics. As a philosophy of science, subjectivism in human sciences draws on a seasoned and proven track record, something Menger thoroughly realised.

Whατ Δo ωΣ (κ)πoω?

Evaluating the scientific tools on their appropriateness is not a task for the tools themselves. Obviously, that decision is a task for the philosophy of science to make. The quality of this philosophy will determine the quality of decision making about science and the quality of thinking within science.

One significant result of the Enlightenment has been a marked narrowing of the field of 'reason' to the sense realm. For pre-moderns, reason included in its field the moral and spiritual dimension of human life. For the majority of Western intellectuals since the Enlightenment reason is restricted to the empirical or quantifiable aspects of human existence.

Since time immemorial, it has been characteristic for human beings to recognise their consciousness as a property of being. It is no surprise then that Aristotle expresses this desire to know as a fundamental drive of human beings to determine their place in the world and even in the cosmos. [1] Humans pursue this need by discerning order in the universe and in their own world. The hunger for knowledge is fundamental.

The quest for certainty of knowledge results in two extreme epistemological positions: the quagmire of scepticism (Hume) or the moral holiday of absolutism (Hegel). Each position reduces the Socratic paradox of knowing that one does not know, to an epistemological fallacy.

Ancient thinkers like Aristotle and Socrates rejected both scepticism and absolutism. They were lovers of wisdom (φιλοσοφοι). Knowledge (ειπιστημη) even when lacking a foundation in apodeictic certainty, was superior to mere opinion (δοcα). To them, noetic knowledge is enabled by consciousness without restrictions.

The contemplative Aristotelian discernment of order was replaced during the Age of Enlightenment by radical rationalisations that dichotomised faith and reason, theology and metaphysics, religion and philosophy as the valid path to epistemic knowledge.

Rationalism did not stop there, for the spirit of human commonality and dignity as a basis for ethics, law and politics was replaced with an agglomeration of posited if not arbitrary human order. This posited order is in sharp contrast to the discerned order of the ancients.

Auguste Comte, Émile Durkheim and Herbert Spencer together representing early Anglo-French positivism, influenced by Saint-Simon who professed the secularisation of the world was in its final stage, did not just change the nature of scientific research in human science, they reversed direction. Characteristic for rationalism in human sciences is the underlying idea of 'liberation' of the human from the imprisonment of his conditions within the professed natural order. Overthrowing existing institutions such as culture, art, science, trade, property, money and religion will ensure the fulfilment of the promise of an infinitely better future, posited order.

Scarcity, to name just one of the natural conditions of the human world had become an unmentionable and contemptuous idea. Technology, at any rate science, will liberate the human condition from all restrictions that humanity endures as a result of people being human instead of divine.

The violent dichotomy of physical and noetic sciences effectively banned Plato, Aristotle and Socrates by restricting the respectability of gained knowledge to the knowledge obtained by empirical methods only. The empirical method has become the only scientific method to obtain valid meaningful knowledge.

The scientific method as we now know it is a circular dependence of methodology and empiricism. Logical positivism, espoused by Russel and Wittgenstein had risen to prominence. The criteria to be satisfied under the scientific method to count as science, are stringent. The scientific method generally requires:

(1) Clearly defined terminology.

(2) Quantifiability.

(3) Highly controlled conditions

A scientifically rigorous study maintains direct control over as many of the factors that influence the outcome as possible. The experiment is then performed with such precision that any other person in the world, using identical materials and methods, should achieve the same result.

(4) Reproducibility.

A rigorous science ably reproduces the same result repeatedly. Multiple researchers on different continents, cities, or even planets should find the same results if they precisely duplicated the experimental conditions.

(5) Predictability and Testability.

A rigorous science proposes testable predictions.

Unwelcome Shift To Method

These characteristics set the bar for strict science high. Climate study cannot be science according to criteria three and four. Although most of physics and chemistry meets the standard, some branches will not. Evolutionary biology does not satisfy the third and forth requirement either.

Although positivism in all its aspects outside physics was discredited, it has not disappeared. It is alive and well in educational institutions, even outside the field of hard sciences. The absurdity of logical positivism at its limits is demonstrated by a Scientific American article, entitled: 'Why Life Does Not Really Exist:' [2]

> " ... Why is defining life so frustratingly difficult? Why have scientists and philosophers failed for centuries to find a specific physical property or set of properties that clearly separates the living from the inanimate? Because such a property does not exist. Life is a concept that we invented. On the most fundamental level, all matter that exists is an arrangement of atoms and their constituent particles. These arrangements fall onto an immense spectrum of complexity, from a single hydrogen atom to something as intricate as a brain. In trying to define life, we have drawn a line at an arbitrary level of complexity and declared that everything above that border is alive and everything below it is not. In truth, this division does not exist outside the mind. There is no threshold at which a collection of atoms

suddenly becomes alive, no categorical distinction between the living and inanimate, no Frankensteinian spark. We have failed to define life because there was never anything to define in the first place.'

The preposterousness of this conclusion renders it beneath refutation. Unfortunately, one finds these quality impaired contributions ubiquitous, bearing testimony to their general and uncritical acceptance, despite the resulting quality impairment of the attribute 'scientific'.

The underlying fallacy of this Scientific American contribution is called the eliminativist fallacy: faced with a problem one cannot solve – in this case the problem of crafting an adequate definition of life – the eliminativist denies the data responsible for the problem. *In casu*, the author denies that life exists.

Seemingly unbeknownst to the author, he denies the very datum that got him thinking about this topic in the first place, rendering his philosophical view inconsistent with his own mode of thinking, lest the author would like to declare himself nonexistent.

Returning to the scientific method, the question wether political, economic or human science could be a science according to these criteria is an obvious negative. Yet it is equally hard to deny that these sciences do *not* provide us knowledge. The problem of applying scientific methodology to the study of human sciences lies not in the inability to adequately quantify the data. Rather, the problem is in the underlying assumptions.

The assumption that the methods of physics are appropriate to study human beings, leads the researcher to pass over the most important issues. The damage in human sciences suffered from the tendency of modernist theoreticians to emulate the criteria of the natural sciences is not necessarily due to an accumulation of irrelevant materials, but to interpretation.

The content of a source may be reported correctly and nevertheless create an entirely false picture because essential parts are omitted. Because the uncritical principles of interpretation do not allow recognising those parts as essential. Hence, uncritical opinion (δοξα) cannot substitute for theory in science.

The principles of uncritical interpretation widely held today (e.g. 'Rational Wiki' or Wikipedia as just two examples) can be highlighted by examining the underlying assumptions on which they rest.

The first assumption is (1) that the theoretician has to separate facts from values. Once the theoretician believes he has separated statements of fact from normative judgments, he tends to uncritically assume that he will be able to attain knowledge which possesses the same status as the kind of knowledge pursued by the natural sciences.

The second assumption is (2) that one can attain knowledge of something like a hard fact when they study human beings, so long as he makes use of scientific methodology.

The third underlying assumption is (3) the assumption that the method utilised in the natural sciences is inherently virtuous.

Finally, still underlying, this further assumption (4) leads one to conclude that the methodology of the hard sciences should be the basis for judging a proposed object of study as 'theoretically relevant'. In other words, because the assumption is made that empirical methodologies are valid, the researcher will be inclined to favour studying those aspects of human existence which are amenable to this method.

Holding this complex of assumptions should strike one as questionable.

Rarely are these assumptions challenged. What should be considered questionable, is the fact that the methodological issues end up determining whether a particular subject being studied is considered worthy of attention, if any.

Constructionism or interpretive sociology, historically rooted in German Idealism, is based on Kant's ideas who laid down its ontological and epistemological foundations by postulating that human actors were directly involved in the process of human sciences. After the romanticism of Goethe and Schiller the concepts of Kant were nevertheless hidden behind the rise of Anglo-French objectivism and positivism.

As a proponent of constructionism, Weber originally articulated the fact-value distinction to distance himself from positivism in the humanities. His distinction is one of the reasons for the above related still widely held opinion that methodology should determine what is studied. It has harmed Western civilisation morally, spiritually and intellectually. The acceptance of the fact-value distinction results in practise to an artificial limitation of the scope of reason so that it ends up dealing merely with those aspects of reality which have no essential relation to humans endowed with reason. The terms 'value judgment' and 'value free' science have not been part of the philosophical vocabulary before the second half of the 19th century. The notion of a value judgment (*Werturteil*) is **meaningless** in itself. It can only gain any meaning by opposing it to a situation calling for judgments concerning facts (*Tatsachenurteile*).

Under positivism only propositions of the objective type can be considered 'scientific', while the propositions of the subjective type should be considered personal preferences and decisions, incapable of critical verification and therefore, devoid of objective validity.

A simple demonstration: to the positivist, the statements ...

▷ that torturing people or animals for fun is morally wrong;

▷ that 'ought' implies 'can';

▷ that moral goodness is a higher value than physical strength;

▷ that might does not make right;

▷ that a punishment must fit the crime;

▷ that a proposition and its negation cannot both be true;

▷ that what is past was once present;

▷ that if A remembers B's experience, then A = B.

(Acknowledgement: I have based these examples on Dr. W. Vallicella's) [3]

...are neither true nor false, but cognitively meaningless. Empirical investigation inspired by positivism as a handmaiden to philosophy, cannot answer normative questions. Positivism conceitedly ditched millenia of collective wisdom.

Internalising the fact-value distinction increases the likelihood that the scientist will equate the scientific method with virtue. The equation of scientific methodology with virtue is capricious and self-sustaining. Judgments about whether the subject matter has any value to human beings are 'subjective' and consequently, not only will such judgments not be made, but questions as to the relevance of the subject matter will not be posed.

Yet these are precisely the judgments and questions that have to be made by any researcher in the social sciences and humanities. There is, However, a catch. If one accepts this definition of 'objectivity' as posited, the theoretician is henceforth unable to question the assumptions he made and which led him to make methodological issues paramount or why he has chosen the particular subject matter that he has. [4]

Insofar as he internalises the fact-value distinction and then makes methodology the determining factor in his approach to research, he will define objects which fall within the method as 'objective' and those which don't as 'subjective' and Hence, not valid for consideration.

The practical consequence is a separation of his own judgment about what matters from the very act of reasoning he is involved in. Once a possible object of study is viewed as a 'fact' and therefore, as scientifically objective or independent of reason itself, the possible irrelevance of the assumed fact to man in his capacity as a human being becomes very difficult to question.

Ironically the most important factor shielding this scientific epistemological approach from scrutiny is precisely the kind of judgment proscribed by the fact-value distinction, namely the a priori identification of the method with virtue. A perfect scientistic trap.

Subordinating the choice of subject matter to be studied to methodology spuriously limits topics considered for serious inquiry. Making methodology the criterion for theoretical relevance requires that the identification of methodology with virtue remain unconscious and merely implicit. If what determines theoretical relevance is not made explicit and if substantive theoretical concerns are then subordinated to issues of methodology, the purpose and meaning of science is perverted.

If the adequacy of a method is not measured by its *usefulness to the purpose* of science and if *a contrario*, the use of a method is made the criterion of science, then the meaning of science as a truthful account of the structure of reality, as the theoretical orientation of man in his world and as the great instrument for man's understanding of his own position in the universe is *lost*.

Carl Menger understood only too well that restricting knowledge to *epistemology* threatened not only the quality of human and economic science, but also the philosophy of science that underpins the validity of meaningful knowledge.

Ignoring other than epistemologically valid knowledge is debilitating the theoretician and is highly inconsistent for his reasoning, for there are questions of general metaphysics or ontology. Among them: questions about existence, identity, properties, relations, modality. To illustrate, consider these two claims:

(1) Principle of the Rejection of Nonexistent Objects: Necessarily, for any x, if x *has* properties, then x *exists*.
(2) Principle of the Rejection of Unpropertied Objects: Necessarily, for any x, if x *exists*, then x *has* properties.

Both are true propositions of general metaphysics. They are items of knowledge about the structure of any possible world and therefore, items of knowledge about the structure of the actual world. But we do not know them by any empirical method: they do not belong in an empirical science. The principles are not truths of pure logic either. For their negations are not logical contradictions. They are irreducibly ontological truths. They belong to *metaphysica generalis* or ontology.

Menger in his rejection of positivism and constructionism and by embracing the ancient time honoured wisdom, was and still is only too right.

Harmful Ideologies

Ideologues have a long standing problematic relationship with 'control'. [5] Eugen von Böhm-Bawerk already discussed the control problem in his *Control or Economic Law*. Eric Voegelin treated the philosophical aspect of the general control issue extensively in *Modernity Without Restraint*. [6]

The ideologists' control problem reduces in essence to an estrangement from and rebellion against reality. Such estrangement comes clearly to the fore in the American Scientific article (above), however, in economic science, ideological infections seem ubiquitous! Perhaps the 'Econometrics Laboratories' are not as pristinely disinfected as previously thought.

We propose a good scrub with Sunlight. ©

Richard Hooker And The Representation Of Truth

The first pages of Hookers' *Praefatio* in his *Ecclesiastical Polity*, analyse the type of the Puritan of his time. He also lists the psychological manipulation techniques by which Gnostic mass movements operate. Gnosticism, a subject in the field of theology, falls outside the scope of economic science, except when it encroaches on economic science. Then the true scientist may make it his business to analyse the phenomena affecting his field. In brief, Gnosticism describes an ancient religious movement of people thinking of themselves as 'those in the know'. Essentially, for those ancient gnostics, the world was created by a demiurge, not God and therefore, it could not be perfect. Hooker analyses the gnostics of his time as a group where somebody requires a 'cause', a word invented by the Puritans. Belly-aching about all the evils of society and in particular of the upper class, some 'cause' or another needed advancement. Repeated performances in front of audiences will induce the idea that these men just have to be of singular integrity. Next, they will channel society's ill-will towards the established authorities of society. When moods are ripe, they will promote themselves as the natural 'new and better' authorities.

In consolidating their position, gnostics rely on written sources; the Scriptures did serve this purpose back then, nowadays it would be some other White Paper written by a Scientist with a White Lab Coat. E.g. Al Gore's *Inconvenient Truth* or, say, Keynes' *General Theory of Interest and Employment*. Naturally, the content of the Scripture incompatible with their cause, will be ignored. Next, 'They will experience themselves as the elect; and this experience breeds 'high terms of separation between such and the rest of the world'; so that mankind will be divided into the 'brethren' and the (lower) 'worldlings'. The gnostics have officially turned dualistic ... [7]

Unshaken

Gnostic dualists by ideological persuasion will be, characteristically, next to impossible to convince by argument. Voegelin summarises Hooker: [8]

> " Let any man of contrary opinion open his mouth to persuade them, they close their ears....

They are impermeable to argument and have their answers well drilled. Suggest to them that they are unable to judge in such matters and they will answer:

> " God has chosen the simple.

Show them convincingly they are talking nonsense and they answer:

> " Christ's own apostle was accounted mad'.

Anything else thrown at them will evoke a response in the form of casting themselves in the role of:

> " innocency persecuted for the truth.

In brief, the gnostic dualist ideologue's attitude remains unassailable and iron-clad against all argument.

Many parents recognise in this refusal of argument, the position of toddlers throwing a tantrum and covering their ears whenever their desires are frustrated by an accompanying parent in, say, a candy shop. Young adolescents have reportedly the same inner experience of frustration in certain of their wishes. Enough puerility apparently has survived to exponentially grow into the intellectual defects of the gnostic dualists to destroy the social function of persuasion. The most infamous examples of our time being the terrorist movement Al Qaeda or ISIS, yet the SS of Hitler would fare no better nor would any so-called Red Brigade.

Cuckoo's Camouflage

Richard Hooker surgically dissects Cromwell's Puritans as seeking justification for 'some cause' vastly different from scripture. However, gnostic dualist movements will abuse scriptures when it suits them and ignore passages incongruent with its 'cause'. Scriptures, therefore, provide camouflage. To render camouflage effective, two techniques were singled out by Hooker.

The first technique involves some form of *codification* of the scriptures. Hooker immediately points to John Calvin and his *Institutes*. A work like the *Institutes* provides the function of guide for the perplexed with an authentic formulation of truth, rendering thereby a recourse to earlier scripture unnecessary and superfluous. John Calvin, according to Hooker's witty description, was 'brought up in the study of civil law' meaning he wasn't even a man of the cloth. [9] In the 18th century we find Diderot and d'Alembert who claimed to have produced the 'definitive' *encyclopédie*. Nobody would need to read any other work predating theirs. [10]

In the 19th century Karl Marx graciously provided his faithful flock with his own scriptures, supplemented by patristic literature of the hand of Lenin and others.

The 20th century saw the birth of Chairman Mao Zedong's *Red Book*. And of course, to return to that other field of political science called economics: the *General Theory of Interest and Employment*, by the Prophet. The ancient roots of gnosticism provided by a Bible or a Koran (literally: 'the Law') readily demonstrate the religious roots of such gnostic dualism. No doubt exists on how modern gnostic dualism branched out with a secular trend from its religious roots, probably stretching all the way back to the texts of *Hermes Trismegistus*, [11] popularised under the name of Hermeticism.

Modern Spells

Codifying the truth as a gnostic technique of insulation against other scriptures except their own may eventually result in a desired and socially relevant mass of faithful followers. Members of such flock will not touch any other literature which is well known to argue against their own position. The device of codification for prevention of critical study can count on a voluntary self-censorship of its adherents. If not, the thought police or an anti-defamation association will remind its 'subjects' of the heinous crime against 'the law' such deviant revisionism amounts to. [12]

Nevertheless, to prevent embarrassing if not crippling criticism, a second technique has been proven an evergreen. By putting a taboo (or a fatwa or a listing on the *index prohibitorum*) or any other undesirable stain, [13] criticism of the position promulgated may be neutralised effectively. As Voegelin points out, in the light of the Reformation, the taboo had to fall on classic philosophy and scholastic theology. [14] Since Western intellectual culture relied heavily on these sources, it was ruined insofar the taboo had effect. Unfortunately, the destruction was so thorough, Western culture never completely recovered. Modern 21st century variants of a taboo may be recognised in e.g. things like the 'Panama Papers' where a strong condemnation is made palpable concerning those who dare not contribute taxes in a quantity deemed sufficient for the 'general wellbeing'. [15]

Richard Hooker, a man of considerable erudition, found himself outwitted when confronted with the Puritan's attitude of non-communication. Rational debate with his opponents proved impossible, because they *do not accept logical argument*. [16] Parallels with the 20th century exist abundantly. Today, we are confronted by even more sophisticated sophisms in the same vain, most of them developed by members of the so-called Frankfurt School or by some aberrant Islamic schools of theology. Although outwitted, Hooker was not desperate. One of the ideas he entertained can be reconstructed from his letters just before he died, among them, a passage from Averroës:

> "*...Discourse (sermo) about the knowledge which God in His glory has of Himself and the world is prohibited. And even more so is it to put it in writing. For the understanding of the vulgar does not reach such profundities; and when it becomes the subject of their discussions, the divinity will be destroyed with them. Hence, discussion of this knowledge is prohibited to them; and it is sufficient for their felicity if they understand what they can perceive by their intelligence.*'

In this passage Averroës reached for a solution under an old Islamic constellation of society. Considering the destruction of divinity or the 'murder of God' one has to admit, coming back to Western societies, that Averroës had a point. [17] Nietzsche made that much abundantly clear.

Not A Suicide Pact

However that may be, the structure of society is not at the disposal of its individual members. Although Richard Hooker wrote down this passage, Western society took a different direction from the Eastern and the debate amongst the '*populo vulgaris*' was well under way at the time. Hence, Hooker had to contemplate a different solution in which he appealed to governmental authority. [18] Since his opponents did not constitute partners in a debate, but rather a political revolutionary action group, appealing to government seemed beyond reproach. Hooker

perfectly grasped the situation that gnostic propaganda constitutes political propaganda under camouflage, not so much theoretical debate.
Gnostic dualism, moreover, has a nihilistic component, diagnosable in
the expressions such as 'the absolute command of Almighty God, must
be received, although the world by receiving it should be clean turned
upside down.' Hooker correctly points out that 'herein lieth the greatest danger of all.' In formulating the *'things turned clean upside down'*
sentence, we are reminded of many occasions and of writers, especially
the pamphleteer Marx, who is singularly famous for using such phra-
seology – *Dinge auf den Kopf stellen*. In the four volumes before you, we
have made several direct references and indirect endnotes pointing to
revolutionary gnosticism, Marx being exemplar for the past, the global
climate alarmists being exemplar for the present.

Finally, according to Hooker, a government (in his time at least) is
not supposed to betray the trust given to it nor abdicate its authority.
Voegelin points to a contemporary U.S. Constitutional court appeal
called the 'Terminiello case' (available on line). [19] The case crucially
hinges on the right of free speech, fixed in the U.S. Bill of Rights, but
massively abused by gnostic activists, in casu a showdown between a
Catholic priest, suspended however, from all duties by a bishop and
a rowdy communist crowd outside the venue of his speaking engage-
ment, throwing stones into windows:

> " ...*This Court has gone far toward accepting the doctrine that civil liberty
> means the removal of all restraints from these crowds and that all local
> attempts to maintain order are impairments of the liberty of the citizen.
> The choice is not between order and liberty. It is between liberty with order
> and anarchy without either. There is danger that, if the Court does not
> temper its doctrinaire logic with a little practical wisdom, it will **convert
> the constitutional Bill of Rights into a suicide pact.***

Justice Jackson – dissenting

A government entrusted with public powers is not supposed to stand
by and tolerate its own overthrow through allowing gnostic activists to
proliferate in the shelter of a muddy interpretation of civil rights.

Language Matters

So far, the rule of no betrayal suffers any exception for governments,
entrusted with public power. However, as individuals, we escape not.
Besides exciting the public against other people and breaching the
peace or even public order, the other favourite past time of the gnostic
dualist consists of destroying morals by destroying language. It is a

favourite of the members of the Frankfurt School, camouflaging their 'cause' under the academic flag of 'Critical Thinking.' We better expose the destructive meaningless jargon of this lot, lest the perpetrators feel licensed by our silence. Here is what E. Voegelin had to say:

> " … *If anything is characteristic of ideologies, it is the destruction of language, sometimes on the level of intellectual jargon, on the high level of complication, sometimes on the vulgarian level. When we go beyond Marx, into the ideological epigonai of the late 19th and early 20th centuries, we are already far below the intellectual level that formed even the background of a Marx….* '[20]

Karl Kraus was known to Carl Menger as a colleague from his journalistic days, but also to Voegelin, who attended Vienna University from 1918. Kraus published *Die Fackel* (the Torchlight), which appeared at irregular intervals in Vienna and appeared to be widely read there. It gave a critical understanding of politics and of the function of the press in the disintegration of German and Austrian society, preparing the way for National Socialism. Karl Kraus was the great artist of language who would defend the standards of language against its corruption in the current literature and especially through the journalists.

> " … *Regaining language meant recovering the subject matter to be expressed by language and that meant getting out of what today one would call the false consciousness of the petty bourgeois (including under this head positivists and Marxists), whose literary representatives dominated the scene.* [21]

Hence, the use of language forms part of a resistance against ideologies, which destroys language inasmuch as the ideological thinker has lost contact with reality and develops language for expressing –not reality –but his state of alienation from it. To penetrate this phoney language and restore reality through the restoration of language was the work of Karl Kraus as much as of Stefan George and his friends at the time. And on the economic front, Carl Menger did his part, not so much in language as in restoring sanity in thinking.

Today, gnostic language of destruction has taken on comical proportions, just as it did in Germany and Austria at the time of Carl Menger. Unfortunately today, unlike in pre-war European conditions, ideologists have had their 'long march' into our venerable institutions and have infected all its levels, taking pride in reducing great works of art, literature or science to 'power relations' among 'race, class and gender,' or else denying they have any independent meaning at all... Consider the attack of so-called 'social-justice-warriors' [22] – a quote from the Student Assembly for Power and Liberation:

" ... As has become increasingly obvious to us since we arrive at Western, we cannot count on the University to follow through for hxtorically oppressed students. These demands come out of a long hxstory of oppression played out at all levels of schooling and just like the events of last quarter, these demands do not come out of nowhere. Rather, they come from careful consideration of what students need. We build these demands and this sense of 'need' on the understanding that all of these forms of oppression are racialized and are built on the continued expropriation of Native land and life, the enslavement of bodies and the forced exploitation of people across the world.

Phoniness

Particularly influential was Kraus' great drama of the First World War, *Die Letzten Tage der Menschheit*, with its superb sensitivity to the melody and vocabulary of phoniness in politics, war patriotism, denigration of enemies and ochlocratic name-calling.

The second Kraus' great works dealing with the major catastrophes of the twentieth century was Dritte Walpurgisnacht, treating the phenomenon of Hitler and National Socialism. A restrained version of this work was published in the last year of his life in *Die Fackel*. [23] The unrestrained text of the Dritte Walpurgisnacht was published posthumously after the war by Kösel Verlag in Munich as volume 1 of Die Werke, which run into sixteen volumes.

No serious study of National Socialism, [24] which we may just as well diagnose as a gnostic dualist pneumopathology, is possible without recourse to the *Dritte Walpurgisnacht*, because the intellectual morass that must be understood as the gnostic dualist background against which a Hitler could rise to power, comes to life in that text.

The phenomenon of Hitler is not exhausted by his person. His success must be understood in the context of an intellectually or morally ruined society in which personalities who otherwise would be grotesque, marginal figures can come to public power because they superbly represent the people who admire them. [25]

This internal destruction of a society – and science with it – did not finish with the Allied victory over the German armies in World War II. Judging from the influences in our Universities by the 'critical' Frankfurt School members, [26] such destruction still goes on. There is yet no end in sight so far concerning the intellectual and moral ruination of society.

Personal Responsibility

And we could do no better concerning other theoretical garbage in what passes today for 'economic science' or even the education of our toddlers or youth. We quote the Aquinas specialist E. Feser concerning the Self Ownership Proviso (SOP), when gnostic dualist indoctrination, in economic science or otherwise, threatens the moral and intellectual integrity of our children, who cannot be deemed to come up for themselves.

> " *If our offspring is to flourish in this world, we ought not only to feed, shelter and clothe our children and dependents, we better also teach them to be self-sufficient where physical needs are concerned as well as providing moral and spiritual instruction. Failing to provide proper moral and spiritual instruction constitutes a clear violation not only of the civil law in many countries and before common sense judges, but also of the SOP on philosophical grounds, for it effectively constitutes a nullification or disablement of the child's innate capacities.* [27]

The Origins Of Trouble

In his New Science of Politics, Eric Voegelin notes that the period between the disintegration of the Roman Empire in the West and the High Middle Ages would be characterised on a sociological level by its 'de-divinisation of existence.' This de-divinisation meant that the worship of people redirected to a transcendent God instead, whose non-interference in daily life guarantees freedom of conscience and self-responsibility. The pagan worship of objects with obligatory quid pro quo demands for divine interference, proved without result by the general experience of conquest and defeat of the order of the world, first under Alexander the Great, then under Roman Generals.

The new experience of the divine as a transcendent ground, did, importantly, postpone 'demands for certainty,' a perennial human characteristic. The imperfections of the natural world and the social order might be redeemed, but not in this life, where only degrees of amelioration seem possible. Men simply must reconcile themselves to the limitations inherent in worldly existence. Eschatological uncertainty nevertheless afflicts some people with terrific anxiety; when these anxious characters could not fall back upon pre-Christian alleged certainties and worship practices, [28] which had gradually disappeared, they availed themselves of 'the Gnosis' that formed 'an accompaniment of Christianity (in the West) from its very beginnings.'

To be sure, Voegelin notes there was and still is a Pagan Gnosis, a Jewish Gnosis, as well as a Christian Gnosis [29] in the West; in each case, the Gnostic position defines itself by its implacable enmity against the prevalent normative stance of transcendency of divinity; the insurrection, in Voegelin's analysis, must be total, because the rebel against reality, determined to erect his second reality, [30] can tolerate no remnant of that which he despises, lest it reminds him of his own shortcomings.[31]

When Plato or his followers maintain that one should love the Creator-Deity and attune oneself most graciously to the beauties of his gift, i.e. creation, then the Gnostic dualist insist that one better not. The Creator-Deity is an usurper and one ought to revile the many debased phenomena of this usurpers creation. [32] When Plato and his followers maintain that it feels good to have been born in a beautiful world, then the Gnostic dualist insists that such view comes across as insufferable; 'enlightened' folk want nothing less than to redeem themselves from the universal miasma, alternatively they will dedicate themselves to detoxifying existence. [33] When Plato argues for a universal humanity, then the Gnostic dualist insists that humanity is not single, but dual: there is a vast cohort of the unsalvageable barbarians who surely belong in Hell where Fate has consigned them and that, set apart from those fools, there is an elect of the enlightened and salvageable, who can either escape from the Hellish world or transform it back into its pristine state before the usurper polluted it. [34] And herewith the theme of Paradise-on-Earth a.k.a. Utopia emerges. Beware of those who insist of saving and changing the world ... When Plato and his followers maintain that the world is at least contingently knowable, that it is, more or less, as our senses and our mental operations report it to be, then the Gnostics insist that phenomena are false, or worse yet, deliberately falsified and that the world is a lie concealing a hidden truth to which they alone have access. [35]

Diagnostic Tools

'The revolution of the Gnostics,' according to Voegelin, 'has for its aim,' one at least among others, 'the monopoly of existential representation.' It tolerates no challenges nor competition to itself. In addition, to this, the Gnostic assault on reality seeks 'a change in the nature of man and the establishment of a transfigured society.' [36] Finally, according to Voegelin, Gnostic agitation inclines its followers to conceive of existence as 'a struggle by the world of darkness' wickedly to nip their own luminous 'universality' in the bud.

In short, at least six symptoms betray a gnostic dualist syndrome:

(1) Dissatisfaction with present situation – we need to improve this world from its design faults; existence is a horror and we urgently need escaping it.

(2) [Cosmogony] The reason for the dissatisfaction is to be found in the 'wickedness of the world.' If not the Demiurge's fault, then, one may assume with that other French gnostic, Sarte: l'enfer, ce sont les autres.

(3) [Soteriology] Salvation from the evil and shortcomings of the world is possible – the sky is the limit, better yet: there's no limit! No attuning necessary...

(4) The change to a better world must be a historical process. Look at me, mom, I am making history!

(5) [Eschatology] Not many people grasp the problem, just one in a million maybe. But Man's own effort makes all change possible. Indeed, I am your Man. No others know the secret.

(6) [Systemisation] The Gnostic will come out with a 'formula' or 'system' for self– and world salvation. However, do not ask questions, because that would expose the assumptions and lay bare its Gnostic character of denial of reality. Systemisers like Auguste Comte betray the Gnostic character of their thinking.

It is difficult not to see the phenomena that Voegelin describes in his Collected Works as being prominently active in our times.

Applying this tool to the field of economic science, the gnostic dualist acts most ingeniously. His bigotry leads to what I would call the 7th characteristic: (limited perhaps to economics):

(7) [Parasitism] The Gnostic Dualists has as aim to disenfranchise people. You will find most of these Gnostics in positions where tax proceeds flows to, one way or another. If they are in high positions with an enterprise, it will find itself typically, on the receiving end of government largesse – big time.

Let me also recapitulate the main **techniques** used to camouflage the truth of reality:

(1) codification of truth in scriptures ("The science is settled we have scientists in white lab coats to prove it")

(2) social engineering of consent (taboo, fatwah, social sham-

ing, etc. and YOU are just a sad little conspiracy theorist).
Obviously, there may exist more techniques, different from the above.
We now know the means, but what about motive ? Why would anyone hide the truth or live in another reality. Unfortunately, the answer
may never be known, althought it may be knowable. Almost always,
the perpetrator has a 'cause' as Hooker adequately put it. Perhaps the
estrangement from reality leads to a pathological condition of the mind
or the soul, evidenced by a *libido dominandi*. The pathological need of
a control freak. It does not explain why the libido exists , nor does it
explain the cause of the estrangement in the first place. For all intents
and purposes, we may never know why; for now it suffices to know
it happens and we also identified the techniques and diagnosed the
symptoms. The charge of a conspiracy theory evaporates as soon as it
becomes clear the charge is a defence mechanism in the form of a taboo
to silence dissenters from the violently imposed New Truth.

Keynes & Friedman: Gnostic Warriors

Knowledge of camouflage and spells helps in deconstructing ideologies, born from a 'cause' by uncovering and subsequently exposing
the techniques; one may even progress to discover the ultimate 'cause'
that underlies all ideologies. Applied to economic science, the general
strategy of codification with obligatory glorification of its authors and
subsequent taboo on dissent can be recognised in e.g. Keynes' General
Theory. To underline its gnostic dualist ideology it may be stressed that
in economic terms, the world is an 'evil copy' (of paradise), plagued by
uneven income distribution and other afflictions. Aggregate demand
for goods could stagnate, heaven forbid! (Volume II: Keynes' Massive
Fail, p. 151)

   To that end, the so-called omnipotence of God and his creation
needs to be found wanting (that's the easy part) and man's skill to
help himself (a trifle harder) seems to be eagerly called for. The latter objective seems fine, without the hubris or the palace revolution
banning God from his own creation. Unfortunately, Nietzsche already
murdered the Occupant of the Throne of Omnipotence, so he says.
Naturally reconstruction involves plans to be found in the filing cabinet
under the letter U of Utopia or P of Paradise.

Theological Roots

Modern gnostics deny their religious roots. They deny occupying the
vacant throne previously occupied by God. Yet, in full view of all to

see, the same vacant throne becomes occupied again with some United Authority On Earth, claiming Universality. It even has its own Global Bank. To expose the fraudulent denial, it suffices to distill the common characteristics, such as suggested in diagnostic tools (above). Like theological scriptures, modern gnostic dualists in the field of economics equally rely on a written source such as The General Theory of Money, Interest and Employment. That is the new Sacred Scripture not to be doubted or attacked. Bishops and cardinals will protect the flock of followers against inroads made against the scriptures. The favourite tools of the gnostic warriors today is the policy of 'engineering consent' (à la Edward Bernays) by abusing public education and media. Dissenters will be tabooed. (E.g. the scandalous contributions in the New York Times by Krugman and consorts). Of course, cardinals and bishops wear special attributes and sycophants bestow them with titles; they even speak Gnostic Language (a.k.a. some pseudo-intellectual jargon without any substance).[37] Sycophants infiltrate societal institutions such as government and hijack it for private purposes. Since the State divorced its bride, the Church, in 1648 at Westphalen, it has found a new mistress named Science, given away at the altar by Francis Bacon. Hence, today we find Barry Eichengreen, donned in a white lab coat, working in the Econometrics Laboratory of Berkeley University, no doubt pursuing a place in the Hall of Fame, like Francis Bacon promised. Eichengreen and Krugman play the flock's bishops. Their message contains all the hallmarks of discontent with gold as money, for it is deflationary and there is hardly enough around. Moreover, the public, who have no idea what they are doing, exercise full control over interest rates. It only makes sense to escape this intolerable situation by all means possible. Even Reverend Fisher said so: 'we can make our own money.' The miller (Chapter 12, Volume I) our faithful member, has already followed up on his sermon. Soon the days of shortages will be over. Very soon... Of course, being a historical process, in which you all partake, it will be an arduous road before we get there, but look yonder...our president is on television making the necessary announcements. Yes, good times have arrived . .! We just need to find an optimum formula. Where 's my alchemy book again ...? Oh here it is... by bishop Friedman. Why 4 % inflation, you ask? ...it's complicated. One day, when you're ready, I may tell you.[38]

Hope

Again, it is difficult not to see the phenomena betraying gnostic dualism, described above, as being hyperactive in our current society. We have no intention, however, to induce a state of universal pessimism with our readers. Quite *au contraire*.

> Because Gnosticism is a pneumopathology, at war with reality, that does its level best to seal itself inside the bubble of its 'dream world' it cannot, over any long term, succeed.[39]

For one thing, when 'the critical exploration of cause and effect in history is prohibited... the rational co-ordination of means and ends in politics is impossible.' When emergent factors pierce the bubble, or at least impinge on the membrane, Gnostic leaders vaguely acknowledge them, but respond irrationally 'by magic operations in the dream world, such as disapproval, moral condemnation, declaration of intention, resolutions, appeals to the opinion of mankind, branding of enemies as aggressors, outlawing of war, propaganda for world peace, world government,' and so on. One can predict, generally, that the radical spasm through which Europe and North America are now passing will eventually remit. De-creation can only be called creation for so long before the fraud becomes undeniable and the masses become disenchanted with their formerly charismatic leaders. The trouble for all of us is that, in the meantime, in 'the weird, ghostly atmosphere of such a lunatic asylum,' as Voegelin writes, the agitating 'elites' can wreak enormous harm. But we can return the compliment. We simply emulate Karl Kraus and expose their behaviour as total lunacy. After all, it is funny.

Endnotes to Chapter 48

[1] Aristotle Met. [980a] [21] 'Πάντεj a1nqropoi tou e1idenai o2regontai fusei'

[2] Acknowledgement: reported by Dr. W. Vallicella on his weblog 'maverick philosopher', 2008 on which a portion of this contribution is based.

[3] Dr. W. Vallicella blog 'maverick philosopher', 2008

[4] If you wondered how a Faustian pact looks like, this is it!

[5] See Appendix -Exhibit B

[6] The Climate Change – previously known as Global Warming gnostic movement has been scandalised so many times by proven data falsifications, debunking an defections from the scientists ranks, it is hard to accord any credibility to its 'cause'.

[7] See e.g. the perennial complaints by Marxists how true Marxism was debased and catastrophically vulgarised, etc..

[8] Eric Voegelin, *The New Science of Politics, An Introduction*, Chicago, 1952, Chapter V, p. 137.

[9] Could this be a 'poisoning the well' argument? It seems not.

[10] The *Encyclopédie ou dictionnaire raisonné des sciences, des arts et des métiers*, 1759. For the claim to fame see d'Alembert, *discours préliminaires de l'Encyclopédie*, ed. F. Picavet (Paris, 1894) pp. 139-140.

[11] Ancient Greek 'Ermhj 'o Trismegistoj - 'Thrice Greatest Hermes' or even Mercurius ter Maximus. Although Hermes represented the ancient god of writing and alchemy, gnosticism may be the 'popularised' version, Hence, the confusion between hermeticism and gnosticism.

[12] This kind of social engineering is aimed at engineering a consensus of the flock. Social engineering started with Edward Bernays, nephew of Fredu, and grew mature under the Frankfurt School. Today's social engineering of concensus as a way to camouflage the reality can be observed in e.g the global climate change cabal. It suffers no dissenters and members of the flock will engage spontaneously in public shaming of critical positions.

[13] So many ways and means: E.g. Wikipedia uses 'editors' that have clearly no idea what they are doing. For all we know, they may be 14 years of age... Another way of damaging reputations is producing something like the Panama Papers. All of a sudden a handful of journalists, not known these days for their literary acumen, suddenly develop into international tax specialists almost overnight. Such study takes several years... And what to think of the serendipity of publication? Right before an OECD meeting, ready to take action with texts that need months of preparation?

[14] E. Voegelin, *New Science of Politics*, p. 140.

[15] Even a mafia boss like Al Capone was never convicted on his proper crimes, but on charges of 'tax evasion.' In an economic sense, certain people in the U.S.

had paid out golden coins to themselves which, when brought before a Judge, was claimed to amount stated as face value. The face value is the value the Mint gives its own coins. But the judge nevertheless applied the dualist nostrum 'law' and found the defendants guilty of 'fraud'. (see Joslin case in the U.S. Court of Appeals, Tenth Circuit Court, ruling under 26 U.S.C. par. 61 and 26 C.F.R. 1.61-2(d)(1) a.o.)

[16] Gnostic dualism seems to be of all times. Even a theoretical debate with certain Muslims or Zionists, wether inside or outside Israel, would prove sterile.

[17] For the benefit of students, not involved in philosophy, the reference here is to Nietzsche, who is known for his 'Murder of God'.

[18] During Hooker's lifetime, governmental authority did not yet elicit ridicule as it does today. In his political culture, it was clear that the government, not its subjects, represent the order of society.

[19] Retrievable from https://www.law.cornell.edu/supremecourt/text/337/1

[20] E. Voegelin, *Autobiographical Reflections*, Col. Works, vol. 34

[21] E. Voegelin, *ibidem*, Chapter 5, 'Stefan George and Karl Kraus', pp. 47-50.

[22] Justice is justice. But in dualistic language, social justice takes on another form, for no apparent reason, as if social justice differs from simply justice...

[23] The restraint was due to his fear that the full exposition of the swinish catastrophe could hurt people who were potential victims of the man in power.

[24] Consult also the glossary in Volume I for a differentiation of the types of socialism.

[25] To provide contemporary examples will be superfluous, not? There is a good reason why even the founders of a Wikipedia warn the public against its use.

[26] There are six original members, all known in the philosophical world: Max Horkheimer, Theodor Adorno, Herbert Marcuse, Friedrich Pollock, Erich Fromm, Otto Kirchheimer, Leo Löwenthal, Franz L. Neumann and Henryk Grossman. Jürgen Habermas is a later associated member.

[27] Edward Feser. 'Self Ownership, Abortion and the Rights of Children: Toward a more Conservative Libertarianism', Journal of Libertarian Studies, 2004, p. 105.

[28] One such worship would be the Mithras cult. It was still widely practised under Roman soldiers until the 4th century AD, by soldiers from everywhere in the Empire, serving Rome. It gradually disappeared but temple ruins are still found today all over Europe.

[29] Known as the *Hermes Trismegistus*, the *Kabbalah* and simply Christian *Gnosis*.

[30] Since reality is one and not dual, the notion of 2nd reality is to be taken in the sense of an irrealis. Eric Voegelin noted the lack of technical vocabulary in this field. We are not in a position to offer better vocabulary as yet, so we will have to do with some existing vocabulary that, against our wishes, may convey to the reader a notion of 'DoubleThink.' There is no 2nd reality in reality. Reality is what it is. But people with enough willpower will dominate others to comply

with their game, like children playing 'home', create this 2nd version. Philosophy has as yet not developed the necessary technical terms for this situation.

[31] Read, if you can stomach it, Stalin or Lenin. However, for a modern take: think of the themes in the news whereby students demand the covering or even destruction of statutes that 'trigger' something or another such as an imaginary insult. Even Al Qaeda, and before them, Napoleon Bonaparte's Army, used ancient iconographic statues, part of a people's heritage, for target practice...

[32]   Plato Timaeus and the Christian devil, called Satan or Lucifer (bearer of light). Satan may be looked up in the Codex *Gigas*. See also the treatment of Satan as a 'stumbling block or obstruction to human concupiscence or desire. in René Girard, *I See Satan Fall Like Lightning*, 1999, 2001

[33] In Rome, 1954, the First Convention On Population took place, discussing the Malthusian subjects of how this world would quickly become 'unsustainable' (read 'insufferable') with all these people around. Many 'green' movements find the presence of humans on the planet inimical to the Planet's welfare.

[34] A perfect slogan for the Islamic State, isn't it? It was also the beginning of the Catholic Church, but also the hundreds of religious sects like Manicheists, Valentinians, etc...

[35] D. Dennett and e.g. Richard Dawkins belong into this class of gnostic dualists, although they probably are unaware of it themselves; the Scientific American article 'Why life does not really exist' must win the prize of being most exemplar of the Gnostic dualist symptom of denial of reality with escapism to follow on its heels...; concerning the scientist's exclusive right on truth, only the scientist, donned with a white lab coat, can call himself owner of the truth. Only he knows, through years of serf-training, how the scientific method has to be applied. All others are well-willing amateurs, perhaps, but, come on, they are not scientists. The Ph.D documents, all peer reviewed, prove it! And, you know, only government approved universities can call themselves 'true universities'...etc..*ad nauseam.*

[36] The transfigured society can easily be distinguished in its modern form of Artificial Intelligence, which, as is claimed, will soon have a life all by itself...Older gnostic transfiguration movements exists, such as the one by eccentric Jesuit palaeontologist and mystic Pierre Teilhard de Chardin. Chardin in his work The Phenomenon of Man famously suggested the concept of a 'noosphere', a spiritual version of the lithosphere or biosphere; the collective consciousness of all human beings as though it were a physical substance. Chardin posited that this 'noosphere' could only project man into a future humanity of egoless, immortal electrical Christ-energy. Christianity v. 2.0 leads towards an immanentised eschaton of history, an 'Omega Point' brought about by man's 'exteriorisation' of his nervous system through electronic networks. Millenarian gnosticism at its most bizarre.

[37] An interesting experiment has been performed by Prof. Allan Sokal in 1996 by

publising a nonsensical article in a scientific journal. Tere ave been copycats since... very funny.

[38] In his introductory lecture at the University of Munich in 1958, later published as *Science, Politics, and Gnosticism,* Voegelin dropped a bombshell by demonstrating how Karl Marx, Hegel and Nietzsche were accomplished intellectual **swindlers**. Their swindle was the result of them having built in a prohibition of questioning into their intellectual systems (or lack of system, in the case of Nietzsche). For someone like Marx, socialist man simply must not ask a question like, what is the meaning of life? Or what is the origin of one's existence? To the question of origin, Marx argues that man does not exist out of himself, they are simply 'a product of abstraction.' 'When you inquire about creation of nature and man, you abstract form nature and man' To preempt any possibility of a questioner asking proof of existence of abstract man, Marx writes: 'Give up your abstraction and you will give up your question along with it. .... Do not think, do not question me.' K. Marx, Early Writings, Economic and Philosophical Manuscripts, T.B. Bottomore translation, New York, 1964, p. 166. The gnostic swindler does not like his assumptions exposed, nor questions asked...

[39] See e.g. Volume III, phantom profits, p. 19 and 43.

PART 9

IN THE MEAN TIME . . .

~∞ Chapter 49 ~∞

Can We Have Inflation And Deflation At The Same Time?

The Curse Of Electronic Dollars

Helicopter Ben has made a most unpleasant discovery. He has promised that the Federal Reserve will not stand idly by while the dollar 'deflates' and the economy slides into depression. If need be, he will go as far as having dollars air dropped from helicopters.

Time came to make good on those promises in August when the subprime crisis erupted. To his chagrin Ben found that electronic dollars, the kind he can create instantaneously at the click of the mouse in unlimited quantities, cannot be air dropped. They just won't drop.

For electronic dollars to work they have to be able to trickle down through the banking system. The trouble is that when bad debt in the economy reaches critical mass, it will start playing hide-and-seek. All of a sudden banks become suspicious of one another. Is the other guy trying to pass his bad penny on to me? In extremis, one bank may refuse to take an overnight draft from the other and will insist on spot payment. A field day for Brink's. The clearing house is idled and armoured cars deliver FR notes and certified checks on FR deposits in both directions up and down Wall Street.

Under such circumstances electronic dollars won't trickle down. In effect they are frozen. Ultimately, they may be demonetised by the market. How awkward for Helicopter Ben. He would now have to go back to the old-fashioned and cumbersome way of inflating the money supply via the printing press. Literally.

Northern Rock and Roll

He had better and do it double quick. The Northern Rock and roll fever may spill over across the Atlantic from England to the United States. Northern Rock is a bank headquartered in Newcastle with lots of branches in the Northern Counties. It was a high-flyer using novel ways of financing mortgages through conduits and other SIV's, instead of using the more traditional methods of building societies through savings. (SIV or Structured Investment Vehicle is a euphemism for borrowing short, lending long through securitisation). Now a run on the bank has grounded the high flier. As long queues in front of the doors of branch offices indicate, a world-wide run on banks may be in the offing. Bank runs were thought to be a pathology of the gold standard. In England they haven't seen the like of it since 1931 when the Bag Lady of Threadneedle Street went off gold. Surprise, surprise: bank runs are now back in vogue playing havoc on the fiat money world. Depositors want to get their money. Not the electronic variety. They want money they can fold.

There's the rub. Pity Helicopter Ben. It looked so simple a couple of weeks ago. The promise of an air drop should stem any run. It sufficed that people knew he could do it. No reason to mistrust the banks since they are backed up by air drops. Now people have different ideas. The air drop is humbug. Can't be done. Ben is bluffing. As calculated by Alf Field writing in Gear Today, Gone Tomorrow – available online – if only ten percent of the notional value of derivatives is bailed out by dropping $500 FR notes the pile, if notes are stacked upon one another, would be nearly 9000 miles high. Helicopter Ben hasn't reckoned that FR notes do not exist in such quantities. They will have to be printed before they can be dropped. Even if they existed, to drop them all would take years and by that time the shaky house of cards of FR credit might be blown away. And bailing out just ten percent of the derivatives mess is a conservative estimate. You may have to bail out a lot more than that.

Devolution

What does it all mean? At minimum it means that we can have inflation with deflation. I am not referring to stagflation. I refer to the seemingly impossible phenomenon that the money supply inflates and deflates at the same time. The miracle would occur through the devolution of money. This is Alf Field's admirable phrase to describe the 'good money is driven out by bad' syndrome. Electronic dollars driving out FR notes. The more electronic money is created by Helicopter Ben, the more FR notes will be hoarded by banks and financial institutions while passing along electronic dollars as fast as they can. Most disturbing of all is the fact that FR notes will be hoarded by the people, too. If banks cannot trust one another, why should people trust the banks?

Devolution is the revenge of fiat money on its creator, the government. The money supply will split up tectonically into two parts. One part will continue to inflate at an accelerating pace, but the other will deflate. Try as it might, the Federal Reserve will not be able to print paper money in the usual denominations fast enough, especially since the demand for FR notes is global. Regardless of statistical figures showing that the global money supply is increasing at an unprecedented rate, the hand-to-hand money supply may well be shrinking as hoarding demand for FR notes becomes voracious. The economy will be starved of hand-to-hand money. Depression follows deflation as night follows day.

Decoupling Tectonic Plates

Side-by-side of deflation of hand-to-hand money there will be hyperinflation as the stock of electronic money will keep exploding along with the price of assets. You will be in the same boat with the Chinese (and the son of Zeus: Tantalus). You will be put through the tantalising water torture – trillions of dollars floating by, all yours, but which you are not allowed to spend. The two tectonic plates will disconnect: the plate carrying electronic dollars and the plate carrying FR notes, with lots of earthquakes along the fault line. No Herculean effort on the part of the government and the Federal Reserve will be able to reunite them. At first, electronic dollars can be exchanged for FR notes but only against payment of a premium and then, not at all.

The Curse Of Negative Discount Rate

If you think this is fantasy, think again. Look at the charts showing the collapse of the yield on T-bills. While it may bounce back, next time around the discount rate may go negative. You say it's impossible? Why, it routinely happened during the Great Depression of the 1930s. Negative discount rate means that the T-bill gets a premium (or agio), the discount goes into premium even before maturity and keeps its elevated value after. This perverse behaviour is due to the fact that the T-bill is payable in dollars. Yes, the kind you can fold, the kind that is in demand exceeding supply, the kind people and financial institutions hoard, the kind foreigners have been hoarding for decades through thick and thin: FR notes. Thus, T-bills are a substitute for the hard-to-come-by FR notes. Mature bills may stay in circulation in the interbank market, in preference to electronic dollar credits.[1] Why, their supply is limited, isn't it, while the supply of electronic dollars is unlimited! The beauty of it all is that we have an accurate and omnipresent indicator of the premium that cannot be suppressed like M3: the (negative) T-bill rate. This is an indicator showing how the Federal Reserve is losing the fight against deflation.

Inverted Pyramid Of John Exter

The grand old man of the New York Federal Reserve bank's gold department, the last Mohican, John Exter explained the devolution of money (not his term) using the model of an inverted pyramid, delicately balanced on its apex at the bottom consisting of pure gold. The pyramid has many other layers of asset classes graded according to safety, from the safest and least prolific at bottom to the least safe and most prolific asset layer, electronic dollar credits on top. (When Exter developed his model, electronic dollars had not yet existed; he talked about FR deposits.) In between you find, in decreasing order of safety, as you pass from the lower to the higher layer: silver, FR notes, T-bills, T- bonds, agency paper, other loans and liabilities denominated in dollars. In times of financial crisis people scramble downwards in the pyramid trying to get to the next and nearest safer and less prolific layer underneath. But down there the pyramid gets narrower. There is not enough of the safer and less prolific kind of assets to accommodate all who want to 'devolve'. Devolution is also called 'flight to safety'.

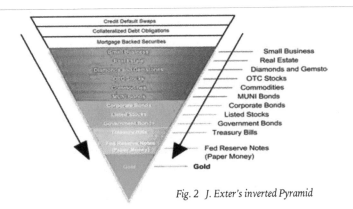

Fig. 2 J. Exter's inverted Pyramid

An example of this occurred on Friday, August 31, 2007, as indicated by the sharp drop in the T-bill rate from 4% to 3%, having been at 5% only a couple of days before. As people were scrambling to move from the higher to the lower layer in the inverted pyramid, they were pushing others below them further downwards. There was a ripple effect in the T-bill market. The extra demand for T-bills made bill prices rise or, what is the same to say, T-bill rates to fall. This was panic that was never reported, still less interpreted. Yet it shows you the shape of things to come. We are going to see unprecedented leaps in the market value of T-bills, regardless of face value! You have been warned: the dollar is not a pushover. Electronic dollars, maybe. But T-bills (if you can fold them) and FR notes will have an enormous staying power. Watch for the discount rate on T-bills morphing into a premium rate!

It is interesting to note that gold, the apex of the inverted pyramid, remained relatively unaffected during the turmoil in August. Scrambling originated in the higher layers. Nevertheless, ultimately gold is going to be engulfed by the ripple effect as scrambling cascades downwards. This is inevitable. Every financial crisis in the world, However, remote it may look in relation to gold, will ultimately affect gold, perhaps with a substantial lag. The U.S. Government destroyed the gold standard 35 years ago, but it could not get gold out of the system. It was not for want of trying, either, as we all know. Gold remains firmly embedded as the apex of Exter's inverted pyramid.

Vertical devolution is not the only kind that occurs in the inverted pyramid. There are similar movements that can be described as horizontal. Nathan Narusis of Vancouver, Canada, is doing interesting research on the Exter-pyramid. He noted that in addition, to vertical there is also horizontal devolution. Within each horizontal layer of the same safety class there are discernible differences. An example is the difference between gold in bar form and gold in bullion coin form, or silver in bar form and silver in the form of bags of junk silver coins. Franklin Sanders in Tennessee is an expert on horizontal devolution of silver and has a fascinating study how the discount on bags of junk silver coins may go into premium and vice versa. There may also be differences between FR notes of older issues and FR notes of the most recent vintage. There are obvious differences between the CD's of a multinational bank and those of an obscure country bank. The point is that movement of assets horizontally between such pockets within the same safety layer is possible and may be of significance as a crisis unfolds and deepens. [2]

Dousing Insolvency With Liquidity

In a few days during the month of August central banks of the world added between $300 and 500 billion in new liquidity in an effort to prevent credit markets from seizing up. The trouble is that all this injection of new funds was in the form of electronic credits, boosting mostly the top layer, *where there was no shortage* at all, if anything, there was a superabundance. Acute shortage occurred precisely in the lower layers.

This goes to show that, ultimately, central banks are pretty helpless in fighting future crises in an effort to prevent scrambling to escalate into a stampede. They think it is a crisis of scarcity [of credit] whereas it is in fact a crisis of overabundance [of quality impaired credit].

We feel strongly that this aspect of research on the denouement of the fiat money era has been lost in the endless debates on the barren question whether it will be in the form of deflation or hyperinflation. Chances are that it will be neither, rather, it will be both, simultaneously. There is a little-noticed and little-studied continental drift between the money supply of electronic dollars and the money supply FR notes. (Continental drift of the geological variety is invisible and can only be studied with the aid of high-precision instruments.) The tectonic plate of electronic dollars will keep inflating at a furious pace, while that of FR notes and T-bills will deflate because of hoarding by financial institutions and the people themselves. The Federal Reserve will be unable to convert electronic dollars into FR notes, as present denominations cannot be printed fast enough physically in times of a crisis. Moreover, if it comes out with new denominations by adding lots more zero's to the face value of the FR notes, then the market will treat these the same way as it does treat electronic dollars.

Genesis Of Derivatives

Alf Field (op.cit.) is talking about the 'seven D's' of the developing monetary disaster: Deficits, Dollars, Devaluations, Debts, Demographics, Derivatives and Devolution. Let me add that the root of all evil is the double D, or DD: Deliberate Debasement. In 1933 the government of the United States embraced that toxic theory of John Maynard Keynes (who borrowed it from Silvio Gesell). [3] It was put into effect piecemeal over a period of four decades. But what the Constitution and the entire judiciary system of the United States could not stop, gold could.

> It was found that gold in the international monetary system was a stubborn stumbling block to the centralisation and globalisation of credit. So gold was overthrown by President Nixon on August 15, 1971 by a stroke of the pen, as he reneged on the international gold obligations of the United States.

This had the immediate effect that foreign exchange and interest rates immediately destabilised and prices of marketable goods embarked upon an endless upward spiral. In due course derivates markets sprang up where risks inherent in the interest and forex rate variations could be 'hedged.' [4] The trouble with this idea, never investigated by the economic profession, was that these risks, having been artificially created, can only be shifted but cannot be absorbed. By contrast, the price risks of agricultural commodities are nature-given and, as such, can be absorbed by the speculators.[not gamblers].

The important difference between nature-given and man-made risks (see above) is the very cause of the mushrooming proliferation of derivatives markets, at last count half a quadrillion dollars strong (or should I say weak?!) Since the risk involved in the gyration of interest and forex rates can only be shifted but cannot be cushioned, there started an infinite regression as follows:

The risk involved in the variation of long-term interest rates we may call x. The problem of hedging risk x calls for the creation of derivatives X (e.g., futures contracts on T-bonds). But the sellers of X have a new risk y. Hedging y calls for the creation of derivatives Y (e.g., calls, puts, strips, swaps, repos, options on futures and, with tongue in cheek: futures on options, options on options, etc.) Sellers of Y have a new risk z. The problem of hedging z will necessitate the creation of derivatives Z. And so on and so forth, *ad infinitum*.

J'accuse

We have to interpret the new phenomenon, the falling tendency of the T-bill rate accurately. Maybe the financial media will try to put a positive spin on it, for example, that it demonstrates the strength of the dollar. (Now that would be really spin that would make any Mengerian student laugh, reducing the newspaper's economic section to the comic section) Just the opposite is the case, of course.

We are witnessing a sea change, tectonic decoupling, a cataclysmic decline in the soundness of the international monetary system. The world's payments system is in an advance state of disintegration. It is the beginning of a world-wide economic depression, possibly much worse than that of the 1930s.

We have reached a landmark: that of the breaking up of centralised and globalised credit, the close of the dollar system.

J'accuse – said Zola when he assailed the French government for fabricating a case of treason against artillery captain Alfred Dreyfus in 1893. It is now my turn:

J'accuse – the government of the United States under president Roosevelt reneged on the domestic gold obligations of the U.S. in violation of the Constitution and violated people's property rights without due process by confiscating gold in 1933;

J'accuse – academentia has been pussyfooting the government by failing to point out the economic consequences of gold confiscation, namely, the prolonged suppression of interest rates that was ultimately the cause of prolonging depression;[5]

J'accuse – the government of the United States under president Nixon reneged on the international gold obligations of the U.S. thereby globalising the monetary crisis in 1971;

J'accuse – cringing academia failed to point out the consequences of gold demonetisation: price spiral of marketable commodities worldwide; roller-coaster ride of long-term interest rates, up to 16 percent per annum and down to 4 percent per annum or lower and back up again; the fact that interest rates may take prices along for the ride;

J'accuse – foreign governments accepted Nixon's breach of faith without demur, apparently because in exchange for their compliance they were given the freedom to inflate their own money supply with abandon on the coattails of dollar inflation;

J'accuse – the banks have embraced the regime of irredeemable currency with gusto and greatly profited from it, instead of protesting that under such a regime it was impossible to discharge the bank's sacred duty to act as the guardian of the savings of the people and the value of the inheritance of widows and orphans;

J'accuse – the accounting profession for their compliance in accepting gravely compromised accounting standards that convert liabilities into assets in the balance sheets of the government and the Federal Reserve.

In the words of Chief Justice Reynolds, in delivering a dissenting minority opinion on the 1935 Supreme Court decision, that upheld president Roosevelt's confiscation of people's gold, 'Loss of reputation for honourable dealing will bring us unending humiliation. The impending legal and moral chaos is appalling.'

No less appalling, we may add, is the impending financial and economic chaos.

Endnotes to Chapter 49

[1] An object lesson in negative T-bill rate is being presented as I [A. Fekete] write this on Thursday, September 20, 2007. The 30-day silver lease rate has gone to minus 0.1 percent. I wish analyst Ted Butler stopped bitching about manipulation and instead of telling fairy tales about raptors and dinosaurs explain to us what the negative silver lease rate means. My own explanation is panic short covering in silver. Normally the price of silver moves in tandem with that of gold. In case the rising price of silver lags substantially behind that of gold, negative lease rate may develop, indicating that silver is delivered faster by the lessees than the lessors are willing or able to take (for example, if the lessors assumed until the last minute that the leases will be rolled over). Under these circumstances the lessor is happy to leave the silver with the lessee even after the lease expired. This seems to explode the myth about an acute shortage of silver, so ardently spread by Butler. The rising price of silver that may well follow the panic short-covering has nothing to do with shortages. Just the opposite.

Concerning the case of a negative T-bill rate, the pinching shoe is on the other foot. Here we do have a shortage, namely, a physical shortage of FR notes in which the bill is supposed to be paid. But since the borrower is the government, there is no presumption of a default, so the mature T-bill is monetised by the market to alleviate the shortage.

[2] Naturally, these horizontal variations may be interpreted in Menger's thinking frame of marketability.

[3] Silvio Gesell, a gnostic warrior, a.k.a. 'social activist' that Keynes compared favourably to Marx. Gesell may be called the polar opposite of Menger, in view of his denial of 'value' in economics. Like the Prophet, he was convinced of the necessity to stop the hoarding of money by introducing deprecating paper coupons with an expiry date. That ought to do the trick of making money circulate. Of course, had he paid attention to Menger, he would have realised that people will fall over themselves to get rid of the * they were holding, only to not accept it any further. The denial of marketability would be instant. Had he paid closer attention to devolution and marketability, he may have realised that people, after getting rid of their coupon-money will hoard anything else that can be hoarded instead and even marginalise coupon money. Gesell may be the personification of the gnostic abyss that 19th and early 20th century science had fallen into.

[4] Or so it was believed. The 20th century generation of gnostic dualist in economics have overlooked to suppress the grain trading handbooks. Basis, contango and backwardation will not be found in their grossly useless economics handbooks. Sending your children to university for an economics degree is tanta-

mount to sending them of to an indoctrination camp in Soviet style. It will take years to recover and you will have learned precisely nothing.

[5] The causal connection between gold confiscation and the prolonging of the Great Depression should be clear. Gold must be seen as the main competitor of bonds. Once the competitor is forcibly removed, bond prices start rising or, what is the same to say, interest rates start falling. Linkage between falling interest rates and falling prices did the rest.

✺ Chapter 50 ✺

The Shadow Pyramid

John Exter, the six-foot tall 'gnome' of the Federal Reserve Bank of New York and one-time custodian of earmarked gold locked up in the Liberty Street fortress in Manhattan, is best-known for his model of the money supply represented as an inverted pyramid. Exter belongs to the school teaching that the current experiment with irredeemable currency is more likely to lead to a deflationary than an inflationary catastrophe.

The inverted pyramid is delicately balanced on a tip of pure gold. Its upper layers consist of money of increasingly greater proliferation such as Federal Reserve notes, T-bills, bank deposits, as well as other bank liabilities. The layers are graded according to safety, going from the safest, gold at the bottom to the least safe, the layer of electronic dollars at the top.

While appearing placid, static and monolithic, the pyramid comes alive every once in a while when a monetary or banking crisis erupts somewhere in the world. There is great commotion and agitation manifested by the scrambling of assets downwards to less prolific layers below, in the wake of owners trying to take a 'flight to safety' — as it has been happening with increasing frequency in the twentieth century, especially during the fourth quarter, after the United States defaulted on its gold obligation to foreign governments in 1971.

The pyramid is deflationary because, although it is increasing at a double-digit rate, it threatens to collapse to its low-lying layers in consequence of repeated monetary crises.

The Derivatives Revolution

Exter's pyramid casts a huge shadow which is increasing even faster than the pyramid itself, as you might expect the shadow of any pyramid to loom ever larger in the sunset. Make no mistake about it, the sun is setting on the irredeemable dollar. The shadow is none other than the derivatives market with its tip consisting of T-bond obligations of the U.S., followed by layers of interest-rate derivatives graded by remoteness from the tip.

In more details, calling the tip or the layer of T-bonds the first, the second layer consists of futures contracts to be settled by surrendering T-bonds below. The third consists of futures contracts to be settled by surrendering obligations belonging to the second layer. And so on, the nth layer consists of future contracts to be settled by surrendering obligations belonging to the $(n-1)^{st}$ layer. It is readily seen that only T-bonds can ultimately liquidate all liabilities. Thus a pyramid of liabilities, which is allowed to grow beyond any limit as n gets arbitrarily large, is being built on a limited supply of T- bonds.

As Floyd Norris writes in The New York Times :

> " ... the transfer of risk was supposed to be the great advance brought to the world by financial engineers in developing exotic derivative products that enabled risks to be sliced and diced in all manner of ways. The risks have been transferred through a bewildering jungle of futures: options, swaps, swaptions, specialised investment vehicles, collateralised debt obligations, variable interest conduits and who knows what other instruments'. [1]

Short Squeeze And Corner

But there is another side to the Derivatives Revolution. The market for interest-rate derivatives is not unlike an imaginary futures market in corn that allows unlimited short selling of the next crop regardless of its size. Of course, there are consequences: short squeeze and, ultimately, a corner – the classical example of the game of musical chairs. Every player is happy – until the music stops.

The origin and growth of the shadow pyramid is the great mystery of 21st century finance. Its layers [2] are subject to the same kind of scrambling during times of crisis as those of Exter's pyramid, only worse. Those who have a long position are trying to swap it for another in the lower layers, closer to the 'real thing', the T-bond. The trouble is that the lower layers cannot satisfy potential demand simultaneously.

But why is the shadow pyramid growing at the break-neck speed of 40 percent per annum? At that rate it doubles every other year, presently representing liabilities in the order of ½ quadrillion or 500 trillion dollars, a sum that boggles the mind. [3] In comparison, the annual GDP of the U.S. is a paltry $14 trillion while that of the world is hardly more than $60 trillion. What is the inordinate size and growth of the pyramid trying to tell us?

Fast Breeder Of Derivatives

It has been suggested that fewer than ten people in the world understand the shadow pyramid and its dynamics. It is further suggested that the $½ quadrillion is merely a 'notional' value. Don't be misled by the semantics. Every dollar of the ½ quadrillion is a real liability: the obligee cannot walk away from it any more than the issuer of a bond can walk away from his – except through default. The shadow pyramid is an ideal hiding place for bad debt. Gold doesn't exist in sufficient quantities to liquidate Exter's pyramid; neither do T-bonds to liquidate its shadow.

Why do managers of the regime of irredeemable currency allow the proliferation of liabilities greatly to exceed the means of settlement? How could such an insane construction come about and continue to prosper, nay, to accelerate, threatening the world with an avalanche of defaults? The question is a taboo by order of government, which pussyfooting economists are only too anxious to observe. Yet monetary science has the answer. We're proud to take the initiative in violating the taboo.

Futility Of Price Control

The irredeemable dollar is not a stable monetary standard. Like all irredeemable currencies in history, the dollar is facing periodic runs that will ultimately wipe out its value. The purchasing power of the dollar is being destroyed through relentless price rises. As long as the rate of average price rises can be kept under control, people don't worry too much about the value of their money. They are lulled into believing that what goes up will come down. The problem, therefore, is whether the government can limit price rises to, say, 3 percent per annum.

Limiting price rises administratively through price control is a non-starter. Black markets would spring up and people would take black market prices as 'real' rather than the managed prices at which supplies were either unavailable or of inferior quality. The government has to resort to a method more sophisticated than that. So it attempts to control prices by taking advantage of the so-called 'linkage', [4] (a.k.a. Gibson's Paradox), the well-observed albeit not so well-understood phenomenon that prices and interest rates are linked. Neither is free to move independently of the other, in particular one cannot, apart from leads and lags, run away while leaving the other behind.

The task facing the government is still daunting. In an inflationary scenario it is not enough to control short-term interest rates. But that is all the central bank is equipped to do: it is quite powerless to control long-term rates. So the government resorts to chicanery. It tries to enlist help from bond speculators to keep interest rates low by letting them bid up the price of T-bonds.

Making Bond Speculation Risk-Free

But how can the government persuade bond speculators, arguably the smartest lot in finance, to do its bidding? Well, that's just the thing. The government has to make bond speculation on the bull side of the market risk free. That is a tall order. How can it be pulled off?

Here is how. Speculators are encouraged to build up large inventories of T-bonds and 'hedge' their long position in the futures market. That's the tricky part. Simple hedging won't do. The hedges must also be hedged.

In effect, the government legalises unlimited short selling of T-bonds thereby creating unlimited demand for them. As any demand for bonds when fine-tuned is expected to result in a declining long-term rate of interest. To guard against the danger of falling interest rates spreading the fire to falling prices, the central bank stands ready to hose down the price-decline with liquidity. The arsonist is girding himself as a fire-fighter.

In the absence of unlimited short selling the value of dollar-denominated bonds would be devastated even before that of the dollar. But as the recent sub-prime crisis has demonstrated, this is not what is happening. There is hardly a ripple-effect in the bond market even after the value of the dollar is shattered. Bond hedges do work. Bond values can be insulated from the vicissitudes of the dollar by the layered structure of the shadow pyramid.

Mendacity Of Mainstream Economics

The question arises why it is that prices of agricultural products can be effectively hedged by first-round control, without constructing an infinite tower of hedges of ever higher order. Here I must point to the mendacious nature of mainstream economics. It teaches that hedging bond prices is no different from hedging agricultural prices. The very same principles apply in bringing about the same desiderata: stable bond prices and stable interest rates.

This teaching is a shameless lie spread by mainstream economists who are paid to know better.

The proof : the Babeldom of interest rate derivatives.

> No infinite tower of hedges is needed to stabilise the prices of agricultural goods; by contrast, simple hedging will not stabilise bond prices.

The fact is that the risks involved in fluctuating gold and bond prices, or fluctuating interest and foreign exchange rates have been artificially created. They are man-made: the same as risks created in gaming casinos. How do we know? Well, under a gold standard all of the above risks were absent. At any rate, variation in the gold and bond prices or in interest and foreign exchange rates were so small that no organised speculation could spring up spontaneously for lack of sufficient volatility.

Speculation Versus Gambling

By contrast, risks involved in the variation of the prices of agricultural commodities are nature-given. Herein lies the fundamental difference between speculation and gambling.

> Speculators address risks that exist in nature.

But risks that are man-made cannot be cushioned by speculation, just as risks artificially created in the gambling casino cannot.

[You may have to read again all our previous instances of the use of the word speculation concerning irredeemable fiat bonds and remember that we ought to have used gambling instead of speculation. However, we did not want to confuse the issue too early. The speculators in the market of commodities are not necessarily gamblers insofar no hedging is involved.]

Instead, risks are shifted (possibly after having been sliced and diced to the point of making them unrecognisable). In destroying the gold standard the government has created the whole gamut of artificial risks, from variable foreign exchange rates to variable interest rates, neither of which can be successfully addressed by speculation as can the risk of fluctuating agricultural prices. In other words, while speculation addressing nature-given risks is stabilising, speculation addressing man-made risks is destabilising. Just as at the roulette table: an increase in the number of players will in no way limit the risk involved in betting. Just the opposite: gambling frenzy will climb and, with it, risk exposure will be rising, too.

The successful speculator correctly diagnoses budding supply shocks. If he anticipates a crop failure, then he buys while prices are

still low(ish). He sells when prices rise after the crop failure has occurred, thereby augmenting supply, tampering the price rise. The consumer benefits. [5] Alternatively, if the speculator anticipates a bumper
crop, then he sells short while prices are still high. He covers his short
position when prices fall after the bumper crop has been brought in,
thereby augmenting demand, tampering the decline of prices. The producer benefits.

> The speculator is a benefactor of society — but only in so far as
> the risk of price-fluctuation is nature-given.

Natural Selection: Central Bank Style

The case is very different when the risk is man-made. Take variable foreign exchange rates. Here central bankers pit their wit against that of
the currency 'speculator' [read gambler]. We may be confident that the
wits of speculators are sharper. After all, they make it their business
to outsmart the central banker. In the process they risk their capital.
The central banker knows that his losses will be covered by the Treasury. The 'natural selection' that shapes the skills of speculators, allowing only the smartest of the smart to survive while the rest, having
lost their 'capital' [read stacks of irredeemable notes] will fall by the
wayside, fails to apply to central bankers. Instead, there is inbreeding
and complacency. Central bankers are on salaries and risk no capital of
their own. No natural selection is at work culling the herd of obtuse
central bankers. The upshot is that central bank intervention in the
futures and derivatives markets is more often a failure than a success.
Nimble and wily speculators routinely win.

Pump-Priming To Make Speculation Self-Fulfilling

Jaw-boning will not persuade speculators to keep buying T-bonds. They
see through and will sell the bonds rather than buying them if they expect interest rates to rise. However, there is something the government
can still do, vicious as though it might be. If the government could only
demonstrate that interest rates will keep falling or, what is the same to
say, bond prices will keep rising, then speculators [read gamblers] will
naturally converge on the bull side of the market and the prediction
of rising bond values will be 'self-fulfilling'. Stable bond prices won't
do. It is necessary for the government to grant risk-free profits to bond
bulls. The backdrop of a falling interest rate regime is essential.

The problem therefore, is reduced for the government to engineer an initial falling bias for the rate of interest. That is a problem of pump-priming. Once a falling trend has been established, speculators will finish the job. They will perpetuate the trend by making bullish bets on bonds self-fulfilling. Pump-priming is deviously accomplished through legalising higher order hedges in the bond market. The demand for T-bonds is artificially boosted.

Just as a Ponzi scheme is fraudulent and dealt with by the Criminal Code accordingly, the infinite proliferation of bond hedges through authorising ever higher order of hedging is no less fraudulent. There is no difference in substance between the two schemes, only difference in form. Payoff is being promised to an ever larger population which cannot possibly be honoured. Both schemes come to a sorry end when the supply of fools is exhausted.

The supply of fools, however, large, is still finite and there is no doubt that the Babeldom of derivatives will ultimately collapse.

Sacrifice On The Altar Of Moloch

To recapitulate, the derivatives market has been created for the sole purpose of perpetuating the regime of the irredeemable dollar. It embodies demand for dollar-denominated bonds that can be augmented without limits. The government creates an infinite pyramid of liabilities that can only be liquidated by a finite supply of bonds.

The dollar-system would have disintegrated in the twentieth century already, but for the demand that has been artificially created for T-bonds. Through the derivative pyramid the demand for bonds is boosted in a seemingly endless merry-go-round. The public is unaware that the T-bonds are rotten to the core. They are, in the words of the late Dr. Franz Pick, 'guaranteed certificates of confiscation'.

Once upon a time T-bonds were the safest investment vehicles on earth. Guardians of widows and orphans wouldn't look at anything else when investing their wards' inheritance. Savings were sacrosanct. But that was another age: the golden age of the gold standard when interest rates and bond values were stable.

Only after the U.S. government single-handedly demolished the international gold standard did interest rates start bouncing up-and-down like a yo-yo. To the eternal shame of academia, the chorus of mainstream economists started parroting the propaganda line that, after all, it was the nature of interest rates to fluctuate wildly, just as it is the nature of prices of agricultural commodities, in response to changes in supply and demand – an unmitigated lie. T-bonds (and the inheritance of widows and orphans) have thus become a plaything in the hands of gamblers. The welfare of innocent children was sacrificed on the altar of Moloch. In the fullness of time, academia and the regime of irredeemable currency will be judged in the light of the Biblical admonition against tormenting widows and orphans.

Playing With Fire

The foregoing explains how bullish bond speculation has been made virtually risk-free by the government through the inverted pyramid of derivatives. The outcome was a falling trend in the yield of 30-year bonds, from 16 percent in 1981 to 4 percent 25 years later, in 2006. Every time the rate of interest is halved, bond prices approximately double. Every time the rate of interest is cut back to one-quarter, bond prices approximately quadruple, as it has between 1981 and 2006. It is quite a windfall, with interest income at the rate of 16 percent kicked in as a bonus. Capital gains like this are not to be ridiculed, especially if they are available risk-free.

It is an open question whether the falling trend of interest rates will continue on its own, or it will be necessary to repeat the prestidigitation of 1980, printing another slate of 30-year bonds with 16 percent coupons attached to them. Let me suggest that the existence of the shadow pyramid makes this unnecessary. The pump has been primed already. The key ingredient, demand for T-bonds, is already given.

To be sure, in encouraging bullish bond speculation the government is playing with fire. Falling interest rates could drag commodity prices down, regardless of injections of new liquidity. Deflation and depression loom large on the horizon. The recent desperate attempt of the Open Market Committee to cut interest rates even in the face of a collapsing dollar shows a rare instance of brinkmanship.

> The U.S. Treasury and the Federal Reserve have sold the nation's birthright for a pottage of lentils. They are no longer in control. Their check-kiting scheme is up. They noisily yank the stick-shift up and down, right and left, all in vain: it is no longer connected to anything.

The future depends on the collective judgment of bond gamblers, especially those not subject to the jurisdiction of the United States, into whose hands the fate of the dollar has slipped. It is a matter of guesswork to say how they will decide.

'China Shrugged'

This may not be the end of the dollar yet. We have the Chinese puzzle wrapped in mystery inside of an enigma to solve. I would certainly, count the Chinese among not just the biggest, but the shrewdest and most skilful bond speculators ever, backed up by their unprecedented kitty of well over one trillion dollars in T-bonds. I would even go so far as suggesting that a large part of this kitty has originated, not so much in trade surplus but, rather, in bond speculation. After all, the Chinese have been active players at the blackjack table where the chips are U.S. bonds, since the early 1980s. They have played their hand quite adroitly. It would be out of character if they all of a sudden turned into dummies.

How can you explain the fact, mentioned by Edmund L. Andrews in The New York Times on October 10, 2007, (see the article entitled U.S. Affects a Strong Silence on Its Weak Currency) that China's central bank has stepped up its already huge purchases of dollar denominated securities? According to recent data, China's foreign exchange reserves have been climbing at a pace of $40 billion a month, or twice as fast as last year. Don't buy the ridiculous argument that China is trying to protect its market share in the U.S. by giving away its goods for next to nothing. Continued Chinese purchases of U.S. securities look more like an opening gambit than a stupid mistake.

Like Atlas carrying the globe on his shoulder, the Chinese carry the globalised dollar on theirs. Let others dump the T-bonds in a rout. The inscrutable Chinese will enter the fray later and clean up. [6]

China's central bank is a big-time bond speculator [gambler for the purists]: the biggest ever in history. Without fanfare it is following a script that promises a huge pay-off on T-bonds – in view of a growing shortage as the shadow pyramid of derivatives matures and demand for T-bonds intensifies.

As long as the payoff remains greater than dollar-depreciation, the Chinese are doing fine.

Who Is Holding Whom To Ransom?

From now on the game of musical chairs is going to continue with the Chinese calling the shots.
The dollar will be stabilised albeit at a level reflecting big losses, but not so big as to jeopardise the mountain of paper profits the Chinese have piled up during the past 25 years. Through their control of the

shadow pyramid the Chinese hold the U.S. Treasury to ransom in spite of appearances, namely, that the U.S. Treasury is holding the Chinese to ransom. That's the good news. The bad news is that this means deflation in the United States and the Western World, confirming Exter's gloomy prognostications: falling real estate prices, falling banks, falling employment.

Don't blame the bond speculators. Don't blame the Chinese. Blame the managers of the global regime of irredeemable currencies for the disaster. First and foremost blame those in the U.S. government who trampled on the Constitution in issuing irredeemable promises to pay. Dollar bills and T-bonds are just that. Irredeemable promises are explicitly ruled out by the Constitution.

At first it appeared a smart thing to flood the world with them as foreigners were showing an insatiable appetite for irredeemable promises. But as it often happens, the smart thing turned into too much of a good thing. The chips started accumulating in one hand, the hand of a smarter guy who knew how to call the shots. We need not worry that the Chinese may never get full value for their exports. We have plenty of mischief to worry about at home.

It is criminal how the managers of the dollar have ostracised gold. It is criminal how they have allowed the debt of the U.S. government to burgeon and private thrift to wither simultaneously. It is criminal how they have let American debt get concentrated in foreign hands, in particular, the hand of the enigmatic Chinese. It is criminal how they have permitted the unlimited proliferation of interest-rate derivatives, in order to protect their power to flood the world with worthless paper – disregarding the possibility that falling interest rates may trigger worldwide depression.

It is criminal how the managers of the dollar have let monetary leadership slip away from the United States.

Endnotes to Chapter 50

[1] The New York Times, October 26, 2007 (see the article entitled Who's Going to Take the Financial Weight?)

[2] The layers of John Exter's inverted pyramid closely resemble the structure of the Continental accounting scheme, regarding assets. In the accounting structure, the marketability (some call it liquidity, which is not the same) is reflected. In the accounting class 1 we find assets such as land and building, whilst in the last class, 5, we find bank deposits, cash on hand etc. Due to this old accounting tradition, John Exter was able to construct his pyramid, which reflects this marketability of assets.

[3] The American quadrillion consists of 0.5 x 1015 or 500.000.000.000.000

[4] See Volume III, Chapter 36, Inflationary and Deflationary phases, pp. 190.

[5] Although most consumers will resent the person called a speculator who sells high. The point is that the speculator sells at the top and actually brings about (at the margin) a turnaround, i.e. a lower price. The resentment may even be ideologically inspired, since 'education' was never at such a low point as now.

[6] Meaning that the Chinese Central Bank will own the U.S.A. and Europe, as they already own large area's of Africa. That is: the debtor's fate lies in the hands of the creditors, short of a shooting war.

✀ Chapter 51 ✀

Waiting for Godot

The original title for this article was Timing Hyperinflation with an overlong subtitle The Saga of Unraveling Global Fiat Money Issued on the Strength of Irredeemable Promises of Governments. On second thought I changed it for fear of turning off serious readers suspecting that it was written by a prankster to be released on next April Fool's Day. So the new title Waiting for Godot stands. It obviously calls for an explanation.

In 1952 Samuel Beckett wrote a play with the title En attendant Godot that has subsequently become world famous. In his play the author demonstrates with unforgettable force the pre-conscious visceral form of expectation, similar to the Jewish peoples' waiting for the Messiah, or Christendom's waiting for the second coming of Christ. The question asked by the impatient 'gold bug' population arises in view of the instinctive waiting for hyperinflation in the wake of the 'latter-day miraculous proliferation of money'. It is motivated by the quantity theory of money (QTM), a faulty doctrine. The superficial observer misses the individual's effort to shape the future and the fact that , to this extent, what is happening is caused by teleological forces (as distinct from forces shaped by causality). The expectation of future always builds on empirical foundations, but regularly exceeds the level of experience. Reasonable monetary policy ought to be able to figure out what consequences follow from government interference.

My readers bombard me with the question: 'How much longer do we have to wait for Godot (read: hyperinflation)'. 'Why has the prognostication for permanent gold backwardation failed to materialise during the past decade? The question is justified.

I have devoted the greater part of my life to the task of studying hyperinflation throughout the ages. For some six decades I was trying to analyse the problem. I have established the New Austrian School of Economics (NASoE) that attracted brilliant students from all over the world and conferred several Master's and Ph.D's. Some of these doctoral dissertations, written under our program have beaten new paths by using such novel concepts as the gold basis and co-basis. Members of our alumnus contributed important new results to monetary science, for example, proving the important theorem that permanent gold backwardation inevitably brings about hyperinflation in its wake.

Personally, I was motivated by my experience of growing up in a family burdened with the memory that the pension of my grandfather, a government engineer, was wiped out in 1926. He lived to be 90 and was condemned to penury to the rest of his life. This was followed, twenty years later, by the pension of my father, a school principal, being wiped out in 1946.

I felt that I was targeted next. My daily experience in paying for food, medical care, legal fees, for tuition of my five children confirmed this intuitive fear. The deprivation caused by the experience of my grandparents and parents left an indelible mark on me.

I decided that I shall not take it lying down. Although I was trained as a mathematician and made a career as a university professor (of mathematics and statistics), I have become an autodidactic monetary scientist specialising in the study of hyperinflation. To my utter amazement I have found that virtually all my colleagues, students of monetary hyperinflation were ignoring the 'endgame' in the gold markets as the drama of destruction of the purchasing power of fiat paper money was unfolding.

There are two approaches to the problem: one is quantitative or statis- tical, the other qualitative. The former is essentially number-crunching. It was quite clear to me that this was a dead-end street. My departure had to be different. I wanted to pass from an inductive to a deductive methodology.

I consider my greatest contribution to monetary science the shifting of the focus from the gold 'price' to the gold basis, that is, the spread between the future and the spot 'price' of gold. Typically, it is positive. The gold 'price' seismographically picks up a lot of 'noise' while missing false-carding in the gold markets. By contrast, the gold basis is a pristine market indicator filtering out noise while revealing false-carding wherever it occurs.

False-Carding In The Gold Market

As readers familiar with the card game bridge well know, rules governing endgame are very different from those governing the middle-game and the pre-game auction. In the endgame the knowledge of the distribution of cards yet to be played is all-important. Players having a better grasp of the constellation of those cards win. Here false-carding designed to fool the opponents come to the fore. Not surprisingly, in the endgame of the hyper-inflationary phase of the saga of the unravelling of irredeemable currency false-carding becomes a favourite ploy frequently applied by the powers-that-be. For example, a gold mining concern may be selling gold faster or more slowly than justified by its output. Also, central and bullion banks and hedge funds publish fake statistics on their holdings of bullion and on their maturing gold lease contracts and forward sales of gold. The reason for leasing gold and selling it forward – a self-defeating manoeuvre per se from the point of view of the gold mines [1] – is justified by the fact that the gold lease market and forward gold sales is the hotbed in which false-carding strives. Forward selling and leasing of gold bullion is also a favourite play field of banks involved in the gold trade.

When a central bank leases gold to a bullion bank it assumes the risk that it may never see its leased gold ever again. The latter promptly sells it to silk-road countries, the bottomless pit absorbing any amount of the precious yellow metal since times immemorial. The former, the central bank knows this, but it also knows that bank examiners accept paper gold as fully equivalent to physical gold, thanks to the corruption of bank examination standards, [2] compromising the process of auditing. (Never mind that the world's banking system has been insolvent since August 15, 1971, the day on which the U.S. defaulted on its short-term gold obligations.)

For many years we have drawn attention to the unique phenomenon of permanent gold backwardation as a foolproof indicator of the progressive scarcity of gold deliverable against maturing futures contracts.

> The endgame drama features episodes of sporadic backwardation of gold, indicated by the gold basis dipping into negative territory for greater or lesser periods.

These episodes are temporary at first, with the gold basis bouncing back into its normal positive range, thus reestablishing normal contango in the gold futures markets (a condition whereby the 'price' of gold for more distant future delivery is necessarily higher than that for nearby future delivery, the opposite of backwardation). The upshot is that the length of sporadic spells of gold backwardation gets progressively longer making physical gold ever scarcer, severely squeezing short interest.

Anti-Keynes

The consensus pushed by mainstream economists almost all of whom are staunch supporters of global fiat money based, as it is, on irredeemable promises of governments, is that the problem of inflation has been disposed of through successful government measures such as QE (quantitive easing), ZIRP (zero interest policy) blowing bubbles in the bond, stock and real estate markets. Governments have also succeeded in their war on gold: the precious yellow has been marginalised. Gold has been put where it belongs: in the dog-house, so they say.

Thus, inflation is no longer a threat thanks to 'wise' government monetary policy in manipulating the rate of interest. This article aims at exploding the myth of government omnipotence by focusing on the outstanding weak point of mainstream economics, i.e., Keynesianism, namely, the denigration of capital and dismissing the problem of capital destruction. However, all that these 'wise' government policies have accomplished was to let the capital structure of the world enter an advanced state of decay. We are witnessing the wholesale progressive destruction of capital. As a result, inflation will come back with vengeance and, ultimately, global fiat money will unravel causing hyperinflation that we may, for the purposes of this essay, may define as the whole destruction of the purchasing power of money.

We shall see that the decay of capital can be put in a time-frame and the coming doomsday can be pinpointed. This will be done through refining our theory of permanent gold backwardation. The theory of primary gold backwardation will be augmented by the theory of secondary gold backwardation.

Endgame In The Gold Market

We all know from logic and from history that fiat currency will fail.[3] Every experiment with it ended in fiasco sooner or later. The fact that the current experiment survived longer than any previous one proves nothing. In addition, the regime of global fiat currency has become the fast-breeder of irredeemable debt. Again, a sense of reality and logic tells us that the construction of such a Babelian Debt Tower cannot continue forever. It will collapse like its biblical forerunner did in the fulness of time, burying the conceited builders under the rubble. The problem confronting the monetary scientist is to predict when this cataclysmic event will take place.

Curiously, that is not how it played out during the past ten years or so. What is going on? Have governments and economists in their pay figured out a way to put economic reality into abeyance? In the past decade the Federal Reserve System of the United States created irredeemable fiat currency in unprecedented amounts counted in quadrillions [4] setting a precedent to a horde of sycophantic fellow central banks without triggering hyperinflation. How is this possible? The short answer is that our analysis in terms of primary gold backwardation must be refined through the introduction of the secondary gold backwardation.

The Gold 'Price' Is Getting Irrelevant

To recapitulate, research at NASoE concluded that the gold 'price' is not per se a reliable indicator of hyperinflation in the making. More reliable is the gold basis and co-basis [of gold]. A negative gold basis makes physical gold progressively scarcer, paving the way towards permanent gold backwardation. Continuing wholesale withdrawal by sellers offering to sell physical gold brings about a situation where no cash gold is available for purchase at any price denominated in an irredeemable currency. Sellers do not see how they can replenish their inventory through ordinary trading of gold futures contracts.

The Mechanism Of Gold Delivery

In what follows I propose to refine the theory of permanent gold backwardation to explain the lag between cause and effect.

> Strictly speaking gold futures markets trade capacity for warehousing-space for gold and the gold basis is just the price of that warehousing space.

We have to familiarise ourselves with the nitty-gritty of making and taking delivery on gold futures contracts. I apologise to my readers for the complexity of the following description of the mechanism of gold delivery on the gold futures markets. Quite possibly this mechanism was made contorted deliberately by the principals of gold futures markets in order to protect trading by erecting a firewall to protect trading against 'predatory' long interest trying to corner the market.[5]

In talking about warehousing we mean allocated gold, in which case the warehouse certificate in the possession of the owner of gold specifies the exact weight, fineness and the serial number of the gold bar covered. There are well-known risks involved in owning unallocated gold, starting with the potential bankruptcy of the warehouse itself.

Even when we limit ourselves to the warehousing of allocated gold, not all gold certificates are created equal. [6] The gold futures exchanges (the largest of which is COMEX in New York) appoint warehouses whose certificates are acceptable in delivery on gold futures contracts.

It may come as a surprise to my readers that delivery on gold futures never involves delivery of physical gold directly. It involves delivery of gold certificates. At any given time there may be 12 gold futures contracts outstanding that correspond to the 12 calendar months. However, only half of them are **actively** traded: February, April, June, August, October, December.[7]

The procedure of taking delivery on a gold futures contract is as follows. Holders of a maturing long contract who intend to take delivery must give notice of their intention on first notice day. At the same time they must capitalise their account with the exchange to 100 percent (zero-margin).[8] Holders of short contracts, of course, are also subject to the zero-margin rule. In addition, they must deposit with the exchange a gold certificate issued by an exchange-approved warehouse.

Now we have come to the crucial point that plays a role in refining our theory of permanent gold backwardation.

Two varieties of warehouse certificates are distinguished:

  ▷   gold certificates on 'registered' gold
  ▷   gold certificates of 'eligible' gold.

There is no difference between gold covered by these two varieties. The difference is in their ACCEPTABILITY in the delivery process.

Certificates on registered gold are acceptable; certificates on eligible gold are not acceptable. I beg the reader to bear with me while I explain this cumbersome and seemingly superfluous provision that is crucial in understanding secondary gold basis and secondary gold backwardation.

Thus, then, there are two markets for gold certificates, one for those on registered gold and another, on eligible gold. Recall that it is arbitrage between the spot gold market and futures gold market that is responsible for primary gold backwardation. Similarly, arbitrage between the market for gold certificates on registered gold and the market for gold certificates on eligible gold is responsible for secondary gold backwardation.

The question arises naturally what motivates market participants to carry an inventory of either variety of gold certificates? The motivation for carrying an inventory of certificates on registered gold is to be first in line for getting the physical gold (recall that physical gold may be in short supply and may even be unavailable in case of permanent gold backwardation.) Not surprisingly, the (fiat) price of certificates on registered gold is higher than that of certificates on eligible gold, in spite of the fact that exactly the very same physical gold is backing either variety....

The market does not directly quote prices of these certificates, but they can be extrapolated from data released by the exchange, such as the number of certificates of either variety *outstanding*. [9] The motivation for carrying an inventory of certificates on eligible gold primarily is *speculation (gambling) on the gold 'price'*.

> Gold certificates moving from the registered to the eligible category reflect the opinion of market participants in the firing line how many gold certificates are in existence for every ounce of physical gold.

Clearly, at any given time there is an overissue, just as airlines are known to overbook seats. When it happens, holders of long gold futures contracts who are bumped are Typically, offered a bribe in the form of a premium on the price of the certificate on registered gold.

The premium [bribe] may move holders of certificates on registered gold to give up their priority. But it is also possible that they do not want to deliver their certificates because they do not see a chance to replace them through the regular trading of gold futures contracts. They may not want to hold the proverbial bag. [10]

> *Secondary* gold contango manifests itself by the condition whereby certificates on registered gold command a premium.

Secondary backwardation means that the price of certificates on eligible gold goes to a premium. Recall that primary gold backwardation is about the scarcity of spot gold relative to gold futures contracts. Likewise, secondary gold backwardation is about the scarcity of certificates on registered gold relative to those on eligible gold that, for the stronger reason means that the scarcity of spot gold relative to gold futures.

> *Thus secondary gold backwardation implies primary gold backwardation.*

It indicates the reluctance of the holders of gold certificates to put their registered gold into harm's way (to risk that their registered gold will be called). Secondary gold basis, as we have seen, is the difference between the 'price' of gold certificates on registered and eligible gold.

I leave it to my students to define secondary gold co-basis and study the interplay between the two. Lest someone think that the emergence of dual gold certificates is due to making arbitrary rules, I point out that it comes about due to the organic development of gold futures trading.

> It is part of the firewall to prevent long interest from engineering a corner.

The system of dual gold certificates is the gatekeeper. When the inventory of gold is getting too low in the exchange-approved warehouses and the long interest is approaching critical mass, the clearing house of the exchange shuffles the gold certificates on registered and eligible gold.

A Short Course On The History Of The Legal Position Of Gold In The U.S.

Under this caption I shall deal with the question why the 'powers that be' allowed gold futures trading to go ahead in the U.S. in 1975.

During the period 1933-1975 the ownership and trading of gold was criminalised in the U.S. pursuant to F.D. Roosevelt's suspension of the monetary clauses of the Constitution. [He used martial law, comprehensively known as the Trading With the Enemy Act or TWEA] Of course, this was trampling on the rights of the citizens and an abominable restriction of freedom. Change occurred in 1975 when the ban was lifted and futures trading in gold was allowed. [11] What is in the background of this change of heart? First of all, it must be emphasised that – as the executive order made it very clear – the easing was on a 24-hour basis.

Since the writ of the U.S. government stops at the water, in foreign countries gold markets continued to trade gold, invariably quoting premium dollar prices, indicating dollar debasement. This was embarrassing.

At first, there was no ban on Americans to own and to trade gold in the overseas markets. Such a ban was imposed later, during the Eisenhower administration.

Mainstream economists (all staunch supporters debt-based fiat money) came to the conclusion that the system leaked like a sieve and suggested that the way to stop the leakage would amount to allowing gold futures trading.

They were hoping that the availability of paper gold suppress the appetite for real gold. They were inspired by a metaphor of Keynes:

> " People want the moon, but, of course, they cannot have the moon. So the government must convince them that blue cheese (sic!) is just as good and order the central bank to produce it galore to make them happy. So why did the U.S. government legalise gold trading? Well, because it saw the proliferation of paper gold an effective (even the only) way to deflect the inevitable hyperinflation.

Such shabby Keynesian musings were used to justify the trampling on the American Constitution.

So why did the U.S. government legalise gold trading? Well, because it saw the proliferation of paper gold an effective (even the only) way to deflect hyperinflation. [12]

Secondary Gold Basis Measuring Capital Destruction

We have seen that the primary gold basis is the price of warehousing space for gold. It measures the ratio of paper and physical gold in existence. What does the secondary gold basis measure? Secondary gold basis measures the ratio of gold certificates on registered and eligible gold in existence. In other words, it indicates how many ounces of gold in certificates have been issued on every ounce of physical gold. When this number reaches a critical mass, a chain reaction ensues. People start scrambling to get out of paper gold and into physical gold. We shall also describe the secondary gold basis as the price of insurance against default on paper gold. In this view, the secondary gold basis is a measure of decay in the capital structure of the world. Recall that gold is the only form of capital that is not subject to decay nor destruction, while all other forms of capital, whether physical or financial are.

To recapitulate, our refined theory of permanent gold backwardation in introducing secondary gold backwardation scrutinises the endgame in the gold markets. It focuses on the jockeying of people to get into position where they have control over the only indestructible form of capital, gold in existence.

The new element is the importance of the endgame in the gold market that has been ignored thus far. I submit that once we make it part of the theory of permanent gold backwardation, we shall have a handle on the problem of timing hyperinflation. Primary backwardation in gold hard on the heels of secondary backwardation heralds hyperinflation, not too far behind.

> Our conclusion is that an early warning system of hyperinflation must involve monitoring arbitrage between the markets for registered and eligible gold certificates on the gold futures exchanges.

So where are we in 2018 in terms of secondary backwardation heralding hyperinflation? Here is my answer: almost every day information surfaces according to which the pyramid of paper gold that is being constructed on each ounce of physical gold held by government Treasuries, central and bullion banks. Just this past week, as reported by Chris Powell, the Secretary-Treasurer of GATA, the Gold Anti-Trust Action Committee on January 31, 2018, Six bank employees have been arrested on charges of rigging the precious metals markets, see Rory Hall's article Golden Rays and Silver Linings. [13]

Just confirmed by the Senate the new Chairman of the FED Jerome Powell by a vote of 84-13 remarkable because of its wide margin. He is on record to favour a 'weak dollar' along with President Trump. This raises the question what can we expect when the sitting president and his chief monetary advisor both publicly declare that they both 'like the weak dollar'. Think about it: Shouldn't the President be impeached for high treason on charges that he is urging a monetary policy of a weak dollar on his FED Chairman, which is tantamount to endorsing the embezzlement of the funds of the people entrusted on the member banks of the FED?

What does it say about the paper-gold pyramid constructed on every ounce of physical gold in existence? How will gold traders in the market for paper gold and gold certificates react to such a rotten state of monetary affairs in the U. S. and in the world? Is the monetary system of the world not running headlong into self-destruction?

A Final Word...

In the previous paragraphs, the idea of 'secondary backwardation' was introduced, which is related to the interplay between eligible and registered gold certificates. Any long holder of futures claiming delivery is entitled to a certificate on registered gold, not gold itself. [But with the certificate, he actually can claim his bars from the warehouse] As gold open interest increases, Comex managers have to bring in bullion 'to cover' the market's liability on gold in lieu of the market being able to cover themselves. When the stress indicator is rising, it shows that as registered certificates on bullion are handed over to long contract holders, bullion from outside Comex is being brought in by managers to satisfy potential claim liabilities from increased open interest.

As can be seen on the chart showing the indicator for Comex gold, there's been a noticeable, sharp increase since end January'18 in the context of a gradual rising trend since June 2017. The trend for Comex silver looks similar.

Why would people be looking to 'get into gold' as interest rates rise? Surely such a move would be suicidal? It's to do with 'capital values.' Any increase in interest rates hurts perpetuities' (long dated bonds) capital [principal] values the most and shortest-dated the least. Stocks/bonds compared to gold/silver are the longest dated 'assets' possible – if they are truly 'assets' in the same sense as 1,000 grains of gold – which they are not!

In terms of metal ratios, industrial metals still continue to massively outperform gold as expected and are likely to continue doing so.

For example:

Gold: nickel/zinc/tin has fallen from 1: 3367/12446/2062 at the end of January to 1: 3182/12054/1982 now.

However, this doesn't mean anything negative for gold's 'price' per se (gold's exchange against fiat) as has been explained above.

SANDEEP JAITLY

Spring 2018.

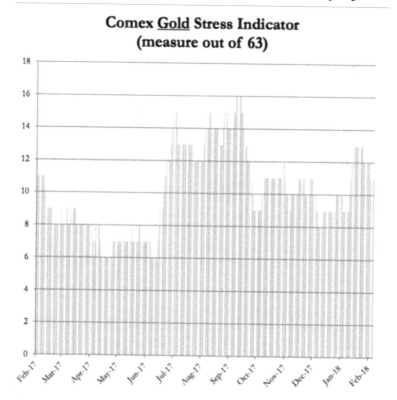

Fig. 3 *Comex Stress Indicator for gold futures*

Endnotes to Chapter 51

[1] See the chapter on the economics of gold mining, supra.

[2] The gnostic dualist zombie flock does not accept anything outside its own scriptures i.e. laws, rule books, manuals, guidelines, auditor reports, academic text books are of course sacred scriptures. Alas, there is nothing in those academic handbooks that is worth knowing.

[3] We may be accused of jumping to conclusions regarding history. History has not been concluded and 'black swans' do exists. We may even be accused of using our own, perhaps arrogantly deemed infallible logic. Yet to our knowledge, not a single person has as yet defeated Menger's arguments or ours for that matter. But perhaps, that time will come.And maybe that person exists or will exist, but it won't be a gnostic warrior with a 'cause' though. In the interim, we hold our position, fallibly. Unlike some other gnostic dualists.

[4] The use of such large numbers shows the meaninglessness of it all. People can not fathom its size, thus becoming 'academic numerology'.

[5] There is no symmetry, of course, on the short side of the trade. I.e. the bias against gold became larger. Cornering the gold market would precisely translate into that other word: hyperinflation.

[6] Heaven forbid, no. Gnostic dualists have a pneumopathological need for conjuring up a split of what is essentially one into two different things. It takes the form of hairsplitting with them on the 'good side' and you not.

[7] These contracts have their own ticker codes on the exchanges.

[8] For the first notice day, look at the rules of the exchange. Topping up the account for delivery is nothing but logic. A long delivery will require full payment...

[9] Please do not confuse this with short or long interest.

[10] In other words: either they are 'chicken' or they know something...

[11] The same martial law was not repealed, it is still in operation.

[12] Gnostic dualists deal with embarrassment by hiding and distorting reality. If that does not help, only the bigger embarrassment of hyperinflation could convince them to allow trading- reluctantly.

[13] On the website www.Gold-Eagle.com, see also video, https://youtube/c47XZ-MvdqoM.

PART 10

ANTHOLOGY OF MONETARY
CRANKS

~≈ Chapter 52 ≈~

The Gold Bug Variations

The Gold Standard – And The Men Who Love It.

PAUL KRUGMAN

The legend of King Midas has been generally misunderstood.
Most people think the curse that turned everything the old mi-
ser touched into gold, leaving him unable to eat or drink, was a
lesson in the perils of avarice. But Midas' true sin was his failure to understand monetary economics. What the gods were really telling him is
that gold is just a metal. If it sometimes seems to be more, that is only
because society has found it convenient to use gold as a medium of
exchange – a bridge between other, truly desirable, objects. There are
other possible mediums of exchange and it is silly to imagine that this
pretty, but only moderately useful, substance has some irreplaceable
significance. [1]

But there are many people – nearly all of them ardent conservatives
– who reject that lesson. [2] While Jack Kemp, Steve Forbes and Wall
Street Journal editor Robert Bartley are best known for their promotion
of supply-side economics, they are equally dedicated to the belief that
the key to prosperity is a return to the gold standard, which John Maynard Keynes pronounced a 'barbarous relic' more than 60 years ago.
With any luck, these latter-day Midases will never lay a finger on actual
monetary policy. Nonetheless, these are influential people – they are
one of the factions now struggling for the Republican Party's soul – and
the passionate arguments they make for a gold standard are a useful
window on how they think. [3]

There is a case to be made for a return to the gold standard. It is not
a very good case and most sensible economists reject it, [4] but the idea
is not completely crazy. On the other hand, the ideas of our modern
gold bugs are completely crazy. Their belief in gold is, it turns out, not
pragmatic but mystical. [5]

The current world monetary system assigns no special role to gold;
indeed, the Federal Reserve is not obliged to tie the dollar to anything.[6] It can print as much or as little money as it deems appropriate.

[7] There are powerful advantages to such an unconstrained system.[8] Above all, the Fed is free to respond to actual or threatened recessions by pumping in money. [9] To take only one example, that flexibility is the reason the stock market crash of 1987 – which started out every bit as frightening as that of 1929 – did not cause a slump in the real economy. [10]

While a freely floating national money has advantages, however, it also has risks. For one thing, it can create uncertainties for international traders and investors. Over the past five years, the dollar has been worth as much as 120 yen and as little as 80. [11] The costs of this volatility are hard to measure (partly because sophisticated financial markets allow businesses to hedge much of that risk),[12] but they must be significant. Furthermore, a system that leaves monetary managers free to do good also leaves them free to be irresponsible – and, in some countries, they have been quick to take the opportunity. That is why countries with a history of runaway inflation, like Argentina, often come to the conclusion that monetary independence is a poisoned chalice. (Argentine law now requires that one peso be worth exactly one U.S. dollar and that every peso in circulation be backed by a dollar in reserves.)[13]

So, there is no obvious answer to the question of whether or not to tie a nation's currency to some external standard. By establishing a fixed rate of exchange between currencies – or even adopting a common currency – nations can eliminate the uncertainties of fluctuating exchange rates; and a country with a history of irresponsible policies may be able to gain credibility by association. (The Italian government wants to join a European Monetary Union largely because it hopes to refinance its massive debts at German interest rates.) On the other hand, what happens if two nations have joined their currencies and one finds itself experiencing an inflationary boom while the other is in a deflationary recession? (This is exactly what happened to Europe in the early 1990s, when western Germany boomed while the rest of Europe slid into double-digit unemployment.) Then the monetary policy that is appropriate for one is exactly wrong for the other. These ambiguities explain why economists are divided over the wisdom of Europe's attempt to create a common currency. I personally think that it will lead, on average, to somewhat higher European unemployment rates; but many sensible economists disagree.

So Where Does Gold Enter The Picture?

While some modern nations have chosen, with reasonable justification, to renounce their monetary autonomy in favour of some external
standard, the standard they choose these days is always the currency
of another, presumably more responsible, nation. Argentina seeks salvation from the dollar; Italy from the deutsche mark. But the men and
women who run the Fed and even those who run the German Bundes-
bank, are mere mortals, who may yet succumb to the temptations of
the printing press. Why not ensure monetary virtue by trusting not in
the wisdom of men but in an objective standard? Why not emulate our
great-grandfathers and tie our currencies to gold?

Very few economists think this would be a good idea. The argument against it is one of pragmatism, not principle. First, a gold standard would have all the disadvantages of any system of rigidly fixed
exchange rates – and even economists who are enthusiastic about a
common European currency generally think that fixing the European
currency to the dollar or yen would be going too far. Second and crucially, gold is not a stable standard when measured in terms of other
goods and services. On the contrary, it is a commodity whose price is
constantly buffeted by shifts in supply and demand that have nothing
to do with the needs of the world economy – by changes, for example,
in dentistry.

The United States abandoned its policy of stabilising gold 'price's
back in 1971. Since then the 'price' of gold has increased roughly ten-
fold, while consumer prices have increased about 250 percent. If we
had tried to keep the 'price' of gold from rising, this would have required a massive decline in the prices of practically everything else –
deflation on a scale not seen since the Depression. This doesn't sound
like a particularly good idea.

So why are Jack Kemp, the Wall Street Journal and so on so fixated
on gold? I did not fully understand their position until I read a recent letter to, of all places, the left-wing magazine Mother Jones from
Jude Wanniski – one of the founders of supply-side economics and
its reigning guru. (One of the many comic-opera touches in the late
unlamented Dole campaign was the constant struggle between Jack
Kemp, who tried incessantly to give Wanniski a key role and the sensible economists who tried to keep him out.) Wanniski's main concern
was to deny that the rich have gotten richer in recent decades; his letter
is posted on the Mother Jones Web site and makes interesting reading.
But, particularly noteworthy was the following passage:

" ... First let us get our accounting unit squared away. To measure any-thing in the floating paper dollar will get us nowhere. We must convert all wealth into the measure employed by mankind for 6,000 years, i.e., ounc-es of gold. On this measure, the Dow Jones industrial average of 6,000 today is only 60 percent of the DJIA of 30 years ago, when it hit 1,000. Back then, gold was $35 per ounce. Today it is $380-plus. This is another way of saying that in the last 30 years, the people who owned America have lost 40 percent of their wealth held in the form of equity. ... If you owned no part of corporate America 30 years ago, because you were poor, you lost nothing. If you owned lots of it, you lost your shirt in the general inflation.

Never mind the question of whether the Dow Jones industrial average is the proper measure of how well the rich are doing. What is fascinat-ing about this passage is that Wanniski regards gold as the appropriate measure of wealth, regardless of the quantity of other goods and ser-vices that it can buy. Since the dollar was de-linked from gold in 1971, the Dow has risen about 700 percent, while the prices of the goods we ordinarily associate with the pursuit of happiness – food, houses, clothes, cars, servants – have gone up only about 250 percent. In terms of the ability to buy almost anything except gold, the purchasing pow-er of the rich has soared; but Wanniski insists that this is irrelevant, because gold and only gold, is the true standard of value. Wanniski, in other words, has committed the sin of King Midas: He has forgotten that gold is only a metal and that its value comes only from the truly useful goods for which it can be exchanged.

I wonder whether the gods read SLATE. If so, they know what to do. For a lesson from the Golden Boys, see Jack Kemp's Wall Street Jour-nal op-ed touting the gold standard and Steve Forbes' piece, 'A Case for Sound Money.' Or, check out Jude Wanniski's Polyconomics Home Page. 'Clad in the armour of a righteous cause,' William Jennings Bryan holds forth against these gentlemen's claims. See his famous 'Cross of Gold' speech from the 1896 Democratic National Convention. To judge for yourself the competence of an unhampered Federal Reserve, see its home page.

***

Excerpted above, Wanniski's letter was written in response to Krug-man's recent piece for Mother Jones on income inequality. Read the letter in its entirety, the article that precipitated it and Krugman's re-sponse to the letter.

Endnotes to Chapter 52

[1] Krugman presumably cites Aristotle *Politics I, 9, 1257B.* where the story of Midas is related as if it were a philosophy of money. However, Aristotle the philosopher, retells the peoples' opinions on the nature of money. Sentence 11 reads:

"ὀτὲ δὲ πάλιν ληρος εἶναι δοκεῖ τὸ νόμισμα καί νομος παντάπασι, φύσει δ' ουθέν, ὄτι μεταθέμενων τε των χρωμένων οὔθενός ἄξιον οὐδὲ χρήσιμον πρὸς οὐδὲν των ἀναγκαίων ἐστί, καί νομίσματος πλοῦτων πολλάκις ἀπορήσει τῆς ἀναγκαίας τροφης. "

The English translation of this text reads:

"Others maintain that coined gold is a sham, an unnatural thing, and conventional only, because it is not useful as a means to any necessity of life. and he who is rich in gold coin may often find himself in want of necessary food."

This last sentence is key, for it tells the people story of the wisdom of exchange and the drama that ensues when wealth and income exchangs are no longer possible.

A gnostic dualist, worth his salt, selects his sacred scriptures scrupulously.(See Hooker). Self censure (i.e. taboo, fatwa or whatever you call it) ensures a greater and longer membership of The Flock of Faithful. Krugman 'forgets' in his lesson to mention that it is not Aristotle's opinion, but those of 'others' - presumably the sophists, with whom Aristotle wiped the floor. Apparently Krugman gives the text, which he doesn't quote, yet another meaning, presumably under poetic licence, for Krugman obviously does not quote King Midas nor Aristotle.

Aristotle in this section of Politics is indeed describing the art of making a living for oneself, without the obsessional character of hoarding excessive wealth for its own sake. Aristotle puts a limit to a healthy preoccupation of making a living and the unbridled and unlimited compulsive obsessive behaviour of certain people. For the sake of completeness, Aristotle even praises the art of exchange (with coined money) !

[2] It is not the lesson of the myth, neither is it the lesson of Aristotle. Krugman misrepresents the legend of King Midas, for in reality it relates to compulsive obsessive behaviour and the consequences of not being able to exchange wealth for income and income for wealth. The philosopher Aristotle, like all wise men, knows that one has to make a living. Life's purpose is not to hoard without limits... The story of Midas tells the story of the limits, rather than what Krugman makes him say. A strawman fallacy.

[3] And what can be said about people who revile the men in favour of honest money ...?

[4] Krugman defines 'sensible' as 'thinking like Krugman'... a bit tendentious, no?

[5] We are awaiting proof of the contention. However, for brevity's sake, we have compiled a diagnostic tool identifying gnosticism and dualism as a pneumopathology. And Mr. Krugman, has been diagnosed positively!

[6] Krugman jumps straightaway to The Highest Authority of the Universe, housed in the Temple of the Paper Mill near the Potomac, where its High Priests reign supremely. We are not apologising for not being impressed

[7] 'It' can print... whereby 'it' seems to be a reification or objectification of some bureaucrats, under the leadership of the Pontifex, following the Scriptures of Prophets Keynes and Krugman.

[8] The 'powerful advantages' are for the parasites only, not for the common people. Of course, 'system' is a word that is often used by Gnostics. They produce them all them time. The most ardent 'producer of systems' could be Auguste Comte, positivist and indeed, Pontifex Maximus of the Temple of Positivists, celebrating mass in the Religion of Humanity..

[9] There we go again: invalid mechanical comparisons from the field of engineering, of the kind that would impel C. Menger to write his diatribe against such ill-conceived ideas from the field of hard sciences. Besides, Krugman takes his concept of what constitutes money rather for granted.

[10] With this sentence, Krugman admits that the task of the Federal Reserve is something different than purported. The Fed's task is to keep the stock exchanges (read : the people behind it who run and participate this show) afloat. Thanks all the same, but we study theoretical economics, not shenanigans per se. And what is this real economy as oposed to unreal ? Gnostic dualism like social and other justice as if there's a difference ?

[11] Measuring a rubber band using another as benchmark or yardstick is very good engineering science, isn't it?

[12] Hedge ? Streak you mean !

[13] Mr. Krugman, that law is not recent, it dates back to the time Kemmerer and consorts came to promote the gold backing standard, like Ricardo invented. Pre-World War I, when the U.S. dollar was officially still redeemable for an ounce of Au.

~~ Chapter 53 ~~

Chrysophobia

Here's Where Gold Enters The Picture...!

This is a rejoinder to a piece of the same title by Paul Krugman, MIT professor (now at Princeton) and staff writer of The New York Times. It was posted on the internet on November 22, 1996, with a note saying that it was to be composted two weeks later, on December 6. It wasn't. I came across it a few weeks ago while surfing the internet. At first I thought that it fully deserved to be composted in short order. But on second thought I decided that it called for a careful rejoinder. Bad-mouthing the gold standard is a periodically returning pastime for mainstream economists. Their arguments have never been put to rest by an authoritative rejoinder, which I therefore, venture to present.

Krugman's piece was part of a series entitled 'The Dismal Science'. If I continue with these variations, which I am rather tempted to do, then I shall call my series 'The Dismal Monetary Science'. I apply this name to the monetary science, so called, of the Krugman variety, more precisely, the demand-side theory of money according to Prophet Keynes, as well as the Quantity Theory of Money according to Nobel laureate Milton Friedman, also known as monetarism.

In the sequel, quotations (containing what Krugman deems persuasive arguments) are under the caption 'Argument' and our rejoinder under 'Refutation'.

King Midas

" ...The legend of King Midas, the original goldbug, has been generally misunderstood. Recall that his prayers were answered by the gods: everything he touched turned into gold. The catch was that 'everything' included food and drinks as well and the poor king was starving to death as his system could not ingest gold. The gods wanted to teach him a lesson. Most people think that the lesson was in the perils of avarice. This is a mistake. Midas' true sin was his failure to understand monetary economics. What the gods were telling him was that gold was just another metal. If it sometimes seemed to be more, that was only because society has found it convenient to *use gold as a medium of exchange – a bridge between other, truly desirable, objects.*

Refutation

Krugman is cutting down the difference between 'sometimes' and 'always' to microscopic size. Gold has been the preferred means of exchange since time immemorial. After barter was phased out as inefficient and after a relatively brief period of experimentation with other goods such as oxen, shells and tobacco to mention but three of them, the marketability of gold (and silver) snowballed relative to that of other contenders. Gold became king and silver the queen. Gold would still be king but for a coup d'état overthrowing the Constitutional monetary order in the United States and imprisoning the king.

In 1933 it took all the violence and duplicity a government could muster against its own people to grab the gold belonging to them. There was wholesale confiscation of monetary gold, under false pretences. No sooner had the U.S. government laid its hands on the people's gold than it wrote up its value. This piece of chicanery was used to conceal the act of robbery. People were 'compensated' for the confiscated gold in the form of paper money. In 1935 the Supreme Court of the United States dismissed charges that value was taken from the people without due process of law arguing that paper money continued to have the same purchasing power as gold coins. This flies in the face of the fact that the loss of purchasing power of the dollar abroad was instantaneous. Domestically it was gradual and by the 35th birthday of the irredeemable dollar it amounted to 90 percent, an unprecedented monetary destruction in the history of the republic up to that point. (Much worse was to follow during the next 35 years.)

Gold's forcible removal as the monetary metal was done in two convenient steps, 35 years apart.

(1) In 1933 the U.S. government defaulted on its domestic monetary obligations, including the dishonouring of the promise printed on every Federal Reserve note, to pay bearer gold coin of the specified weight and fineness upon demand and the repudiation of the gold-bonded public debt held by its own citizens. To be sure, it was repudiation. If you contract debt payable in gold and then at maturity you pretend to pay off your debt with another promise payable in never-never land in the never-never future, then you have repudiated the debt, haven't you? And the pretence

that you have discharged the obligation has made the repudiation worse, hasn't it?

(2) In 1968 the U.S. government defaulted on its gold obligations to foreigners as well (the initial *de facto* gold embargo was made official in 1971). To add insult to injury, the U.S. government (after some behind-the-scenes arm-twisting) put a gag-order into effect. The injured party was not allowed to call a spade a spade. An international obligation, solemnly agreed to at an international conference enjoying the widest publicity, duly ratified by Congress and subsequently affirmed by four sitting Presidents, was unceremoniously and unilaterally abrogated by a stroke of the pen. Foreign creditors of the United States, the primary victims, were not allowed to say 'ouch'. They were ordered to call it an 'enlightened monetary reform,' dropping nothing more substantial than the trappings of a 'barbarous relic', in the words of John Maynard Keynes. Such a level of bad faith in monetary dealings, compounded by the gag-order, was surely unprecedented in the financial annals. Previously a defaulting government had to bear the shame and live it down before it could rejoin the exclusive club of credit-worthy nations. Now the offender's deserts were not only high praise for a courageous deed in fighting superstition, but also license to keep on plundering its neighbours' natural and human resources through the fiat money system.

Even today textbooks refrain from calling the 1933 and 1968 repudiation by its proper name, default. A new breed of professors, including Krugman (who was born after these defaults have taken place) lionise the U.S. for cheating its domestic and foreign creditors and plunging the nation and the world into the worst experimentation with fiat paper. Some dismal monetary science, indeed!

Gold? Insignificant!

" There are other possible mediums of exchange beside gold and it is silly to imagine that this pretty, but only moderately useful, substance has some irreplaceable significance.

Refutation

It is incredible that this monetary economist has apparently never heard of marginal utility. Every substance, In addition, to its main applications, has a marginal application (which determines its marginal utility), as well as several submarginal applications. Bread, for example, has its main application as staple food for humans. The marginal application of bread was inadvertently found by Queen Marie Antoinette of France who later paid with her head for her discovery on the scaffold during the French Revolution. When she had heard that people had no bread to eat, she asked: 'Well, why don't they eat cake?' Accordingly, the marginal utility of bread is determined by its marginal application which is to be eaten for dessert, instead of cake, if you have it. But bread could also serve as fodder to animals and it could be used as fertiliser of agricultural land. If it isn't, it's because it is far too valuable for these 'submarginal' applications.

It is no different with gold. Its main application is to serve as the monetary metal. Marginal application is in jewellery. But the list of the submarginal applications of gold is endless, thanks to its fine physical and chemical properties such as malleability, ductility, conductivity, non-corrosiveness, among others. It is the last-mentioned property of gold which Lenin's fertile imagination used, dangling it before the hungry eyes of his starving subjects, [1] to illustrate the blissful conditions prevailing under Communism. Lenin observed that there was no better material with which to plate public urinals. It was precisely this application to which the 'capitalist metal' would be put after the final victory of Communism, Lenin said. You may object that gold is far too valuable for this submarginal application and, as a consequence, the gold plating of public urinals would be picked just as quickly as they were installed, by the beneficiaries of the Soviet paradise. Lenin, of course, would have an answer ready to meet this objection. The Cheka (secret police) would take care of saboteurs who picked the gold plating of public urinals and would shoot them on sight. To say that gold is only moderately useful betrays ignorance of Himalayan proportions. Ignorance of technology but, no less, ignorance of microeconomics.

Whether gold is irreplaceable or not as money remains to be seen. It will not be decided by quacks and imposters posing as doctors who have banned the use of gold as a thermometer, expecting that the patient will not run a temperature if he remains blissfully ignorant about his feverish condition. Can it be reasonably doubted that the patient, if he survives, will chase the quacks away and rehabilitate the thermometer to its former use?

Mystical Gold Bugs

" ... *There is a case to be made for a return to the gold standard. It is not a very good case and most sensible economists reject it, but the idea is not completely crazy. On the other hand, the ideas of our modern gold bugs are completely crazy. Their belief in gold is, it turns out, not pragmatic but mystical.*

Refutation

I do not speak for the gentlemen named by Krugman as 'modern gold bugs' but I am happy to present the case for the gold standard as I see it. I am prepared to submit it for general discussion before any competent and impartial forum to judge whether it is 'completely crazy' or not.

The gold standard has nothing to do with stabilising the price level that is neither possible, nor desirable. It has to do with the stabilisation of the rate of interest at the lowest level compatible with savings and production, which is both possible and utterly desirable. Under a gold standard there is no bond speculation, just as there is no foreign exchange speculation. There are no derivatives markets in interest-rate futures the size of which, as measured by the liabilities of speculators, is in the hundreds of trillions of dollars, which is more than the market capitalisation of the entire globe (or soon it will be). Under a gold standard talent must find outlet in productive enterprise rather than in gambling.

Bond speculation is the heel of Achilles for the regime of irredeemable currency, that will cause its self-destruction in due course. Like an incubus, it sucks all the economic resources of the world and robs it of the best talent. The tricksters who grabbed the gold belonging to the people of the United States and its foreign creditors were unaware that their looting would let the genie of destruction, bond speculation, out of the bottle. How can we explain this colossal oversight?

Interest rates were stable under the gold standard and the small variation in bond prices did not admit a profitable opportunity to speculate in bonds. But bond speculation started as soon as the gold anchor was cut in 1971, on the dot. The 'brain trust' of apologists for irredeemable currency can develop theories about bond speculation, suggesting that it has a stabilising influence on interest rates, just as commodity speculation has on the prices of agricultural goods. Let us bypass, for the sake of argument, the fact that this stabilisation was automatic under the gold standard. Any effort to prove that speculation has an analogous stabilising influence in both the commodity and the bond market is doomed to failure. It ignores the fact that the supply of bonds is controlled by man, in contrast with that of agricultural goods which is controlled by nature. The analogy is flawed beyond the hope of repair. Commodity speculation is self-limiting. It is limited by the size of available supply. By contrast, bond speculation is not self-limiting. It is self-aggrandising. The more it grows, the more bonds will be printed. Or, to save the cost of printing, the more bond-derivatives (futures, call options, put options, options on futures, etc., ad libitum) will be invented. Thereby an avalanche is set into motion which will bury innocent villages down there in the valley. There is nothing that the protagonists of 'managed money' can do about it. Bond speculation introduces distortions into the economy that will inevitably cause the downfall of the regime of irredeemable currency. It may or may not be through runaway inflation as in France during the last decade of the eighteenth century. It may be through runaway deflation. In either case, there will be enormous economic pain.

What Krugman calls 'mystical', Keynes called 'psycho-pathological'. Another famous quotation from him is that 'the desire to palm gold is a human aberration that the economist passes on to the psycho-pathologist for study with a shudder.' Well, gold is the ultimate means of payment, such as the regime of irredeemable currency hasn't got and will never get. Gold is voluntarily accepted in final settlement of debts by all creditors. In this capacity, gold can be applied as the agent of the bubble-test. If an individual wanted to make sure that he would not be victimised in a check-kiting scheme, all he had to do was to demand that his check be paid in gold coin. Why is the joy one feels over one's ability to frustrate would-be criminals 'psycho-pathological'? What is 'mystical' about one's desire to protect oneself against check-kiting?

The litmus-test to find out whether a monetary economist serves the cause of the search for and dissemination of truth, or whether he has a hidden agenda such as to cover up for the looting of the people's gold, is to engage him in a discussion on the subject of interest rates under the regime of the irredeemable dollar as opposed to the gold dollar. Apologists for the gold-looting invariably wriggle out.

Nothing More...

" *...Gold is just another metal. If it sometimes seems to be more, that is only because society has found it convenient to use gold as a medium of* *exchange – a bridge between other, truly desirable, objects.*

Refutation

Society has also found it convenient to use gold as a medium of savings. The demand-side theory of money of Keynes has not succeeded, after 70 years of intensive brain-washing and indoctrination, to wean society from the idea that money must unite in itself two properties: those of a medium of exchange and a medium of savings. This gold does admirably well, in fact better than anything that has been recommended in its place. Gold is not just another metal. It is the monetary metal par excellence.

Money promoted by the dismal monetary science of Krugman is a singular failure in that it loses at least 90 percent of its purchasing power in every generation, or 35 years and its protagonists can do absolutely nothing about it. Nor is it wear and tear that is responsible for the miserable record of the irredeemable dollar. The loss of purchasing power has not been dissipated in the universe without a trace. Where has it gone? According to the principle of conservation of matter, it must still exist. This is a question Krugman dare not confront. Well, I have asked it and shall answer it, too. What appears as a loss of purchasing power is value that has been embezzled. That's right, embezzled through a deliberate scheme designed to throw dust into the eyes of the victims. It is the check-kiting scheme between the Federal Reserve banks and the Treasury of the United States.

Check-kiting is a conspiracy, generally between two banks. They are issuing checks which they haven't got the means or the intention to cover. That is to say, the checks are issued fraudulently. They issue them with the criminal intent to tap the float, the mass of checks in the process of clearing and so to defraud the public. The checks issued by Bank A are cleared at the clearing house through earmarking the checks issued by Bank B and vice versa. In more details, the first unbacked check is 'backed' by an infinite string of subsequent unbacked checks.

The gold standard makes check-kiting highly unlikely to succeed. That is one of its chief merits. Every individual using gold substitutes such as checks, bank notes, or bank deposits can apply the 'bubble-test' at any time: he can demand payment in specie. It is a basic human right to protect oneself against would-be criminals. To be able to exercise this right there must be an ultimate means of payment. Under a gold standard it is the gold coin of the realm. The regime of irredeemable currency has no ultimate means of payment, nor can it have one. Before Krugman interrupts me objecting that the Federal Reserve notes are the ultimate means of payment under the monetary system he is pushing, I hasten to add that the Federal Reserve notes themselves are the product of a cleverly designed and disguised check-kiting scheme. Government coercion can make the Federal Reserve notes legal tender, but it can hardly make them the ultimate means of payment. There is a difference. An ultimate means of payment cannot be legal tender because it must be voluntarily accepted in final settlement of debt, while legal tender implies coercion.

To the best of my knowledge no one before has pointed out that the origin of Federal Reserve notes and deposits, as they are presently issued, is fraud and conspiracy that goes by the popular name of check-kiting. I want you to know that I am not making this charge frivolously and I stake my professional reputation in support of it. People in the United States are inclined to believe that it is not possible to cover up theft, fraud and conspiracy by legislation. But it is. I got my education, including the first university degree, under a Communist regime in Soviet-occupied Hungary, where legislation was routinely used to 'justify' the violation of virtually every basic human right. If you think that it cannot happen in your country, then you are kidding yourself.

The original Federal Reserve Act of 1913 nowhere mentions open market operations whereby the central bank can inject new currency into the economy through purchases of government bonds. Monetisation of government debt was not authorised. In fact, government paper was explicitly made ineligible for use as a reserve to back Federal Reserve notes and deposits. Those liabilities had to be covered by gold coins to the extent of no less than 40 percent; and the remainder by short-term self-liquidating commercial paper. If a Federal Reserve bank was short of gold or eligible paper to cover its outstanding note and deposit liabilities and if it used government bonds in its portfolio to make up the shortfall, then a steep and progressive penalty had to be paid. The penalty made it virtually prohibitive to use government paper as cover for the note and deposit liabilities.

Open market operations were introduced clandestinely in violation of the law in the 1920s. It is true that later the Federal Reserve Act was amended to legalise the practice. It is possible that Congress was presented with a fait accompli and had little choice in the matter if it wanted to avoid a financial panic in a fragile international monetary environment. Be that as it may, the introduction of open market operations was a serious violation of the law. As it then stood, the law did not authorise it. And for a very good reason, too. If they had leave to do it, then the Federal Reserve banks could conspire with the U.S. Treasury to start a gigantic check-kiting scheme to defraud the public. The Treasury could sell bonds in the open market which it had neither the resources nor the intention to honour. The Federal Reserve banks could then purchase these bonds in the open market paying for them with newly issued currency which, likewise, they had neither the resources nor the intention to honour.

Guess what, this is exactly what happened once gold has been eased out of the system. The proportion of required gold reserves was reduced from 40 to 25 percent of liabilities, first for Federal Reserve deposits and then for Federal Reserve notes as well. Then gold reserves were eliminated altogether, first for Federal Reserve deposits and then, in 1968 (appropriately enough, on the 35th birthday of the irredeemable dollar), for Federal Reserve notes as well. It was done in carefully staggered stages, through four or five separate amendments to the Federal Reserve Act.

There is no valid argument why the Treasury or the Federal Reserve banks should be given the privilege to issue liabilities which they had neither the means nor the intention to honour while the same, if committed by private parties, is treated as a serious crime punishable by severe penalties as specified by the Criminal Code. On the contrary, in jurisprudence the principle of double standard of justice is rejected, not just because it is unfair but, for the stronger reason, because it is self-defeating.

Refutation Continued

I have said that gold is not just another metal but it is the monetary metal par excellence. Nor is this an opinion, subject to dispute. This is an objective fact as I shall presently show. Today gold is still the monetary metal and as such is immune to efforts by the United States government, or any combination of governments, to 'demonetise' it. All that the governments can do is to deprive themselves and their subjects, of the manifold benefits afforded by gold money.

As money, gold circulates and circulate it may with various velocities, including the zero velocity. It had happened before and it has been the case for the past 35 years, that gold 'circulates' with zero velocity, meaning that monetary gold has gone into hiding. It Typically, happens when the Constitutional order breaks down and the administration of justice becomes arbitrary, so that owners of monetary gold have reasons to worry about the safety of their possession. That is what happened during the last decades of the Roman Empire when the government stopped protecting private property against highway robbers. That is what happened during the final stages of the French Revolution when possession of gold coins was made punishable by death. That is what is happening today in the world when private ownership of monetary gold is on a 24-hour basis. When in 1974 the politicians in the United States restored the citizen's right to own and trade gold, they 'forgot' to give legislative guarantees that this right will not be disturbed in the future again, using any number of possible excuses, including the fight against terrorism.

Do not be misled by the trading of paper gold on a number of commodity exchanges. Very little monetary gold is involved as compared with the size of the commitments of speculators and even that is provided by central banks as a way for them to influence the 'price' of gold. In addition, gold miners are driven into the open embrace of the commodity exchanges. Not only are they denied freedom by their creditors, the bullion banks, to market their product as they see fit including withholding it from the markets, they are also forced to sell forward several years of future output, never mind that it is in violation of the laws governing futures trading in general and the charter of the commodity exchange in particular. I find it hard to lay the blame on the commodity exchanges. They can't very well refuse to honour call options written by a central bank whose balance sheet, showing gold, is supposedly true to fact and open to public scrutiny.

I now come to the proof that gold is still the monetary metal par excellence (albeit with zero velocity of circulation). There is one and only one, fundamental reason for this. It is the fact that gold has constant marginal utility. I am not going to quibble whether the marginal utility of gold is indeed constant, or whether it declines at the slowest rate, by far, among all the substances known to man – a fact that even Paul Krugman cannot deny (that is, provided that he is familiar with the concept of marginal utility). For the purposes of this discussion the two formulations amount to the same. At any rate, it is easier to refer to this property of gold as constant marginal utility, than rattling off the other description, even if it may be more accurate.

The marginal utility of any good used by man declines, with the possible exception of gold. This means that subsequently acquired units of the good in question are earmarked for uses with lower priority than units acquired earlier. Carl Menger, one of the three economists generally credited with formulating this important concept in the late 19th century, gives the following example. Suppose an isolated farmer in the rain forests of Brazil brings in five sacks of corn at the end of the harvest. He earmarks the first sack to cover his and his family's need for food until the next harvest. The second sack is seed corn. The third sack he intends to use as animal feed. The fourth sack is for making beer and vodka. The fifth or marginal sack he will use to feed the birds around his house whose antics are the only entertainment he and his family have. If he had more sacks available, then they would be surplus that could be used for the purposes of barter. At any rate, the value of corn for this farmer would be determined by its marginal utility, that is, the utility of his marginal sack. It follows that if the farmer lost one or more sacks to fire or any other mishap, then the marginal utility of corn to him would go higher. By the same token, if he harvested more sacks, then the marginal utility of corn to him would go lower. The same is true of any other good.

What makes gold coins different is that anyone receiving a number of them will earmark the first and the last coin with the same priority. He can use either one to purchase other goods in the market on exactly the same terms. This property of gold is not due to an accident. It is the result of a long evolution taking several millennia. As gold has been a means of savings In addition, to being a means of exchange and because of its constant marginal utility, the stock of gold in existence is huge relative to the flow of new gold from the mines (defined as the combined annual output of all the gold mines in the world). The stocks-to-flows ratio for gold is a high multiple, variously estimated between 50 and 80. This means that, at current rates of production, it would take 50 to 80 years to produce the same amount of gold that is now in existence. The stocks-to-flows ratio for all other goods (with the possible exception of silver) is a small fraction. For copper, for example, it is around 0.3 meaning that the available supply of copper is equivalent to about four months' production. If the ratio went higher, the price of copper would most assuredly plummet, because of the relatively fast declining marginal utility of copper, even though it is an industrial metal with lots of uses.

To say that gold is the monetary metal of the world is not an expression of opinion. It is an objective observation justified by the size of the stockpiles of gold, the accumulation of millennia, that are known to exist. They are huge relative to the meagre annual flows of new gold from the mines. Indeed, it was an evolution lasting for thousands of years during which the market has made its choice which particular good will have the slowest-declining marginal utility, allowing the accumulation of monetary stocks to take place. By the same token, gold cannot be dumped as the monetary metal by government decree, regardless whether it was countersigned by V.I. Lenin or by F.D. Roosevelt. If gold was really to be demonetised, then the enormous stocks relative to flows would have to be dissipated first through consumption. Literally, you would have to make people eat gold. King Midas couldn't eat it. Lenin and the commander-in-chief of the Cheka with his machine guns could not make people eat it. Not in the 73 years of their control of power in Russia and not in another hundred years.

It is true that the government can outlaw gold as money, or ban the gold market. It can even forbid or discourage the use of gold in jewellery (as the Indian government may be planning to do according to rumours). None of this will address the crux of the matter: the highest stocks-to-flows ratio for gold, which gives people that superb confidence to entrust their savings to gold, rather than to the gentlemen running the central banks and treasury departments of the world.

Not A Good Idea

" ... Why not assure monetary virtue by trusting, not in the monetary wisdom of men, but in an objective standard? Why not emulate our great grandfathers and tie our currency to gold? Very few economists think this would be a good idea.

Refutation

So few economists indeed, that it jumps out as a statistical aberration.[2] This contorsed reasoning is all the more curious given the miserable record of the fiat dollar for the past 35 years while it has been trying to make do without a link to gold. What makes the loser the winner and the winner the loser? My explanation is that the economists have been bribed. The bribe money can actually be tracked as the record is in the public domain. Please bear with me as it takes some time to relate this incredible story.

The Federal Reserve (FR) banks pay dividends at 6 percent per annum of subscribed capital to shareholders, the member banks. The Federal Reserve Act bars them to pay dividends at a higher rate, regardless how profitable the FR banks may be. And as you may have guessed, they are fabulously profitable. So what happens to the undivided surplus? The answer is this: the Federal Reserve banks remit most of the undivided surplus to the U.S. Treasury under false pretences. In the income statement the remittance is called 'franchise tax on the Federal Reserve notes outstanding'. Now every federal tax must be authorised by legislation duly passed by the Congress and signed into law by the President. I urge you to ask your favourite professor of the dismal monetary science to identify the Act and provide the date of its passing, which authorises the franchise tax. But be prepared for a long wait while the professor is doing the search, because such an Act does not exist, has never been proposed or enacted. Incredible, isn't it? [3]

You are a taxpayer. Would you pay a tax that has never been authorised by law, but someone at the IRS invented a catchy name and started collecting it? No, you wouldn't. You would fight the phantom tax in the courts, if need be, all the way to the Supreme Court. Now there are twelve FR banks in the United States. Every one of them has a legal department, well-staffed with well-paid legal counsels. Do you think that one of the twelve might have challenged the unauthorised tax and withheld payment to test the legality of its collection? Surprise, surprise. Not one of them ever has. Moreover, not one shareholder, not one member bank, has spoken out against the arrangement of paying an illegal tax. Why?

The professors of the dismal monetary science are at a loss to give you the answer. But I will. In the check-kiting scheme of the U.S. Treasury and the FR banks the latter are the junior partners.

The allocation of the loot is not on a 50-50 basis. The lion's share goes to the senior partner. The junior partners must be satisfied with the crumbs. But crumbs are plentiful to throw a jolly good party still. Why complain when the FR banks themselves can set the rate at which the 'tax' is assessed? They are free to subtract any and all expenditures on frills before they come to the bottom line, undivided surplus.

And spend on frills they do. One item listed as legitimate expenditure is money subsidising economic research. It is a big item, covering not only in-house research, but also research grants paid to outsiders on contract at various universities and think-tanks. Now please estimate if you will the percentage of research funds that goes to economists analysing the failure of the fiat dollar and studying the possibility of return to the gold standard as a remedy. You've got it: exactly zero percent.

From the point of view of the FR banks the more money they spend on subsidising economic research the less tax they pay. So funds are gushing forth abundantly and are granted generously to subsidise research in dismal monetary science, taking good care to shut out any dissonant noise about the gold standard.

Interlude

Lest my detractors charge that I have 'the sour grapes complex' I mention an episode from my active days. In 1975 I spent a Sabbatical year as Visiting Fellow at Princeton University. By a strange quirk of fate Paul A. Volcker was also at Princeton University at the same time as Senior Fellow. Paul was cooling his heels between two jobs. After having served as Under-Secretary of the Treasury for Monetary Affairs, overseeing the devaluation of the dollar, he was awaiting a new assignment at the Fed. We didn't know it at the time, but soon it turned out to be his appointment as President of the Federal Reserve Bank of New York, the most lucrative job in the entire establishment, certainly, more lucrative, if less prestigious, than that of the Chairman of the Federal Reserve Board, which was to be Volcker's next assignment a few years later. Paul ran a seminar for postgraduate students 'on international monetary stuff' as he would call it. I was an irregular, occasionally dropping in to listen to Paul's lectures and the presentation of papers by students. I even contributed a paper myself, as I recall, on gold in the international monetary system. Paul and I also met outside of the classroom. Once he invited me to dinner at the Faculty Club of which he was a member.

Concerning gold, Paul didn't beat around the bush. He said that there was no objection against gold being the constitutional monarch. But gold must behave and abide by the decisions of Parliament. [4] If gold started asserting itself, if it misbehaved, then it would be ousted and sent into exile. That's what had happened in 1971. Gold would not be tolerated as an absolute monarch.

I did not argue with Paul's anthropomorphism. I could have pointed out that it was not a question of gold being the sovereign but the people holding it, as they should according to the Constitution of the United States.

Paul never had any qualms about the loyalty of other countries following the leadership of the dollar, as vassals follow the feudal lord. Foreign central banks knew full well that their currencies are in the same boat as the dollar. If they scuttle the boat, then they all perish. It was a matter of hanging together lest they hang separately (with thanks to Benjamin Franklin for the felicitous phrase).

Paul of course knew that I was a professional mathematician. He asked me if I would be interested in setting up a differential equation to describe the relationship between the foreign exchange rate and the spread between the rates of interest prevailing in the two countries. I guess if I had said 'yes', then I could have made a career as a contributor of dismal monetary science, with a fat research grant from the FR bank of New York. But I said 'no' adding that, in my opinion, there was no such a thing.

Differential equations describe the relationship of causality. They are quite useless if what you want to grasp is the relationship of tele-ology.

And the relationship between foreign exchange rates and inter-est-rate spreads was a problem of teleology, not one of causality. You can't treat individuals who have free will as if they were inanimate particles in a physics experiment. [5] That's the trouble with macroeco-nomics as opposed to microeconomics. It assumes that economic ag-gregates have their own lives and in their hands individuals are lifeless, inert matter that, like play-dough, could be given any desired shape.

That's how my brush with dismal monetary science ended, needless to say, to the great detriment of my remuneration. Yet I had no regrets. I had not left my native Hungary when Soviet troops overran it in 1956 because I wanted to exchange one sycophancy for another.

Refutation Continued

It should be clear that the funds dished out by the research depart-ments of the FR banks are bribe money subsidising dismal monetary science exclusively, having precious little to do with the search for and dissemination of truth but designed to entrench and aggrandise in-cumbent power. Small wonder that so few economists dare to express views that the regime of irredeemable currency is a disaster of the first magnitude, leading to an economic catastrophe worse than that fol-lowing the experiment with fiat money in France at the end of the 18th century, admirably documented by Andrew Dickson White. [6] Very few economists would express their view in public that tying the dollar to gold is the answer.

Consider once more how profitable the check-kiting scheme be-tween the Treasury and the FR banks is. The latter can buy off an en-tire profession from the crumbs and trickle-down profits and still have money left to award to economists from other countries willing to par-rot the Keynesian demand-side theory of money.

This goes to show the utter insidiousness of the regime of irredeem-able currency. Not only does it allow vampirism plaguing the savers and producers of society through check-kiting while throwing the gates wide open to vote-buying by politicians, it also corrupts the mind and frustrates any impartial discussion of the underlying scientific princi-ples. Irredeemable currency is cancer on the body economic, body pol-itic and body academic as well.

Too Rigid

" ... The argument against the gold standard is one of pragmatism, not one of principle. The gold standard would have all the disadvantages of any system of rigidly fixed foreign exchange rates.

Refutation

Thus according to Krugman pragmatism trumps the Constitution, which mandates a metallic monetary system. Worse still, advocates of the dismal monetary science also think that it is pragmatic not to press for a Constitutional amendment. Why take a chance? People will not notice, still less bother, if their Constitution is trampled in the mud.

The Founding Fathers did not establish a central bank for the United States. They established the U.S. Mint and opened it to silver and gold. In doing so they elevated the principle of free coinage to the level of basic human rights. The power to create or to extinguish money was reserved for the people themselves by the Constitution. It was not delegated to the representatives of the people, nor to so-called experts hired by them. If people thought that there was too little money in circulation, or that interest rates were too high, then they could do something about it. They could take old jewellery and plate, or cause new silver and gold from the mines to flow, to the Mint to be converted into the coins of the realm. Conversely, if the people thought that there was too much money in circulation, or that interest rates were too low, then they could do something about that, too. They could melt down the coins and convert the monetary metals into jewellery and plate, or have them exported along with new gold and silver from the mines.

It is true that the international gold standard confines the foreign exchange rate between two countries adhering to it to a narrow range between the gold export and import points. This is not a drawback of the gold standard; it is one of its main excellence. It is responsible for the promotion of division of labour between countries. Each country will produce the goods and services for which it is best fitted and import other goods and services which can be produced more efficiently abroad. The regime of floating exchange rates (that should be properly called the regime of sinking exchange rates) destroys international division of labour and promotes autarky.

But it destroys division of labour domestically as well. Previously the exporter could concentrate his talent and energies on production, knowing that as long as he is the best, no foreign competitor could harm his business. This is no longer true under floating. Foreign competitors could nail his business on the foreign exchanges. The central banks, as advocated by dismal monetary science, could manipulate foreign exchange rates to his detriment. It goes by the name 'beggar thy neighbour'. To be successful as an exporter it is no longer sufficient to excel in production. The exporter also has to be a skilful speculator in foreign exchange. This is what has killed many a small business during the past 35 years. The principals could not cope with volatility in the foreign exchange market. Big business, on the other hand, decided that it was less risky to export jobs than goods and this is exactly what they did. An unprecedented dismantling of production facilities on American soil was the result, because the price of the imported ingredients rose faster than export earnings, thanks to the deliberate dollar debasement.

Floating exchange rates were a giant step backwards in division of labour, discouraging talent from going into productive enterprise. Talent now goes into financial speculation, as witnessed by the snow-balling derivatives market where the commitment of speculators is estimated at more than two hundred trillion dollars, or more than the market capitalisation of the entire globe.

One of the more imbecile ideas of dismal monetary science is that devaluation of the currency helps the country to export more and import less, thus rectifying the trade imbalance. It is absolutely amazing that economists do not find it repulsive to parrot this trash, apparently on order from the grant departments of the FR banks (in whose interest the policy of currency debasement clearly is). In 1968 the exchange rate with Japan was around 320 yens to the dollar and there was a huge trade deficit run by the U.S. To rectify it a dollar-debasement policy was put into effect promising that it would cure the deficit and turn it into a surplus. That is not what happened. In the next ten years the value of the dollar was pushed all the way down from 320 to 80, or one quarter of the initial, while the trade deficit instead of turning into a surplus ballooned tenfold. The question arises how much more beating does the dollar have to take before a dent is made in the trade deficit?

The explanation for the perverse reaction of the patient to Keynesian therapy as advocated by dismal monetary science is actually quite simple. Naturally, it was never permitted to be publicised by the award- officers at the FR banks. Currency devaluation makes your terms of trade with the rest of the world deteriorate. This means that you can import less for every dollar of export earnings as a result of devaluation.

Virtually all export items have imported ingredients, so devaluation makes them more expensive to produce, not less. While it may let you sell your existing inventory at bargain-basement prices to foreigners, this is fool's paradise. The boost in exports is strictly temporary. It is all at the expense of future production which is put in jeopardy by the higher cost of imported ingredients, as the experience of the American industry for the past 35 years has amply demonstrated.

Currency devaluation is not unlike self-mutilation. You don't cut off one of your arms while trying to compete with foreigners in the world market. Yet this is exactly what America has done to itself. The country's de-industrialisation is the direct result of the deliberate debasement of the dollar for the past 35 years. Keynesian demand-side monetary theory suggests and Krugman agrees, that devaluing the currency has a benefit to offer to the export industry. It is the benefit of the grave. Power is being turned off at factories and plants that once were busy, humming and producing, while providing well-paid industrial jobs for Americans. The once prosperous and productive industrial heartland of America has been turned into a graveyard, thanks to the floating (sinking) dollar.

The trade deficit of the United States is at an all-time high and still increasing. No economist has the courage to say it, but it is caused by the policy of deliberate dollar debasement, now in its 35th year. You have to pursue the argument of dismal monetary science ad absurdum to understand it. If a little bit of devaluation is supposed to be good for the country, then a big devaluation should be even better and, reducing the exchange rate to zero, Nirvana itself. Then the country could give away its goods and services to foreigners free of charge. That, finally, will really perk up exports.

Gold Unstable

" … *Crucially, gold is not a stable standard when measured in goods and services. It is a commodity whose price is constantly buffeted by shifts in supply and demand that have nothing to do with the needs of the world economy – by changes, for example, in dentistry.*

Look Who's Talking…! [7]

Is this the best you can do in defence of Dismal Monetary Science, Krugman? Must the Constitution of the United States of America be dishonoured, besmirched and continuously violated because of your conjecture that, under its provisions, changes in dentistry may cause inflation or deflation?

Here is what dishonouring the U. S. Constitution, implicitly endorsed by Krugman, has given us:

(1) The irredeemable dollar has been losing at least 90 percent of its purchasing power every 35 years.
(2) Interest rates have been destabilised and could reach unprecedented high or low levels.
(3) The volatility of commodity prices has increased explosively and continues to do so.
(4) We are forced to live under the constant threat of disruptive corners, for example, corner in the crude oil market.

The volatility of the price of crude oil has been as high as 1000 percent per annum (i.e., the price increased eleven-fold within a year). It is blamed on the intrigues of OPEC to corner the market. However, this begs the question, as cartels prosper under the regime of irredeemable currency and wither under the gold standard. At any rate there are many other examples of explosive increases in price volatility. The price of sugar went from 6¢ per lb to 75¢ in 1975 (forcing Coca Cola to switch to corn syrup) only to fall back to 10¢ in the following year. The price of coffee underwent comparable gyrations. Nor was volatility confined to imported goods. Soybeans saw wild price movements up and down, as did most cash crops. This type of volatility was simply unheard-of under the gold standard. Also unheard-of was a cartel cornering a commodity such as crude oil, as long as the medium of exchange was gold.

In fact, one of the chief merits of the gold standard is that it eliminates the threat of disruptive corners by reining price volatility back.

Suppose that under an unadulterated gold standard there is an incipient corner in the crude oil market. Arbitrageurs would respond by selling crude oil forward at ever higher prices and keep doing it until the corner is broken. I use the word 'arbitrage' advisedly. A short position in crude oil is balanced by a long position in gold and, as a consequence, the risk of the arbitrageur is limited. Price volatility is reined in through arbitrage long before a corner could materialise. By contrast, under the regime of irredeemable currency a short position in crude oil carries unlimited risk (since there is no obvious limit above which the price may not rise). As a consequence speculators are reluctant to resist price trends and swings.

Volatility Could Become Explosive.

Of course, you could resist the uptrend and keep selling forward crude oil at ever higher prices. But this would no longer be arbitrage. It would be pyramiding naked short positions at escalating losses, a most fool-ish action. No speculator in his right mind would undertake it. For lack of arbitrage corners have become common and volatility is left unchecked. Not just in crude oil. Not just in agricultural products. Also in metals: copper, lead, palladium, you name it. Explosive increases in price volatility are in the making as I write this.

It is ridiculous to argue, as Krugman does, that changes in dentistry could adversely affect the monetary role of gold, presumably by causing deflation in case of an increasing, or inflation in case of a decreasing demand for dental gold. Gold is not merely a commodity. Its highest stocks-to-flows ratio, which is not materially affected by changes in dentistry or in any other marginal application, makes gold the mone-tary metal par excellence.[8]

Interlude

Let me relate my personal experiences concerning gold and dentistry. I can speak with some authority on this matter as a survivor of the Soviet occupation of Hungary in 1945 (which was to last 45 years, until the collapse of the Soviet Union in 1990.) Like most people of the middle classes, my father had gold in his teeth, a relic of more prosperous times. However, gold teeth had not much chewing to do in Soviet-occupied Hungary. The Red Army requisitioned all foodstuff it could lay its hands on for its own use, as well as for shipping it back home – without any regard for the starving local population.

So my father had his gold teeth removed. With the proceeds of the sale of gold he could have false teeth made of cheaper material and still have money left to buy food for his family.

This shows that the demand for gold in dentistry is price-elastic and can even go negative, just as it is in jewellery. Scarcity of money will not cause deflation under a gold standard.

Rather, it will attract gold to the Mint and not only from the mines and jewellery boxes, but also from people's teeth – a further proof of the excellence of gold as monetary metal, contrary to what Krugman thinks.

It is just as silly to suggest that replacing gold in dentistry with oth-er materials could cause the demand for gold decline which translates into inflation under a gold standard. In 1945 dental gold was replaced by cheaper materials in Hungary, without making the demand for gold decline. I remember very vividly the delicate hands of our dentist as he clipped off an agreed portion of the heavy gold chain that used to hold my grandfather's pocket watch. (I still have the remnants of that chain in my possession. The watch itself has been bartered for food during hard times.) In doing so the dentist was taking his fee for professional services, which he simply refused to provide on any other terms. In particular, he contemptuously declined to take his fee in irredeemable currency, However, profusely offered. The dentist did not need the gold in his dental practice as his patients could not afford it. He wanted the gold because he did not trust the value of irredeemable currency. On a more grisly note, high-ranking officials of Nazi Germany as well as of the Soviet Union did not trust it either. They ordered gold teeth to be wrenched from the mouth of the victims they had killed, to be recycled as good-delivery gold bars.

Nicholas Deak, principal of Deak-Perera, a banking firm in New York specialising in precious metals and foreign exchange in the 1970s, was of Hungarian origin. He worked for OSS (predecessor of the CIA) during World War II out of his base in Switzerland. He has told me that agents operating in enemy territory were issued gold coins. Later in the Vietnam War American airmen were also issued gold coins. In each case the idea was that gold might buy them freedom in case they were captured, something that paper money would be decidedly unable to accomplish.

Deak believed that the top brass at the Fed carried part of their personal savings in the form of gold coins. They certainly, appear to understand gold better than Krugman. Chairman Alan Greenspan is on record revealing the 'shabby little secret of fiat money' as an agent of the Welfare State. It enables politicians to promise pie in the sky to the electorate, something they could not do under a gold standard without being found out in short order as imposters. Greenspan is also on record opposing U. S. Treasury gold auctions for reasons that in war the dollar might be useless and gold will be needed to purchase war material abroad to support the fighting men and women of the armed forces. What he did not say was that the dollar could become useless in peacetime, too, under his own watch.

Cadenza

In this Cadenza I give a brief refresher course on the subject of speculation versus arbitrage. The two are very different. In a sense they diametrically oppose one another. The speculator is willing to take large risks in the hope of large profits, while the arbitrageur is interested in reducing risks. The speculator is betting on changes in the price, while the arbitrageur is betting on changes in the spread (difference between two prices). The speculator's basic tools are:

(1) net long position (commitment to buy),
(2) net short position (commitment to sell) at a predetermined price.

The arbitrageur's basic tool is the straddle (combination of a net long and a net short position – see Volume II for illustrations and applications). Every straddle corresponds to a spread, the difference between the prices at which the commitments to buy and sell have been made. Reduction of risk is realised as movement in the spread is often more predictable than that in the price itself.

Unfortunately, the distinction between speculation and arbitrage as a rule is not kept clear and confusion arises frequently. For example, strictly speaking, under an unadulterated gold standard there is no speculation, only arbitrage. What looks like an outright position is really a straddle (in case of a long position, long in the commodity and short in gold; in case of a short position, short in the commodity and long in gold). This fundamental fact is ignored by virtually all authors writing on the subject, thereby obscuring the role of the gold standard as a regulator reining price volatility back. In more details, speculation is less risky under a gold standard than under a regime of irredeemable currency in view of the fact that speculators work with straddles rather than net long or net short positions. Because of the smaller risk, they are not reluctant to resist price swings and trends. By contrast, under a regime of irredeemable currency speculators are often weary to enter a long or a short position because of the greater risks involved. Moreover, speculators seek protection in 'herd instinct'. That is to say, they prefer to jump on the band-wagon in order to ride an established price trend. This is the exact opposite of what they might do under a gold standard where resisting trends may offer a greater profit opportunity than riding them.

To recapitulate, the gold standard has a built-in mechanism to restrain volatility in commodity prices. This is in contrast with the regime of irredeemable currency which is more likely to encourage volatility, as well as the formation of a price trend. By the same token, it is also far more hospitable to cartels than is the gold standard.

It goes without saying that establishment economists, including practitioners of the dismal monetary science, are simply not interested in these problems. The Federal Reserve banks would never sponsor research investigating the fundamental change in the nature of speculation after the dollar has been made irredeemable. This example alone should make it clear that establishment economics has nothing to do with the search for and dissemination of truth. It has to do with the maintenance and aggrandisement of establishment power.

Interlude

The love of paper money may make Krugman the 'modern King Midas in the reverse'. His gods could turn everything he touches, including food and drink, into paper. It is small consolation that the paper he must eat has a long string of zeros following the digit 1 printed on it.

It actually happened, among other places, in Hungary, where bank notes denominated in the billions, trillions and quadrillions circulated in rapid succession in 1946. I know – I have been there. At one point they ran out of prominent people the image of whom could be printed on the bank notes. Luckily, this is no problem in the United States where the supply of professors of dismal monetary science whose image can be printed on the $1 billion, $1 trillion, or $1 quadrillion FR notes is unlimited, thanks to the foresight of the twelve FR banks in making generous research grants to qualified applicants.

Additionally, the game of 'knocking off zeros' can also be played by any country, big or small, with an equal and fair chance to win. The rules are simple. You could declare one New Peso equivalent to, say, one million old pesos, knocking off 6 zeros right there and then with one mighty swoop and a crispy one New Peso note could be printed to replace one million of the old variety. In the game of knocking off zeros the current world champion is Yugoslavia, eliminating 22 zeros in 1994. The runner-up is Argentina that has gone through 13 zeros so far. A recent upstart is Romania with 4 zeros. Not bad, considering that Romania is the only former Soviet satellite having started its 'free market economy' in 1991 with no foreign debt whatsoever!

Unrestrained Goodness

" ... *The current world monetary system assigns no special role to gold. Indeed, the Federal Reserve is not obliged to tie the dollar to anything. It can print as much or as little money as it deems appropriate. There are powerful advantages to such an unrestrained system. Above all, the Fed is free to respond to actual or threatened recession by pumping money. To take only one example, that flexibility is the reason that the stock market crash of 1987 – which started out every bit as frightening as that of 1929 – did not cause a slump in the real economy.*

Refutation

Rub it in, Krugman, rub it in! To the injury of trampling over their Constitution you now add the insult of telling the American people that it makes judicial and economic sense to give a banking cartel the privilege of issuing liabilities it has neither the means nor the intention to honour!

Your example stinks to high heaven. The stock market crash of 1987, just as the one of 1929 before it, were caused precisely by granting privileges without responsibilities to the banking cartel. For damage control you now advocate putting the fox in charge of the chicken coop? Has it not occurred to you that dirt swept under the rug keeps accumulating until it reaches critical mass, at which point damage control no longer works, but further accumulation will start the chain-reaction of dirt explosion?

Poisonous Chalice

" … *While freely floating national money has advantages, however, it also has risks. Countries with a history of runaway inflation often come to the conclusion that monetary independence of the central bank is a poisonous chalice. A system that leaves managers free to do good also leaves them free to be irresponsible and, in some countries, they have been quick to take the opportunity.*

Refutation

'Some'[countries]should read 'all'. First and foremost among those managers were the Officers of the Federal Reserve! Children of a lesser god could not make their fiat money command purchasing power abroad. The United States could. Accordingly, managers of the dollar were double-quick to take the opportunity to be irresponsible with the unlimited power they have usurped, as the diluted dollars still found eager takers abroad, especially in the Third World.

The Constitution of the United States was born of the ashes left behind by runaway inflation, that of the Continental Dollar, although it is not considered polite behaviour to mention this bit of history in the presence of practitioners of the dismal monetary science. Thus, then, following Krugman's logic, we may conclude that the United States has gulped down most of the content of the poisonous chalice. It just takes longer for the poison to act in this case than it would in the case of the children of a lesser god. Be that as it may, we can be sure that there is no way to make monetary managers possessing unlimited power to behave responsibly. Indeed, such a behaviour even defies definition, as the last Interlude below will show.

You just don't delegate unlimited power to anyone, be they politicians elected with large majorities, civil servants, hired experts, appointed judges, or even altruists and saints. You don't calculate the odds whether unlimited power will be exercised responsibly or irresponsibly. If you are sensible, you will adopt a Constitution based on the principle of delegating limited and enumerated powers only, complemented with checks and balances. Then you keep your fingers crossed lest the powers that be won't trample over it. To keep your Constitution alive and well is going to be an uphill battle still. Professors of dismal monetary science may pop in and chalk up differential equations to prove that great danger will befall the world, in the form of over-saving and overproduction, unless their sponsors are granted unlimited power to pump money in rapid response to recessions, actual or threatened. With that power, the professors say, they will be able to abolish the business cycle and, with a little bit of luck, scarcity, too and will wipe out the difference between credit and capital to boot.

Interlude

In the comedy masterpiece written in 1673 by the brilliant French playwright Molière entitled *Le malade imaginaire* the protagonist, Argan, is a hypochondriac. No physician can convince him that there's nothing wrong with his health.

Finally, in desperation, someone suggests that he himself become a Doctor of Medicine. Then he will be able to find out what's really ailing him and what to do about it. Argan takes the advice and the M. D. examination, which may, in a parody, go as follows:

Examiner: What therapy do you apply in case of constipation?

Argan: I prescribe enema.

Examiner: What if it is a stubborn case?

Argan: Definitely more enemas.

Examiner: A most excellent answer! What therapy do you apply in case of diarrhoea?

Argan: I prescribe enema.

Examiner: But what if the condition persists?

Argan: Definitely more enemas, Your Honour!

Examiner: A most excellent answer indeed! Congratulations! You have met the requirements for the Degree of Doctor of Medicine. Welcome to the Club!

Fig. 4 Le Malade Imaginaire

Exactly as in *Le Malade Imaginaire*, dismal monetary science prescribes 'enemas' of new money to be injected into the economy in case of a deflation, actual or threatened, in order to prevent prices from falling. But it also prescribes enemas of new money to be injected into the economy in case of an inflation, actual or threatened, in order to prevent interest rates from rising. In this way money-doctors cannot be held responsible for the treatments they decide on except, perhaps, to suggest that they have failed to administer an adequate number of enemas to their patient.

Gold Spells Deflation

> " ... *The United States abandoned its policy of stabilising gold 'price's back in 1971. Since then the 'price' of gold has increased about 1000 percent while consumer prices have increased only about 250 percent or, roughly, a quarter of the increase in the gold 'price'. If we had tried to keep the 'price' of gold from rising, this would have required a massive decline in the prices of practically everything else – deflation on a scale not seen since the Depression. This does not sound like a particularly good idea.*

Refutation

What the United States did in 1971 was defaulting on its gold obligations to foreign creditors, the biggest act of bad faith in history theretofore. This default and the making of the dishonoured debt money, was the cause of the destabilisation of interest rates, as well as the explosive growth in the volatility of prices that have been plaguing the world ever since and causing ever greater economic distress. Krugman's euphemism in calling the greatest default ever 'the abandoning of the stabilisation policy of the gold 'price' and calling the promotion of the dishonoured paper as money 'a measure designed to prevent deflation and the decline of prices' is doublespeak, the hallmark of dismal monetary science. Krugman suggests that an equilibrium now obtains that didn't before. What we have is not an equilibrium; rather, it is a burgeoning disequilibrium, one that will continue its devastating course.

We must remember that the financial annals do not record a single case in which a default has not been followed by a progressive increase in the discount on the paper of the defaulting banker, until it reached 100 percent – possibly several years or even decades later. Obviously, the defaulting banker would try to slow down the process by hook or crook. However, ultimately economic law was to prevail and the remaining value of the dishonoured paper would be wiped out.

There is no reason to believe that the dollar default will end differently. Suppose that the 'price' of gold is $1520. Let us calculate the discount on the dollar. The gold value of the dollar has been reduced from $1/35$ to $1/1520 = 250/7 \times 35$. Therefore, the loss is 0.98. In percentage terms the loss, also known as discount, is 98 percent (anno 2017). [9]

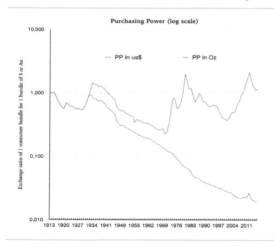

Fig. 5 Loss on the dollar's purchasing power: 98%

Not yet 100, but close enough. Small comfort, as the last 2 percent of the loss, coincident with the death-throes of the dollar, is likely to be most violent and painful, revealing the full extent of the devastation. Remember, the loss affects not only cash holdings, but all dollar-denominated assets, including bonds, annuities, pensions, insurances, endowments, etc. As the discount on the dollar approaches 100 percent, the dollar 'price' of gold will approach infinity. [10] To assert that the dollar is going to escape this fate is tantamount to asserting that the laws of economics and logic have been turned upside down and the penalty for default has been replaced by reward in perpetuity.

Refutation Continued

The discount as calculated above in terms of the 'price' of gold is the leading indicator of the depreciation of the dollar. It is pretty accurate in registering the loss of purchasing power in terms of a wide array of other goods as well. However, it is important to note that the discount on irredeemable currency, although obviously going to 100 percent, is never doing it along a straight line. It goes through fits and starts, sprinkled with ever more violent reversals.

Therein lies a great danger. Reversal confuses people and lulls them into believing that the currency has reached the end of skid-row and is now entering respectable neighbourhood. The explosive growth in the volatility of interest rates and prices is finally over. More astute observers will, however, realise that low interest rates and subsiding volatility won't cure the malady the cause of which, default, has not been acknowledged, still less removed. Nor will asset bubbles cure it. Volatility is bound to return with a vengeance. Like the wrecker's ball, it will keep swinging until the whole financial structure is reduced to rubble.

A reliable measure of destruction is the so-called 'notional size' of the derivatives market trading interest-rate futures, options and swaps. It now stands at a quarter of a quadrillion dollars and is increasing at an accelerating pace. The word 'notional' is a euphemism suggesting that there is nothing to fear about it. As if it were a kind of financial mirage. Well, there is plenty to fear about. It is real enough as it measures the commitments of bond speculators, most of whom are betting that the rate of interest will keep falling in the U.S., too, as it has been in Japan. The bets are well-grounded. They reflect expectation that interest rates will be driven by the Fed into the bargain basement. This is what the Fed did in the 1930s, causing the First Great Depression. This is what it is doing now, causing the second. The Fed buys bonds in the open market when it wants to combat deflation and falling prices, and also buys them when it wants to combat inflation and rising interest rates. If the Fed ever sells bonds, the occasion is few and far in between and it is for window-dressing purposes only. Speculators know this and think that they can't go wrong if they try to preempt or emulate the Fed in buying the bonds.

This raises the question: if the deflationary danger caused by the Fed's open market operations is so great, because it makes bull speculation in bonds risk free, then why don't economists warn us about it? The answer is that dismal monetary science blocks the free flow of information and an impartial scientific debate of the threat (which is caused by the regime of irredeemable currency alternating, as it does, between inflationary followed by deflationary excesses). During the inflationary excess commodity speculation and during the deflationary excess bond speculation is bleeding the economy white, but you are not supposed to know.

Free Floating ...Waffle...

" ... It is true that a freely floating national money can create uncertainties for international traders and investors. Over a period of five years between 1991 and 1996 the dollar has been worth as much as 120 yen and as little as 80. The costs of this volatility is hard to measure but they must be significant.

Refutation

It is disingenuous to say that in 1971 the United States made the dollar 'freely floating'. [11] What the United States did was nothing less than throwing away the yardstick measuring value.

It is truly unbelievable that, in our scientific day and age when the material and therapeutic well-being of billions of people depends on the increasing accuracy of measurement in physics and chemistry, dismal monetary science has been allowed to push the world into the Dark Ages by abolishing the possibility of accurate measurement of value. We no longer have a reliable yardstick to measure value. There was no open debate of the wisdom, or the lack of it, to run the economy without such a yardstick.

To throw away gold, a rigid yardstick and to replace it with a shrinking and elastic yardstick, the dollar, idiotic as though it is, does nevertheless have a rationale as well as a precedent. In less enlightened times the length of the 'foot', as the name of this particular yardstick suggests, was adjusted every time the king died. If the new king's foot was smaller, then the new official unit of length was made shorter. This allowed rope-makers, spinners and weavers to sell a smaller amount of merchandise for the same amount of money. In this way inefficient producers were favoured at the expense of the consumers who were legally short-changed.

The floating dollar does exactly the same. It shelters the inefficient producer who is enabled to sell the same quantity of products at progressively higher prices, to the detriment of the consumer at large.

Interlude

During the course of his travels to many strange lands Gulliver also visited the Country of the Mad Scientists. A government spokesman took him on a guided tour in order to acquaint him with the marvellous achievements and great projects of that land. Among others Gulliver was shown a new procedure under development whereby the erection of buildings would start with the construction of the roof rather than the foundations and proceed from top down. In this way shelter was provided for construction workers in inclement weather.

In another part of Science City, the capital, Gulliver visited an experimental farm where research scientists were simultaneously breeding wool-less sheep and milk-less cows. They were motivated by the idea that the output of sheep milk could be increased greatly through the elimination of wool growing, thus making cow's milk redundant. Wool for clothing could then be replaced by the sturdier cows' hair, that could also be shorn more efficiently.

There was one invention in particular that fascinated Gulliver more than any other. They called it 'floating time'. At the Institute of Horology the director explained that the idea of fixity of time is old-fashioned, even reactionary. In this respect musicians have been more progressive than scientists. They had long ago overthrown constant time, leaving its variation to the discretion of the conductor. Now he could set free the emotive energy implicitly present in the music, the release of which was forbidden by an earlier narrow-minded and reactionary age.

Floating time was implemented by connecting Big Ben in one tower of Parliament Building to Big Barb, the weather vane, in the other. Every time the direction of the wind changed, turning Big Barb one way or another, so did time, as indicated by a slow or a fast Big Ben. The director proudly pointed out that in this way their timepiece was imbued with cosmic power present in the universe, including sun spots and sun flares that have so far been foolishly ignored by clockmakers, but not by the wind.

The director was going to let Gulliver inspect the ingenious mechanism that made floating time possible. It would allow the Chairman of the Board of Time Reserve to overrule the prevailing wind whenever justified. At the Parliament Building they ran into the picket line of workers demanding higher wages. At that moment the town clerk announced that the direction of the wind has just turned Westerly, meaning that Big Ben would run fast, cutting the hour down from 60 minutes to 50. The workers burst into joyous cheering. They understood that the working day has been instantaneously shortened 16 percent by the change of the wind, without reduction in pay. The strike was called off. The director turned to Gulliver and winked: 'See what I mean? Floating time is helpful even in settling labour disputes!'

Finale

The great 20th century economist Ludwig von Mises famously predicted, shortly after the consolidation of Bolshevik power that, unless private ownership of the means of production was reestablished, the economy of Russia would collapse. Without valid market prices for the means of production businessmen could not do the necessary economic calculations as to what, when and where to produce and how much to invest in production facilities, so rational allocation of scarce resources was no longer possible. For a while the economy could limp along but, eventually, the compounding of bad economic decisions would lead to so great an economic distortion that sudden death would become inevitable. Well, it took three and a half score of years to reach the threshold beyond which economic abuse caused by bad decisions could no longer be tolerated and the prophecy was duly fulfilled.

Mises made another famous prediction. If the United States left the gold standard and failed to stabilise the dollar in terms of gold soon thereafter, then a 'crack-up boom' would follow and the dollar would lose all its purchasing power, first internationally, then domestically. This prophecy has not yet been fulfilled but, as the Soviet example shows, sometimes you have to be patient when waiting for Mises' predictions to come true.

Unfortunately, Mises justified his prophecy about the dollar in terms of the Quantity Theory of Money, which is a linear model and is not applicable in a non-linear world such as ours. He should have argued in exactly the same way as he did in predicting the demise of the Soviet Union. If the United States threw away the yardstick measuring value, namely the gold dollar, then businessmen could not do the necessary economic calculations as to what, when and where to produce and how much to invest in production facilities, so rational allocation of scarce resources would no longer be possible. For a while the economy could limp along but, eventually, the compounding of bad decisions would lead to so great an economic distortion that sudden death would, in the fullness of time, become inevitable. We don't know where the threshold is beyond which the economic abuse caused by bad decisions can no longer be tolerated. What we do know, however, is that economic abuse cannot continue indefinitely, as the Soviet example so convincingly demonstrates.

***

The trouble with Krugman's dismal monetary science is not that it can err. The trouble with it is that it functions as a 'thought police'. It intimidates people in their pursuit of searching for and disseminating truth and it bribes others to push propaganda as science.

Endnotes to Chapter 53

[1] Gnostic dualist rulers have no 'people,' only subjects, i.e. dumb peasants that need to be told what to do. Exemplar is the contention of Averroës (supra).

[2] So if almost all people are convinced the Earth is flat and you think otherwise, you are a statistical abberation and therefor you are wrong...!?

[3] Why would anyone pay a voluntary tax, unless there exists already some sort of 'understanding' between parties to share the loot, that is?

[4] Do you recognise the control issue of the gnostic warrior? See Chapter 48, Deconstructing Ideologies, in Part 8.

[5] Too bad if you just bought a new white coat for the Econometrics Lab, isn't it?

[6] Andrew Dickson White, Fiat Money Inflation in France. How it Came, What it Brought, How it Ended, 2005, e-book available online.

[7] Prof. Fekete sets out a legal argumentation against Krugman, based on the U.S. Constitution. For the benefit of all others, we add a scientific argument: why on earth is nobody questioning Krugman's measuring device: the U.S. Dollar a.k.a. Spandex © (with apologies) or rubber band? See Vol. I.

[8] Modern economic textbooks, including the one by the Prophet, lack any insight on speculation, such as we have provided here.

[9] In 2005 we calculated the same in The Goldbug, Variations V, 2005, with a gold 'price' of $ 420 and a loss of 91.66%

[10] Things may not go as 'fast' as you would like? It's no fun, though, even if one possesses gold or silver coins, that everybody will want from you...! See also the Chapter 'Waiting for Godot'.

[11] The free floating euphemisms for sinking are again, typical language destruction, characteristic for gnostic dualists. It makes no difference at what level this language destruction takes place. The master of this game of language destruction was Friedman.

Chapter 54

Religious Roots of Chrysophobia [1]

The Anti-Gold Gospel According To Rev. Kaletsky

Anatole Kaletsky is the author of the most recent Anti-Gold Gospel. He is an establishment journalist, Associate Editor (formerly Economics Editor) of The Times. He says that he instinctively dislikes gold because 'historically gold has been a terrible investment and, even in the short term, gold has failed as a store of value'. I am satisfied to leave this statement to stand on its own and wish Kaletsky good luck in seeking a better store of value in fiat currencies.

It is patently disingenuous and unfair to compare the gold 'price' to stock indexes. It would be fairer to compare stashed-away gold to passbook savings. A portfolio of equities takes managing. It may be beyond the reach of most wage-earners and pensioners while their savings is the main target of the pilferers who run the nation's banks and monetary system. Who said pilferers were after wealth invested in the stock market?

I strongly object to the idea that 'gold is an investment'. Gold is better described as a non-investment, more precisely a place where you park your savings when you cannot find satisfactory investment outlets either because interest rates are too low, or because the risk of holding equities is too high, e.g., after a bull run of the stock market driven by printing-press money. Gold is not an investment any more than a fire-insurance policy is. Governments have a sacred duty to protect the value of funds of the weak, who cannot fend for themselves in the investment arena. Without protection their funds would melt away like butter left in the blazing sun. Governments have failed miserably in discharging this sacred duty. The Biblical curse is upon them for 'tormenting widows and orphans'.

Kaletsky, like everyone before him preaching the Anti-Gold Gospel, studiously *avoids* the question why the Treasury and the Federal Reserve should have the privilege of issuing obligations that they have neither the means nor the intention to honour. If anyone else tried to run a business on that basis, he would land in jail like Charles Ponzi did in the 1920s.

Kaletsky also *dodges* the fact that gold is the only balancing item in the asset column that has no countervailing liability in the balance sheet of someone else. It is this feature that makes gold impervious to defaults, devaluations and deliberate debasement of the currency. For this reason gold is universally sought after as a safe haven, especially when the seas get rough. There is simply no substitute for gold in this regard. [2]

Gold is the indispensable regulator of debt in society. Kaletsky apparently believes that *government bureaucrats should determine* how much debt society is able safely to carry and they should regulate the level of debt accordingly. [3] Well, we have just tried this and found that whenever irredeemable promises are to be liquidated by issuing more irredeemable promises, debt proliferates beyond any limit. The derivatives monster and its bastard offspring, 'bond insurance,' is the beacon luring the boat of the national economy to its doom on the reefs. Clearly, debt existing in the world today will *never* be liquidated through the normal processes of debt-retirement, that is, without detours into deflationary or inflationary territory (i.e., through default or depreciation). It is lunacy to think that the debt-pyramid can continue to grow indefinitely without causing a major catastrophe further down the line. All debt will be liquidated in the same way as subprime mortgages: through default – or else, it will be inflated away.

By the way, did it ever occur to Kaletsky that there is absolutely no need for bond insurance under a gold standard? The reason is that interest rates and, hence, bond prices are confined to such a narrow range that bond speculation becomes unprofitable. Under a gold standard capital and talent are freed to pursue socially desirable goals. [4]

> Kaletsky's argument that there is not enough gold in the world to serve as a means of exchange in our sophisticated global economy is the old war-horse of the Anti-Gold Gospel.

All the output of the gold mines for the past half-century, plus all the monetary gold disgorged by the central banks in a futile effort to contain the gold 'price', has been gobbled up by gold hoarding. This is an unmistakable sign that people do not trust the integrity of government promises, nor do they buy the academic claptrap about gold being a barren asset and a barbarous relic. Obituaries of gold money have been premature. The golden corpse still stirs. People who sought refuge in gold have been amply rewarded for their foresight. More rewards are on the way. Others who did not avail themselves of the opportunity will have occasion to regret it. They are to be victimised by the welfare-warfare state and its unconstitutional power-grab in issuing irredeemable dollars. These dollars could not have been issued under a system of government of limited and enumerated powers. All present dollars have been issued unconstitutionally. They are the corpus delicti: proof of usurpation of unlimited power.

If constitutional money were re-established, then gold would come out of hiding and make itself available as a means of exchange. There is plenty of gold in existence to support a gold standard, provided that confidence in promises is re-established. There is no rigid rule limiting the amount of sound credit that can be safely built upon a given gold base, especially in this age of instantaneous and free communication. However, multiple credit construction and borrowing short to lend long as a banking technique must be renounced.

The last word whether gold is destined once again to become the pivot of the international monetary system, or whether it is hopelessly antediluvian and incompatible with economic progress, will not be pronounced by detractors of gold and devotees of fast-depreciating fiat money. Their time is up. Their schemes and nostrums have been tried. Now it is the turn of their victims to have their day in court to pass judgment on the fiat money experiment. 'He laughs who laughs last'. The annals of monetary history do not know one single instance in which irredeemable currency survived the test of times. Either the currency was returned to its gold anchor in good time and its value stabilised, or it plunged to worthlessness within a generation. We are skirting these limits right now. The present experiment with the irredeemable dollar has been going on for just about a generation. You will not have to wait decades to witness the failure of this experiment.

The dollar is haemorrhaging on two counts: one is the trade deficit and the other is the budget deficit. Both the political will and the economic know-how are missing to stop the bleeding. The U.S. is borrowing $800 billion annually from foreigners to fund its consumption of foreign-produced goods and commodities. The federal government is running an annual budget deficit of almost $600 billion. At one point foreigners will refuse to finance the burgeoning twin deficit, forcing the Federal Reserve to monetise all the additional debt.

The danger is real that the value of the dollar, both international and domestic, will collapse at that point. [yes the H-word] Kaletsky says that the gold standard is totally anachronistic in our age of rapidly advancing technology and growing populations. [5] He might as well say that good faith behind promises have been rendered obsolete by technological progress and the more people there are the more the government is justified to cheat them out of their savings through currency debasement.[6] Kaletsky is entitled to his belief that people will meekly continue in their assigned role of being victimised by spendthrift governments. However, the New Year 2008 brought with it signs aplenty that the open season of governments' preying upon savers and producers of real goods and real services is coming to an end. People wake up and realise that they are surrendering real goods and real services in exchange for irredeemable promises.

The consequences of this awakening will be most painful. The responsibility for the coming credit collapse in the wake of the unconstitutional paper dollar rests with the U.S. Treasury and its partner-in-crime (partner-in-check-kiting if you will) the Federal Reserve. It may serve as a useful reminder to recall that the French, some seventy years before their bloody revolution, experimented with irredeemable currency under the management of the Scottish adventurer, John Law of Lauriston. When Law's system unraveled people wanted to lynch him. He had to leave Paris in a hurry. Under the cover of night. In a disguise. Disguised As A Woman.

The finance capital of the world, denominated as it is in dollars, is in danger of being wiped out. There is only one way to take out insurance against this contingency: buying gold. As I have explained above, the reason can be found in the balance-sheet concept of gold. The only financial asset that will survive any consolidation of balance sheets, any default, any devaluation, any depreciation is gold.

Gold holdings are the most negatively-correlated asset class to traditional financial assets. Portfolio-diversification can be achieved by balancing financial assets such as bonds, equities and currencies by holding gold. The best timing to set up a gold hedge is when cyclical trends change, as they do right now. The Dow/gold ratio is presently indicating a change. It has turned from increasing to declining mode, which is a red-alarm signal warning wealth-holders that it is time to hedge financial assets and even to go overweight in gold.

The rising gold 'price' and its implications have been largely ignored by the financial press and the investing public so far. The proposition that gold is still a monetary metal and still has a monetary role to play is ridiculed, while some central banks around the globe (e.g., that of Russia, China, India, Argentina, Brazil, to mention but the most important ones) are quietly remonetizing gold as they diversify out of dollars and build gold reserves from scratch. They keep this activity under cover as much as possible since it is not their intention to upset the golden apple-cart.

It is not too late to set up gold hedges as portfolio insurance. Private and institutional investors (including pension funds and insurance companies) have investments to protect worth some $180 trillion. Not more than $600 billion worth of gold bullion is presently earmarked as hedges for portfolio insurance. (Note that gold-mining shares are not eligible for this purpose.) In other words, only about one-third of one percent of all the investments is protected by gold hedges while more than 99 percent is unprotected. Even this is a gross overestimate because most of the hedged portfolios are heavily overweight in gold, leaving that much less gold for the unprotected and thinly protected ones. Be that as it may, if global investors decided to allocate even a modest three percent of their assets to purchase portfolio insurance, the consequence would be that $6 trillion paper assets would be chasing gold bullion worth $0.6 trillion, or one-tenth, at the present 'price' of gold. This means ten bidders for every ounce of gold available. Portfolio insurance is still cheap, but the cost may quickly go up ten-fold or more, once the stampede starts.

Kaletsky would serve his readership better if he advised caution at this juncture. It is still too early to dismiss the possibility that the Titanic of the world economy, having collided with the derivatives iceberg tearing a subprime hole in the hull, may go down. Golden lifesavers may yet come handy.

The Anti-Gold Gospel According To Bishop Frieden

Jeff Frieden is professor at Harvard focusing his research on the politics of international monetary and financial relations. He has been quoted as saying that, if once more on a gold standard,

> " The United States would be unable to respond quickly and effectively to sudden economic shocks. Recessions would be deeper and longer and the economy would be biased towards deflationary spirals. Witness the fact that the United States, which remained on the gold standard till 1933, had a much longer and deeper recession than Britain which had gone off gold in 1931. [7]

If the above quotation by Barron Young Smith is accurate, then the Harvard professor writes his monetary economics while standing on his head. [8] He also has a side job as Bishop in the Church of Gnostic Dualism. Take a look at the evidence throughout the text. He is ascribing a bad condition to a hypothetical gold standard, but the same condition presently obtains in an undiluted form as a direct consequence of the regime of the irredeemable dollar. The U.S. economy is presently biased towards a huge deflationary spiral in consequence of a long cycle of falling interest rates that started from the level of over twenty percent per annum in the early 1980s and still has not run its course. As is well-known, falling interest rates must ultimately culminate in falling prices. If we haven't seen much evidence of actually falling prices yet, it is because policymakers have made the unforgivable mistake of using the irredeemable dollar as a tool to dismantle America's industrial fortress. In other words, falling prices are present in disguise through the proxy of the wholesale shutdown of production and the elimination of entire industries. We already have the ultimate effects of a deflationary spiral, usually transmitted through falling prices, but in this instance brought about directly through falling interest rates.

Other proxies of a falling price level are also present. Most important is the loss of pricing power. Some firms have so far survived the hecatomb inflicted upon American industry by policymakers, for example, in the auto industry. But auto-makers have definitely lost pricing power. It is possible that, lately, they have been selling cars at a loss. This loss has been made up by the lucrative business of car-financing, at least prior to the subprime crisis. It is highly unlikely that auto-makers can long continue their subprime car financing business. Not at zero percent interest.

In the meantime American exports fall, in spite of the ongoing debasement of the dollar, with the exception of exporting highly-paid industrial jobs to low-wage countries. But much worse is to come. The real scourge on the economy of the falling interest rate structure has not yet shown up: wholesale bankruptcies of midsize businesses in the United States. I have been writing on this subject for some eight years, but failed to alarm public opinion.

Declining interest rates bestow huge unearned profits upon bond speculators. These profits do not come out of nowhere. They are being siphoned off from the capital accounts of the producers. We are looking at vampirism by the financial sector sucking the blood of the producing sector. It has been made possible by the regime of the irredeemable dollar as it destabilised interest rates. Under the gold standard with stable interest rates there is neither bond speculation nor vampirism. Under the gold standard the producing sector is the dog and the financial sector is the tail. The regime of the irredeemable dollar has turned things upside down: now the financial sector is the dog and the producing sector is the tail which, moreover, is in danger of being cut off altogether. The most appalling part of this vampirism is that producers are not aware that they are being victimised. Their capital is siphoned off stealthily and unobtrusively. Producing firms are paying out phantom profits to shareholders, further weakening their capital.

To understand this process fully we must make an excursion into accounting. Persistently falling interest rates decimate capital values as the present value of debt keeps increasing. The resulting capital loss should be recorded in the balance sheet and made up in the form of charges against future earnings. But nobody does it, as everybody prefers to listen to the sweet siren song: 'falling interest rates are good for you!' In fact, the Fed's policy of serial interest rate cuts is an insane policy cutting the ground under the producers further and providing a tailwind to bond speculation. It confuses a low interest rate structure with a falling one. While the former is beneficial to business, the latter is lethal as it is the root cause of depressions. Professor Frieden's blaming the gold standard as being deflationary is entirely misplaced. So is his title: it should read bishop or sidekick of the Prophet.

Open market operations of the Fed – introduced as an illegal practice* in the 1920s and legalised retroactively in the 1930s – is thoroughly destructive as it makes bond speculation risk-free. Bond speculators stalk and forestall the Fed as it is making its regular trips to the bond market to purchase its quota of bonds. The Fed is helpless: it must purchase the bonds in order to increase the money supply. This illegal regime of risk-free profits to bond speculators was scandalously cheered on by mainstream economist, who declared that 'taxation for revenues is now obsolete'. From now on, they rejoiced, taxation can be used to manipulate the taxpayers and 'the economy.'

Professor Frieden's suggestion that Britain escaped two years of recession in 1931 because it went off gold that much earlier is not valid. In Britain there was no confiscation of gold in 1931. (That particular leaf from the book of the U.S. was borrowed by the British later.) One consequence of the confiscation of gold in 1933 was the falling interest-rate structure, the root cause of the Great Depression. In the eyes of the most conservative investors gold was the only competition for bonds. As this competition was forcibly removed, demand for bonds increased. This made bond prices rise and interest rates fall. Without gold confiscation interest rates would not have kept falling in the 1930s and the Great Depression would have been avoided. Deflation in the U.S. was self-inflicted through the instrument of the gold ban.

> " The gold standard, if introduced, would increase government regulation of the economy. With no Fed, inexpert Congress will bear the onus of alleviating economic suffering. [9] With deeper, longer recessions, Congressmen will inevitably succumb to pressure for more spending and regulation of the economy - as they did during the Great Depression. [10]

If the above quotation by Barron Young Smith is accurate, then Professor Frieden is putting on a poorly fitting garb and mask as a defender of the free market. But his hidden agenda cannot be masked: he wants to preempt at all costs a free and uninhibited discussion [11] of the proposition to abolish the Fed. If he succeeds, a great opportunity will have been lost. The Fed has become conceited and obtuse. Its open market operations are kept above criticism by both the Keynesians and Friedmanites. Yet open market operations are not only deflationary but counter-productive as well. The new 'money' pumped into the economy to prevent prices from falling flows to the bond market and makes interest rates fall. Prices fall as a consequence, contrary to purpose.

> " The gold standard, if introduced, would increase our reliance on foreign credit and ship yet more jobs overseas. Ron Paul says 'our economy and our very independence as a nation is increasingly in the hands of foreign governments such as that of China and Saudi Arabia.' But adopting the gold standard would actually exacerbate the problem, not alleviate it.

Assuming that this quotation is accurate, Bishop Frieden is guilty of scarce-mongering. Besides his argument is disingenuous. Our reliance on foreign credit cannot be further increased as this source of credit is more than exhausted, courtesy of the irredeemable dollar [which he promotes] and its 'spend now, pay later' ethos. It was the regime of the irredeemable dollar that has landed the U.S. economy in a corner where the very independence of the nation is increasingly in the hands of foreign governments. It would have never happened under the gold standard. The only escape route from the corner is through the gold standard, provided the U.S. opens the Mint to gold and silver before the Chinese and the Russians open theirs.

Shipping jobs overseas is not a characteristic of the gold standard. It is a characteristic of the regime of irredeemable currency as it destroys capital so that industry can no longer compete with foreign labour. The lion's share the outstanding marketable debt of the U.S. government is now in the hands of foreign governments such as that of China and Japan, mentioning but the two greatest concentrations. Such a development could have never taken place under the gold standard and no self-respecting government should have ever allowed this to happen.

> " Insofar as it helps anybody, the gold standard would favour Wall Street bankers over entrepreneurs, businesses and workers. Ron Paul likes to rail against Wall Street complaining that our money is being 'inflated at the behest of big government and big banks' who 'cause your income and savings to lose their value'.

If this quotation is accurate, then Professor Frieden betrays his fundamental ignorance [12] about the nature of the gold standard which is the most even-handed monetary system that has ever existed, making *all* playing fields level. Under the gold standard people are the boss and the banks are the servant. The latter can be disciplined by the former withdrawing bank reserves in the form of gold. People have lost this power when the gold standard was forcibly overthrown by the government, which was also irritated by the control over the public purse that people could exercise through gold withdrawals. Under the regime of the irredeemable dollar the banks are the boss and they plunge people into debt-servitude. Control over the public purse by the people has also been removed, giving rise to endless budget deficits.

It is preposterous to suggest that the gold standard would favour bankers over entrepreneurs, businesses and wage earners. If it ever looked that way in the past, it was because of a double standard in contract law and not because of the gold standard per se. The banks were granted immunity from forcible liquidation in case they failed to perform on their contracts. The government declared a bank holiday if a number of banks became insolvent and could not pay gold on their sight liabilities. To add insult to injury, the defaulting banks' paper was promoted to the status of legal tender in place of gold. So much for the perverse incentive system favouring banks bent on credit expansion. While the banks enjoyed immunity, the force of contract law was always applied in full force against other entrepreneurs, businesses, wage earners and home-makers. But what can one expect from gnostic dualists:

- ✓ Dualistic double standards
- ✓ Cosmogonic fault finding with the world
- ✓ Soteriological salvation thanks to 'our own' invention: the-paper dollar
- ✓ Eschatological survival: only one in a million knows, that's us, we know better, not you!
- ✓ Parasitical ways of predatory practices (privileges etc.)
- ✓ Taboo on dissenters (social engineering, funding hall of fame...)

Endnotes to Chapter 54

[1] Text by Antal Fekete, edited with poetic license by P. Van Coppenolle.

[2] See Volume II, Marginal utility of gold as the most marketable good, whose marginal utility over time declines the least.

[3] As is typical for gnostic dualists, only they 'know' the secrets...

[4] See Volume II, on tools and also the Sinking Fund protection every self-respecting bond-issuer ought to install.

[5] Please see Chapter 48 on Deconstructing Ideologies: a gnostic flock is self-censured and will not deviate from their own Sacred Scripture. (SS) The keep repeating the same nostrums like a mantra.

[6] It is probably what he means, but refuses to say out loud.

[7] Like the Biblical Gospels, who apparently were largely copied from each other, we find the same content in the sacred gnostic scriptures like those by Frieden as we find similarities with those of that other bishop, named Barry Eichengreen.

[8] *Dinge auf dem Kopf setzen* [turning things on their head] is a speciality of Marx and his gnostic dualist flock. Just count the times this sentence occurs in any of his writings. Eye-opening linguistic statistic! Aside from linguistic statistics, turning things upside down in current affairs would be the prerogative of hooligans, gangs and other misfits.

[9] ...alleviating economic suffering....? smacks of gnostic 'liberation' doesn't it?

[10] Without FED's what would poor Congress do...? Only the Federal Reserve speaks Latin and they own White Lab Coats, you know! ... This passage oozes gnostic dualism, pulled straight from the Sacred Scriptures according to Cardinal Frieden!

[11] And another typical characteristic of gnostic dualism we can tick off on our checklist: No Dissent From the Sacred Scripture [of Keynes or Krugman]!

[12] Either he is ignorant, which does not bode well for a salaried academic, or he does know better, but admitting to the latter turns him into a liar. We prefer to go with the bumbling ignorant version. But he's free to demonstrate otherwise...

Chapter 55

What Constitutes A Money Crank?

PHILIP PILKINGTON

(Excerpted from: blogger@nakedcapitalism.com, April 8, 2014.
The author is a research assistant at Kingston University in London.)

What constitutes a money crank? A money crank is a person who views the money system from a position in which [he] has a substantial emotional investment. Was Keynes a money crank? I think not...Were Milton Friedman and Anna Schwartz money cranks? I would answer in the negative...Murray Rothbard is, I believe, a money crank. But he is of a more soft-core variety. On the left is Silvio Gesell, albeit he is [also of] a more soft-core variety.

Antal Fekete is what I would consider a hardcore money crank. In his poorly written work The Gold Standard Manifesto: 'Dismal Monetary Science' he writes:

> *"Governments and academia have utterly failed in discharging their sacred duty to provide a serene environment for the search for and dissemination of truth regarding economics in general and monetary science in particular. This failure has to do, first and foremost, with the incestuous financing of research ever since the Federal Reserve System was launched in the United States in 1913... Under the gold standard government bonds were the instrument to which widows and orphans could safely entrust their savings. Under the regime of irredeemable currency they are the instrument whereby special interest fleeces the rest of society.'*

Or, again,

> *"Unknown to the public, at the end of the day the shill alias the Federal Reserve, is obliged to hand over her gains to the casino owner alias the United States Treasury. There is nothing open about what is euphemistically called 'open market operations'. It is a conspiratorial operation. It has come about through unlawful delegation of unlimited power, without imposing countervailing responsibilities. It was never authorised by the Federal Reserve Act of 1913. It defies the principle of checks and balances.*

> *It is immoral. It is a formula to corrupt and ultimately to destroy the Republic.'*

Such passages are pretty off-the-wall. The money system is portrayed as a vast conspiracy set up to defraud widows and orphans. Here we see that Fekete is far more hardcore than Rothbard. Whereas both agree that the government 'meddles' with money and this is undesirable and leads to some sort of personal injury, Fekete goes one step further and portrays the system as an organised conspiracy set up against the vulnerable.

***

Infra dignitatem

How is it that a lame man does not annoy us while a lame mind does?

…

Because a lame man recognises that we are walking straight, while a lame mind says that it is we who are limping.

BLAISE PASCAL
Pensées nr. 98.

Addendum

Exhibit - A

Source: *Foreign Relations of the United States, 1969-1976, Volume XXXI, Foreign Economic Policy, 1973-1976,(Washington: Government Printing Office, April 25, 1974),*

Document 63.

Minutes of Secretary of State Kissinger's Principals and Regionals Staff Meeting [1]

Washington, April 25, 1974, 3:13–4:16 p.m.

[Omitted here is discussion unrelated to international monetary policy.]

Secretary Kissinger: Now we've got Enders, Lord and Hartman. They'll speak separately or together. (Laughter.)

Mr. Hartman: A trio.

Mr. Lord: I can exhaust my knowledge of gold fairly quickly, I think.

Secretary Kissinger: Now, I had one deal with Shultz–never to discuss gold at this staff meeting–because his estimate of what would appear in the newspapers from staff meetings is about the same as mine.

Are you going to discuss something–is this now in the public discussion, what we're discussing here?

Mr. Enders: It's been very close to it. It's been in the newspapers now–the EC proposal.[2]

Secretary Kissinger: On what–revaluing their gold?

Mr. Enders: Revaluing their gold–in the individual transaction between the central banks. That's been in the newspaper. The subject is, obviously, sensitive; but it's not, I think, more than the usual degree of sensitivity about gold.

Secretary Kissinger: Now, what is our position?

Mr. Enders: You know what the EC proposal is.

Secretary Kissinger: Yes.

Mr. Enders: It does not involve a change in the official price of gold. It would allow purchases and sales to the private market, provided there was no net purchase from the private market by an individual central banker in a year. And then there would be individual sales between the central banks on–

Secretary Kissinger: How can they permit sale to the private market? Oh, and then they would buy from the private market?

Mr. Enders: Then they would buy.

Secretary Kissinger: But they wouldn't buy more than they sold.

Mr. Enders: They wouldn't buy more than they sold. There would be no net increase in gold held by the central banks that was held by the EEC. It could be held by others.

I've got two things to say about this, Mr. Secretary. One is: If it happens, as they proposed, it would be against our interests in these ways.

Secretary Kissinger: Have you accepted it or is this just a French proposal?

Mr. Enders: It's an informal consensus that they've reached among themselves.

Secretary Kissinger: Were they discussed with us at all?

Mr. Enders: Not in a systematic way. They're proposing to send over to Washington the Dutch Finance Minister and the Dutch Central Governor would talk to the Treasury.

Secretary Kissinger: What's Arthur Burns' view?

Mr. Enders: Arthur Burns–I talked to him last night on it and he didn't define a general view yet. He was unwilling to do so. He said he wanted to look more closely on the proposal. Henry Wallich, the international affairs man, this morning indicated he would probably adopt the traditional position that we should be for phasing gold out of the international monetary system; but he wanted to have another look at it. So Henry Wallich indicated that they would probably come down opposing this. But he was not prepared to do so until he got a further look at it.

Secretary Kissinger: But the practical consequence of this is to revalue their gold supply.

Mr. Enders: Precisely.

Secretary Kissinger: Their gold reserves.

Mr. Enders: That's right. And it would be followed quite closely by a proposal within a year to have an official price of gold–

Secretary Kissinger: It doesn't make any difference anyway. If they pass gold at the market price, that in effect establishes a new official price.

Mr. Enders: Very close to it–although their–

Secretary Kissinger: But if they ask what they're doing–let me just say economics is not my forte. But my understanding of this proposal would be that they–by opening it up to other countries, they're in effect putting gold back into the system at a higher price.

Mr. Enders: Correct.

Secretary Kissinger: Now, that's what we have consistently opposed.

Mr. Enders: Yes, we have. You have convertibility if they–

Secretary Kissinger: Yes.

Mr. Enders: Both parties have to agree to this. But it slides towards and would result, within two or three years, in putting gold back into the centerpiece of the system–one. Two–at a much higher price. Three–at a price that could be determined by a few central bankers in deals among themselves.

So, in effect, I think what you've got here is you've got a small group of bankers getting together to obtain a money printing machine for themselves. They would determine the value of their reserves in a very small group.

There are two things wrong with this.

Secretary Kissinger: And we would be on the outside.

Mr. Enders: We could join this too, but there are only very few countries in the world that hold large amounts of gold–United States and Continentals being most of them. The LDC's and most of the other countries–to include Japan–have relatively small amounts of gold. So it would be highly inflationary, on the one hand–and, on the other hand, a very inequitable means of increasing reserves.

Secretary Kissinger: Why did the Germans agree to it?

Mr. Enders: The Germans agreed to it, we've been told, on the basis that it would be discussed with the United States–conditional on United States approval.

Secretary Kissinger: They would be penalized for having held dollars.

Mr. Enders: They would be penalized for having held dollars. That probably doesn't make very much difference to the Germans at the present time, given their very high reserves. However, I think that they may have come around to it on the basis that either we would oppose it–one–or, two, that they would have to pay up and finance the deficits of France and Italy by some means anyway; so why not let them try this proposal first?

The EC is potentially divided on this, however, and if enough pressure is put on them, these differences should reappear.

Secretary Kissinger: Then what's our policy?

Mr. Enders: The policy we would suggest to you is that, (1), we refuse to go along with this–

Secretary Kissinger: I am just totally allergic to unilateral European decisions that fundamentally affect American interests–taken without consultation of the United States. And my tendency is to smash any attempt in which they do it until they learn that they can't do it without talking to us.

That would be my basic instinct, apart from the merits of the issue.

Mr. Enders: Well, it seems to me there are two things here. One is that we can't let them get away with this proposal because it's for the reasons you stated. Also, it's bad economic policy and it's against our fundamental interests.

Secretary Kissinger: There's also a fundamental change of our policy that we pursued over recent years–or am I wrong there?

Mr. Enders: Yes.

Secondly, Mr. Secretary, it does present an opportunity though–and we should try to negotiate for this–to move towards a demonetization of gold, to begin to get gold moving out of the system.

Secretary Kissinger: But how do you do that?

Mr. Enders: Well, there are several ways. One way is we could say to them that they would accept this kind of arrangement, provided that the gold were channelled out through an international agen-cy–either in the IMF or a special pool–and sold into the market, so there would be gradual increases.

Secretary Kissinger: But the French would never go for this.

Mr. Enders: We can have a counter-proposal. There's a further propos-al–and that is that the IMF begin selling its gold–which is now 7 billion–to the world market and we should try to negotiate that. That would begin the demonetization of gold.

Secretary Kissinger: Why are we so eager to get gold out of the system?

Mr. Enders: We were eager to get it out of the system–get started–be-cause it's a typical balancing of either forward or back. If this pro-posal goes back, it will go back into the centerpiece system.

Secretary Kissinger: But why is it against our interests? I understand the argument that it's against our interest that the Europeans take a unilateral decision contrary to our policy. Why is it against our interest to have gold in the system?

Mr. Enders: It's against our interest to have gold in the system because for it to remain there it would result in it being evaluated periodi-cally. Although we have still some substantial gold holdings–about 11 billion–a larger part of the official gold in the world is concen-trated in Western Europe. This gives them the dominant position in world reserves and the dominant means of creating reserves. We've been trying to get away from that into a system in which we can control–

Secretary Kissinger: But that's a balance of payments problem.

Mr. Enders: Yes, but it's a question of who has the most leverage in-ternationally. If they have the reserve-creating instrument, by hav-ing the largest amount of gold and the ability to change its price periodically, they have a position relative to ours of considerable power. For a long time we had a position relative to theirs of considerable power because we could change gold almost at will. This is no longer possible–no longer acceptable. Therefore, we have gone to special drawing rights, which is also equitable and could take account of some of the LDC interests and which spreads the power away from Europe. And it's more rational in–

Secretary Kissinger: 'More rational' being defined as being more in our interests or what?

Mr. Enders: More rational in the sense of more responsive to world-wide needs–but also more in our interest by letting–

Secretary Kissinger: Would it shock you? I've forgotten how SDR's are generated. By agreement?

Mr. Enders: By agreement.

Secretary Kissinger: There's no automatic way?

Mr. Enders: There's no automatic way.

Mr. Lord: Maybe some of the Europeans–but the LDC's are on our side and would not support them.

Mr. Enders: I don't think anybody would support them. Secretary Kissinger: But could they do it anyway?

Mr. Enders: Yes. But in order for them to do it anyway, they would have to be in violation of important articles of the IMF. So this would not be a total departure. (Laughter.) But there would be reluctance on the part of some Europeans to do this.

We could also make it less interesting for them by beginning to sell our own gold in the market and this would put pressure on them.

Mr. Maw: Why wouldn't that fit if we start to sell our own gold at a price?

Secretary Kissinger: But how the hell could this happen without our knowing about it ahead of time?

Mr. Hartman: We've had consultations on it ahead of time. Several of them have come to ask us to express our views. And I think the reason they're coming now to ask about it is because they know we have a generally negative view.

Mr. Enders: So I think we should try to break it, I think, as a first position–unless they're willing to assign some form of demonetizing arrangement.

Secretary Kissinger: But, first of all, that's impossible for the French.

Mr. Enders: Well, it's impossible for the French under the Pompidou Government. Would it be necessarily under a future French Government? We should test that.

Secretary Kissinger: If they have gold to settle current accounts, we'll be faced, sooner or later, with the same proposition again. Then others will be asked to join this settlement thing.

Isn't this what they're doing?

Mr. Enders: It seems to me, Mr. Secretary, that we should try–not rule out, a priori, a demonetizing scenario, because we can both gain by this. That liberates gold at a higher price. We have gold and some of the Europeans have gold. Our interests join theirs. This would be helpful; and it would also, on the other hand, gradually remove this dominant position that the Europeans have had in economic terms.

Secretary Kissinger: Who's with us on demonetizing gold?

Mr. Enders: I think we could get the Germans with us on demonetizing gold, the Dutch and the British, over a very long period of time.

Secretary Kissinger: How about the Japs?

Mr. Enders: Yes. The Arabs have shown no great interest in gold.

Secretary Kissinger: We could stick them with a lot of gold.

Mr. Sisco: Yes. (Laughter.)

Mr. Sonnenfeldt: At those high-dollar prices. I don't know why they'd want to take it.

Secretary Kissinger: For the bathroom fixtures in the Guest House in Rio. (Laughter.)

Mr. McCloskey: That'd never work.

Secretary Kissinger: That'd never work. Why it could never get the bathtub filled–it probably takes two weeks to fill it.

Mr. Sisco: Three years ago, when Jean [3] was in one of those large bath-tubs, two of those guys with speakers at that time walked right on through. She wasn't quite used to it. (Laughter.)

Secretary Kissinger: They don't have guards with speakers in that house.

Mr. Sisco: Well, they did in '71.

Mr. Brown: Usually they've been fixed in other directions.

Mr. Sisco: Sure. (Laughter.)

Secretary Kissinger: O.K. My instinct is to oppose it. What's your view, Art?

Mr. Hartman: Yes. I think for the present time, in terms of the kind of system that we're going for, it would be very hard to defend in terms of how.

Secretary Kissinger: Ken?

Mr. Rush: Well, I think probably I do. The question is: Suppose they go ahead on their own anyway. What then?

Secretary Kissinger: We'll bust them.

Mr. Enders: I think we should look very hard then, Ken, at very sub-stantial sales of gold–U.S. gold on the market–to raid the gold market once and for all.

Mr. Rush: I'm not sure we could do it.

Secretary Kissinger: If they go ahead on their own against our position on something that we consider central to our interests, we've got to show them that that they can't get away with it. Hopefully, we should have the right position. But we just cannot let them get away with these unilateral steps all the time.

Mr. Lord: Does the Treasury agree with us on this? I mean, if this guy comes when the Secretary is out of the country

Secretary Kissinger: Who's coming?

Mr. Enders: The Dutch Finance Minister–Duisenberg–and Zijlstra. I think it will take about two weeks to work through a hard position on this. The Treasury will want our leadership on the hardness of it. They will accept our leadership on this. It will take, I would think, some time to talk it through or talk it around Arthur Burns and we'll have to see what his reaction is.

Mr. Rush: We have about 45 billion dollars at the present value–

Mr. Enders: That's correct.

Mr. Rush: And there's about 100 billion dollars of gold.

Mr. Enders: That's correct. And the annual turnover in the gold market is about 120 billion.

Secretary Kissinger: The gold market is generally in cahoots with Arthur Burns.

Mr. Enders: Yes. That's been my experience. So I think we've got to bring Arthur around.

Secretary Kissinger: Arthur is a reasonable man. Let me talk to him. It takes him a maddening long time to make a point, but he's a reasonable man.

Mr. Enders: He hasn't had a chance to look at the proposal yet.

Secretary Kissinger: I'll talk to him before I leave.[4]

Mr. Enders: Good.

Mr. Boeker: It seems to me that gold sales is perhaps Stage 2 in a strategy that might break up the European move–that Stage 1 should be formulating a counterproposal U.S. design to isolate those who are opposing it the hardest–the French and the Italians. That would attract considerable support. It would appeal to the Japanese and others. I think this could fairly easily be done. And that, in itself, should put considerable pressure on the EEC for a tentative consensus.

Mr. Hartman: It isn't a confrontation. That is, it seems to me we can discuss the various aspects of this thing.

Secretary Kissinger: Oh, no. We should discuss it–obviously. But I don't like the proposition of their doing something and then inviting other countries to join them.

Mr. Hartman: I agree. That's not what they've done.

Mr. Sonnenfeldt: Can we get them to come after the French election[5] so we don't get kicked in the head?

Mr. Rush: I would think so.

Secretary Kissinger: I would think it would be a lot better to discuss it after the French election. Also, it would give us a better chance. Why don't you tell Simon this?

Mr. Enders: Good.

Secretary Kissinger: Let them come after the French election.

Mr. Enders: Good. I will be back–I can talk to Simon. I guess Shultz will be out then.[6]

Mr. Sonnenfeldt: He'll be out the 4th of May.

Mr. Enders: Yes. Meanwhile, we'll go ahead and develop a position on the basis of this discussion.

Secretary Kissinger: Yes.

Mr. Enders: Good.

Secretary Kissinger: I agree we shouldn't get a consultation–as long as we're talking Treasury, I keep getting pressed for Treasury chairmanship of a policy committee. You're opposed to that?[7]

Endnotes to Exhibit

[1] Source: National Archives, RG 59, Transcripts of Secretary of State Kissinger's Staff Meetings, 1973–1977, Entry 5177, Box 3, Secretary's Staff Meeting, April 25, 1974. Secret. According to an attached list, the following people attended the meeting: Kissinger, Rush, Sisco, Ingersoll, Hartman, Maw, Ambassador at Large Robert Mc-Closkey, Assistant Secretary of State for African Affairs Donald Easum, Hyland, Atherton, Lord, Policy Planning Staff member Paul Boeker, Eagleburger, Springsteen, Special Assistant to the Secretary of State for Press Relations Robert Anderson, Enders, Assistant Secretary of State for Inter-American Affairs Jack Kubisch and Sonnenfeldt.

[2] Meeting in Zeist, the Netherlands, on April 22 and 23, EC Finance Ministers and central bankers agreed on a common position on gold, which they authorized the Dutch Minister of Finance, Willem Frederik Duisenberg and the President of the Dutch central bank, Jelle Zijlstra, to discuss with Treasury and Federal Reserve Board officials in Washington. (Telegram 2042 from The Hague, April 24 and telegram 2457 from USEC Brussels, April 25; ibid., Central Foreign Policy Files)

[3] Jean Sisco was Joseph Sisco's wife.

[4] From April 28 to 29, Kissinger was in Geneva for talks with Soviet Foreign Minister Andrei Gromyko.

[5] France held a Presidential election on May 19.

[6] George Shultz's tenure as Secretary of the Treasury ended on May 8, when he was replaced by William Simon.

[7] The summary attached to the front page of the minutes notes that 'The Secretary is inclined to oppose the proposal on grounds of non consultation by the Europeans as well as on the proposal's merits. The Secretary agreed to talk to Arthur Burns in this sense.'

Bibliography (Cumulative I to IV)

Titles mentioned here are in English or refer to the English translation. Some of these titles may be difficult to obtain for the reader.

Anderson, B.M., *Economics and the Public Welfare, A Financial and Economic History of the United States, 1914-1946*, Princeton, D. Van Nostrand, 1949, New York.

_____ *The Value of Money*, Macmillan, New York, 1917, 610 p.

Bell, J.W., Spahr, W.E., *A Proper Monetary and Banking System for the Unites States*, Ronald Press Company, New York, 1960, 240 p.

von Böhm-Bawerk, E., *Capital and Interest, A critical History of Economical Thought*, Transl. W. Smart), MacMillan, London, 1890.

_____ *Karl Marx and the Close of His System: A Criticism*, London, 1898.

_____ *Control or Economic Law*, LVMI, 2010, first appeared in 'Zeitschrift für Volkswirtschaft, Sozialpolitik und Verwaltung,' Volume XXIII (1914): 205–71; (tranlation. J.R. Mez)

Campagnolo, G., *Criticism of Classical Political Economy*, Menger, Austrian economics and the German Historical School, Routledge, New York, 2010.

De Roover, R., *The Rise and Decline of the Medici Bank, 1397-1494*, Cambridge, Mass. 1963.

_____ *Money, Banking and Credit in Mediaeval Bruges*, Cambridge, Mass. 1948.

Denniger, C., 'Bernanke Inserts Gun in Mouth', March 20, 2009 market-ticker.denniger.net

Einaudi,L., *Money and Politics : European Monetary Unification and the Gold Standard (1865-73)*, Oxford , 2001.

Eichengreen, B., and Temin, P., 'Fetters of Gold and Paper,' Econometrics Laboratory, Berkeley, California.

Feser E., 'Self Ownership, Abortion and the Rights of Children: Toward a more Conservative Libertarianism', Journal of Libertarian Studies, 2004.

Fetter, F. A., *The Principles of Economics*, New York, 1905.

Fisher, D.H., *The Great Wave Price Revolutions and the Rhythm of History*, Oxford University Press, 1996

Foster, R.T., *Fiat Paper Money - The History and Evolution of our Currency*,

ISBN 978-0-964-3066-1-5

Franz, M., *Eric Voegelin and the Politics of Spiritual Revolt: The Roots of Modern Ideology*, Baton Rouge: Louisiana State University, 1992.

Friedman, M., *Optimum Quantity of Money*, 1912.

_____ *Money Mischief*, New York, 1992.

Fullarton, J., *On the Regulation of Currencies*, New York, A.M. Kelley, 1969.

Gillespie, A.M., *The Theological Origins of Modernity*, University of Chicago Press, Chicago and London, 2009.

Girard, R., *I see Satan Fall Like Lightning*, Orbis Books, 2001.

Grice-Hutchinson, M., *The School of Salamanca, Readings in Spanish Monetary History 1544-1605*, Oxford, Clarendon, 1952.

Gonczy, A.M.L. et al. 'Two Faces of Debt', Federal Reserve Bank of Chicago, 5th Rev. 1992.

Guttierrez, C., 'No Time For T-Bonds', March 28, 2009 forbes.com

Hayek, F.A., *Prices and Production and Other Works*, LVMI, 2008.

_____ 'Commodity Reserve Currency', Economic Journal, vol. LIII, no. 210 (1943), reprinted in Individualism and Economic Order, by F.A. Hayek

_____ *The Counter Revolution of Science*, Studies on the Abuse of Reason, MacMillan, London, 1955.

_____ *The Road To Serfdom*, Routledge, London, 1944

Hidy, R. W., *The House of Baring in American Trade and Finance, English Merchant Bankers at Work 1763-1861*, Harvard University Press, Cambridge, Mass., 1949, 631 p.

Hinshaw, R. (ed), *Monetary Reform and the Price of Gold*, Baltimore, 1967

Hunt, I.L., (Col.) American Military Government of Occupied Germany 1918-1920 - Report of the Officer in Charge of Civil Affairs, Third Army and American Forces in Germany, U.S. Government Printing Office, Washington, 1943.

Jastrow, M. Jr., *The War and the Bagdad Railway*, Philadelphia and London, J.B. Lippincott Company, 1918.

Keynes, J.M., *A Treatise on Money*, Vol I and II, MacMillan, 1914.

_____ *The General Theory of Employment*, Interest and Money, 1935.

Kisch, C.H., *The Portuguese Bank Note Case*, London, 1932.

Kolko, G., *The Triumph of Conservatism, A Reinterpretation of American History, 1900-1916*, Quadrangle Paperback, 1967. (ASIN B00251OE9K)

Krugman, P., The Madoff Economy, available online www.nytimes.com, December 19, 2008.

Laughlin, L., *The History of Bimetallism in the United States*, Appleton, New York, 1896.

Lips, F., *Gold Wars, Will Hedging Kill the Goose Laying the Golden Egg?* New York: FAME, 2001.

Lorton & White, *The Art of Grain Merchandising*, White Commercial Corp, 1994.

MacIntyre, A., *Whose Justice? Which Rationality?* Univ. Notre Dame, 1989.

Martin, J. S., *All Honorable Man - The Story of the Men on Both Sides of the Atlantic Who Successfully Thwarted Plans to Dismantle the Nazi Cartel System*, Little Brown, 1950. (ASIN B0000EEK-BR)

Menger, C., *Principles of Economics*, NYU Press, 1981, originally published in German in 1871 as Grundsatze der Volkswirtschaftslehre.

von Mises, L., *The Theory of Money and Credit*, Yale UP, New Haven,1953, translated by H.E. Batson.

_____ 'Economic Aspects of the Pension Problem', The Commercial and Financial Chronicle, February 23, 1950.

_____ *Planning for Freedom*, 3ed. Libertarian Press, 1950

_____ *The Anticapitalistic Mentality*, D. Van Nostrand Inc, 1956.

_____ *Human Action, A Treatise on Economics*, LVMI, 1998.

Nagel, Th., *Mind and Cosmos, Why the Materialist Neo-Darwinian Conception of Nature is Almost Certainly, False*, Oxford University Press, 2012, 130 p.

Palyi, M., *The Twilight of Gold, 1914-1936*, Chicago, Henry Regnery, 1972.

Perkins, J., *Confessions of An Economic Hit Man*, Berrett Koehler, San Fransisco, 2004.

Pigou, A.C., *The Theory of Unemployment*, Macmillan, 1933.

Rist, Ch., *History of Money and Credit Theory from John Law to the Present Day*, 1940. Willis, H.P., A History of the Latin Monetary Union A study of International Monetary Action, Chicago Press, 1901.

Rohmer, R., *Golden Phoenix: The Biography of Peter Munk*, Key Porter Books, 1999.

Röpke, W., *International Order and Economic Integration*, Reidel, Dordrecht,1959

Salsman, R.M., *Gold and Liberty*, Great Barrington, 1995.

Selgin, G., *Good Money: Birmingham Button Makers, the Royal Mint and the Beginnings of Modern Coinage (1775-1821)*, Institute of Economic Affairs, 2008.

Schumpeter, J.A., *History of Economic Analysis*, New York, 1954.

Shelldrake, R., *The Science Delusion*, Hodder & Stoughton, London, 2013

Smith, A., *An inquiry into the Nature and causes of the Wealth of Nations*, 1776.

Spahr, W. E., *Our Irredeemable Currency System, The Federal Reserve System and the Control of Credit*, Macmillan, 1931

_____ *A Proper Monetary and Banking System for the United States*, Ronald Press Co, NY, 1960.

Strachan, H., *The First World War*, Vol. I., To Arms, Oxford University Press, 2001, 1227 pages.

Sutton, A.C., *Wall Street and the Bolshevik Revolution*, Arlington House, New York, 1974.

_____ *Western Technology and Soviet Economic Development*, Hoover Institute, Stanford University, 1968.

Sykes, E., *Banking and Currency*, 4th Ed., Butterworth, London, 1920, 314 p

Vieira, Edw. Jr., *Pieces of Eight: The Monetary Powers and Disabilities of the United States Constitution*, Sheridan Books, 2nd ed. , 2002.

Voegelin, E., *From Enlightenment to Revolution*, Duke Univ. Press, 1975.

_____ *Modernity Without Restraint*, Collected Works, Vol 5. University of Missouri Press, Columbia and London, 2000.

Warburton, P., *Debt and Delusion : Central Bank Follies That Threaten Economic Disaster*, World Meta View Press, 1999.

Wicksteed, P. H., *The Common Sense of Political Economy*, vol.I., London, Routledge & Keagan, 1933.

Willis, H.P., *A History of the Latin Monetary Union A study of International Monetary Action*, Chicago Press, 1901.

Withers, H., *The Meaning of Money*, London, 1910.

GERMAN

The titles mentioned here refer to German or Austrian works.

Moll, B., *Logik des Geldes*, F. Enke, Stuttgart, 1914.

_____ *Die modernen Geldtheorien und die Politik der Reichsbank*, F. Enke, Stuttgart, 1917.

Palyi, M., *Der Streit um die Staatliche Theorie des Geldes*, Duncker & Humblot, München & Leipzig, 1922, 95 p.

Rittershausen, H., *Arbeitslosigkeit und Kapitalbildung zugleich ein bankpolitischen Programm zur Bekämpfung der Wirtschaftskrise*, Jena,

Verlag, Gustav Fischer 1930. (Unemployment as a Problem of Turnover Credits and the Supply of Means of Payments, Jena, 1930)

Index of Names

Prepared by D. van der Linden

Index of Subjects

Prepared by D. van der Linden

CPSIA information can be obtained
at www.ICGtesting.com
Printed in the USA
LVHW071808180723
752687LV00037B/1309/J